When War Becomes Personal

When War Becomes Personal

Soldiers' Accounts from the Civil War to Iraq

Edited by Donald Anderson

UNIVERSITY OF IOWA PRESS   IOWA CITY

University of Iowa Press, Iowa City 52242

Copyright © 2008 by the University of Iowa Press

www.uiowapress.org

Printed in the United States of America

Design by Omega Clay

The University of Iowa Press is a member of Green Press Initiative
and is committed to preserving natural resources.

Printed on acid-free paper

Library of Congress Cataloging-in-Publication Data
When war becomes personal: soldiers' accounts from the Civil War
to Iraq / edited by Donald Anderson.
    p.   cm.
    Includes bibliographical references.
    ISBN-13: 978-1-58729-680-2 (pbk.)
    ISBN-10: 1-58729-680-2 (pbk.)
    1. United States—History, Military—Anecdotes. 2. Soldiers—
United States—Biography—Anecdotes. 3. United States—
Armed Forces—Biography—Anecdotes. 4. Soldiers' writings,
American. I. Anderson, Donald, 1946 July 9–.
    E181.W565 2008   2008010125
    355.00973—dc22

08 09 10 11 12 P 5 4 3 2 1

"They're trying to kill me," Yossarian told him calmly.

"No one's trying to kill you," Clevinger cried.

"Then why are they shooting at me?" Yossarian asked.

"They're shooting at *everyone*," Clevinger answered.

   "They're trying to kill everyone."

"And what difference does that make?"

JOSEPH HELLER, *Catch-22*

Contents

D O N A L D   A N D E R S O N

War, Memory, Imagination *A Prologue*

> Writing is not apart from living. Writing is a kind of double living. The writer experiences everything twice. Once in reality and once more in that mirror which waits always before or behind him.
>
> CATHERINE DRINKER BOWEN

> When you have done your best, it doesn't matter how good it is. That is for others to say. . . . An act of the imagination is an act of self-acceptance. . . . Writing is a way of saying you and the world have a chance.
>
> RICHARD HUGO

I didn't serve in Vietnam, but my nation did. Because of my "memory" of what had happened—and was happening—to America and Vietnam, I made decisions. For one thing, I joined the air force to avoid the walking tour of Southeast Asia. I meant to beat the draft: it was not my imagination that more soldiers were being buried than airmen. I went on to serve for twenty-two years in the air force, but the point is my initial enlistment had everything to do with the war and hardly would have surfaced as a career choice without the war. That I could imagine the war—its pointlessness borne out in time—was why I worked to avoid it. We have, each of us, factual histories and imagined histories, backfilling, always, when memory proves deficient, though "it's a poor sort of memory," Lewis Carroll's Queen says, "that only works backwards."

Remember back far enough or imagine ahead and you'll find war—or it'll find you. All our lives are framed by war. My father had wanted to serve in World War II, but because of a damaged eye, could not. He'd wanted to sign up with his best friend, Sidney. The navy was signing up pals for the same ships, same assignments. Had my father had his way, he would have signed up and served with Sidney. Sidney died at Pearl Harbor. Whatever might have happened to my father, with Sidney, aboard the USS *Arizona* would have happened more than four years before my birth. Seventy percent of the ship's crew perished. Are my feelings about these facts and potentialities memory or imagination?

Of my four children, one son served as a force recon marine. He managed to just miss Somalia. All during his hitch, I worried the administration would find some foolish place for my son to go. What was I doing, imagining a possible memory?

It gets complicated. What is remembered or imagined *becomes* reality. And: if we don't create our personal versions of the past, someone else will do it for us. This is a frightening and political fact. How many books, for instance, seek to refute the fact of the Holocaust, complete with footnotes? And who can forget the opening pages of Milan Kundera's novel *The Book of Laughter and Forgetting*, which describe a photograph from which a party official has been airbrushed from history?

Then there is Cynthia Ozick's short story "The Shawl," a strafing account of a death-camp murder of a stick-limbed child. Though born in time to have been interned in a death camp, Cynthia Ozick wasn't; she was, at the story's fictional time, a cheerleader in high school in New Jersey. Memory and imagination are the *what* and *how* we have as artists and readers and citizens. To which we must cling, as if to luck or safety.

In the long haul of history, a stone ax crushing a skull is no different from a Tomahawk missile except in its efficiency. We have as much to learn—perhaps even more—from the *Iliad* as we do from *Black Hawk Down*. War and art have reflected one another forever, and it is this intersection of war and art that the journal I edit—*War, Literature and the Arts: An International Journal of the Humanities*—has sought to illuminate. Over the years, *WLA* has welcomed a range of materials: poetry, fiction, commentary, interview, photography and visual art, critical essay, personal essay, and memoir. I am pleased to offer here select personal accounts from our first twenty years of publication, accounts that confront a soldier's or a loved one's singular solitariness in American wars from the Civil War to the current strife in Iraq. The accounts have

reedited and are arranged in the order of the conflicts to which they
rally refer.

it seems to fall to the historian to make distinctions among wars and
var's larger means and ends, the trajectory for the artist, regardless
ture or time, seems to fall toward an individual's disillusionment,
eans and ends of war played out in the personal. For the individual
er, the sweeping facts of history are accurately written not in the
scient, third-person plural but in the singular first. We live in a cul-
hat values the individual. Our works of art about war mirror this
ne bias.

Of course, art and life are different—if they weren't we wouldn't need
art. And if art generally strains toward making sense, most of us have
lived long enough to know that life is under no such obligation. W. H.
Auden, who came into his fullness as a poet while fascism was creep-
ing across Europe, wrote about that scourge and then concluded that
"poetry makes nothing happen," that nothing he ever wrote saved one
Jew from the gas chambers. Yet, works of art convey authority. Why else
would officials at the United Nations have decided to cover the tapestry
of Picasso's *Guernica* as council members met to discuss the start of Gulf
War II?

At their best, war memoirs testify to the power of word and image and
to the human craving for meaning. And if one of the functions of art is to
disturb the status quo, to force us to view the world anew, to consider our
capacities to build or tear down, then we welcome those disturbances.
This collection would, however, be dismissive of the complexity of the
subject it seeks to explore if it did not reflect John Stuart Mill's notion
that war, although an ugly thing, is not the ugliest of things. More spuri-
ous, Mill instructs, is the person who is unwilling to fight for anything
larger than his or her own personal safety.

Thus, *When War Becomes Personal* includes voices from many perspectives. Tim O'Brien hits the mark when he writes as follows in "How to
Tell a True War Story":

War is hell, but that's not the half of it, because war is also mystery and
terror and adventure and courage and discovery and holiness and pity
and despair and longing and love. War is nasty; war is fun. War is thrill-
ing; war is drudgery. War makes you a man; war makes you dead.

And:

You can tell a true war story if it embarrasses you. If you don't care for ob-
scenity, you don't care for the truth; if you don't care for the truth, watch
how you vote. Send guys to war, they come home talking dirty.

Aristotle's notion that history accretes but only poetry unifies is a notion worth subscribing to. Art grants access to a larger world, allows us
to live other lives, allows us to examine the quality and meaning of our
own lives. Whose very earliest recollections do not include the request,
Tell me a Story? The human race needs stories. We need all the experience we can get. Before we made fire, before we made tools, before we
made weapons, we made images. Art, at its deepest level, is about preserving the world.

Visions of War, Dreams of Peace

In 1991, a collection of poems titled *Visions of War, Dreams of Peace: Writings of Women in the Vietnam War* was published by Warner Books. This poetry was written by women who had served in Vietnam, most of them as battlefield nurses. In a foreword to the book, W. D. Ehrhart (an editor himself of two acclaimed collections of poetry by Vietnam War veterans) praises Lynda Van Devanter and Joan A. Furey for their persistence in assembling women veterans' voices:

When Lynda Van Devanter first told me about this book in July 1990, just about the first thing I said to her was: "I wanted these poems. I tried to find them for *Carrying the Darkness*. Why didn't anyone send me anything?"
"Of course they wouldn't send you their poems," she replied. "You're a man."
"But I'm not that sort of a man," I protested, wounded by her reply.
"Yes, but they don't know that."
What they [the women vets] know . . . is that the U.S. government, to this day, can't even say how many of them actually served in Vietnam. What they know is that the Vietnam Women's Memorial Project has met with stiff resistance from people—men—who keep insisting that The Wall and the three male figures cast in bronze beside it is recognition enough for women. Small wonder that these women wouldn't send me their poems. Thank God or whatever you believe in that they've been willing to send them to Lynda Van Devanter and Joan Furey. . . . These are voices that need to be heard. These are voices we need to hear. The experience of Vietnam in particular and war in general cannot be complete without them.

That the editors and publisher of *Visions of War, Dreams of Peace* turned to a male poet-editor to validate their book in a foreword only punctuates the difficulty women veterans faced in getting their voices heard. Sadly, *Visions of War, Dreams of Peace* is out of print, as is Lynda Van Devanter's fine Vietnam memoir, *Home before Morning*.

Any reader will note that of the thirteen personal accounts reprinted in this volume none was written by a woman. Of course, fewer women than men serve in the armed forces (even at present, women make up less than 20 percent of the total), but there must be additional cause for the disproportionate representation. In twenty years of publication, *WLA* has received a fair number of critical essays and poems by women but virtually no war memoirs or personal essays by women. Perhaps the interview with Joan A. Furey will help move toward some explanation.

Joan Furey served as a nurse in Vietnam, where the war—the worst of war—was brought to her and her colleagues daily. Furey and her peers suffered the consequences of combat—both to themselves and the damaged soldiers to whom they ministered—in a far greater proportion than did the male support troops. (In most circumstances, less than 25 percent of any fighting army actually faces frontline battle.)

Despite the medical corps' daily exposure to carnage, few females later spoke of their experiences, much less wrote them down. Like many WWII veterans, Joan Furey and her sisters kept quiet after their war, soldiering on. Perhaps as time passes, female veterans will more willingly share their stories. Meantime, I am pleased to reprint Joan Furey's interview, first published in 1999. I believe it aptly frames the personal accounts that follow.

—Donald Anderson

WLA: Where and when did you serve in Vietnam?

FUREY: I served in Vietnam from January 29, 1969 to January 27, 1970, in the Seventy-first Evacuation Hospital in Pleiku.

WLA: How long after Vietnam did you resign from the army?

FUREY: I had four months left. I returned from Vietnam and was stationed at Kimbrough Army Hospital at Fort Meade, Maryland. Then I got out.

WLA: I don't think it's been written about much, but in some of the reading I've come across, women in the armed forces serving in Vietnam not only had the enemy to fear, but there was trouble with our own soldiers. Women were vulnerable to assault. How much of this is accurate?

FUREY: Certainly what I can say outright is that during the time I was in Vietnam I don't recall any incidents where people were assaulted. Women—American women—were very few in number. We were surrounded by thousands of men who were very interested in developing relationships with us, so there was tremendous social pressure on us to be entertaining, caring, or to get romantically involved. That, in and of itself, was a degree of stress that most women, by the end of their tour, wanted to remove themselves from. I removed myself early by going on permanent nights. I figured out if I worked nights I didn't have to deal with all the other demands that were around. I should say, though, that some people developed relationships, very solid, caring relationships. It may have been an effective mechanism, too: if you belonged to someone, other people left you alone. Then again, we have to remember it was the sixties, and we didn't talk about issues like sexual harassment and date rape. I can't deny that such pressures existed, but these concepts were not in our social thinking at the time. If women were sometimes pressured into experiences such as I've mentioned, they probably wouldn't have interpreted it the way we might today.

WLA: Not only were women fewer in number, but I would think generally you were outranked as well.

FUREY: Absolutely. The majority of women were first and second lieutenants. I think there has been some writing about the fact that sometimes we were asked by our superiors and then actually helicoptered to parties. To be "the female companionship," or whatever. I think that happened, and, again, we have to remember we are talking about women in their early twenties who might have seen such requests as part of their duties. On the other hand, when you have spent twelve hours in a surgical or intensive care unit dealing with people who've been blown up, or have lost limbs, or are dying, bleeding, crying, screaming—sometimes the last thing in the world you may have wanted to do was to be sociable, to be nice and smile, or to even be with other people. Although to have that kind of attention—I suppose there is an element of attraction to it as well. I don't think there is any easy way to describe social pressures in wartime. I suspect most people who went through it would share my ambiguous feelings.

WLA: The point I was trying to get to was that I think women—their experience and the level of stress they may have experienced in Vietnam—are very, very often overlooked, with a kind of Clara Barton veneer.

FUREY: I'm one of those people who believe, once a nurse, always a nurse. And you bring nursing with you. I think I believe all that I have learned over my years in nursing is a significant part of what I do now. I still do actually have a lot of veteran contacts, helping people deal with issues, so that my nursing knowledge, my medical knowledge, my interpersonal skills, are really credible. I don't think I could do what I'm doing without the background I have.

WLA: How long have you been director of the Center for Women Veterans?

FUREY: Five years.

WLA: Is it an appointment position?

FUREY: Yes it is. It didn't start out that way. Originally I was career VA [Veterans Affairs]. The position I now hold was originally a career position that I was promoted into. Then it became an appointed position when Congress passed a law creating a Center for Women Veterans. I had been the director of the Office of Women Veterans.

WLA: Do you read Vietnam War literature?

FUREY: I do so less now than I have in the past, but I've read extensively. There was a time when Vietnam War literature was all I read. I've tended to move myself away from it more in the last couple of years.

WLA: Can I put you on the spot and ask you your two or three favorite writings from the Vietnam War experience?

FUREY: My most favorite is Tim O'Brien's "How to Tell a True War Story" from *The Things They Carried*. Hands down, it's the one—I don't even have to think about it. For me, the story captures the war experience an individual might have and then the way that person might be moved to interpret the experience later. Phil Caputo's *A Rumor of War* is way up there too, though my selection of *A Rumor of War* may be shaded by the fact that it was the first piece of Vietnam War literature I read.

WLA: It was the first piece a lot of people read. Can I say you've named two pretty "male" books?

FUREY: Yes, but I was about to mention another one, one by a woman, Elizabeth Scarborough—*The Healer's War*. It's a science fiction book.

WLA: Science fiction? About Vietnam?

FUREY: Yes. I read a review about this book, then bought it. Elizabeth Scarborough was a nurse in Vietnam. She is now a well-known science fiction writer. *The Healer's War* is about a nurse in Vietnam and the metaphysical journey she experiences while there. The parts about Vietnam are so authentic that as soon as you read them you know this woman has been there, that she is real, that she has caught it all. Even in the science fiction part, the book has to do with her journeys through the jungle with a GI. I was attracted to Scarborough's book because I really felt it was a psychological journey that most of us experienced with the soldiers.

WLA: How is that science fiction?

FUREY: The characters were on a quest. The nurse goes into the jungle with the GI and they have some magical metaphysical experiences.

WLA: That doesn't sound much different from O'Brien's *Going After Cacciato*.

FUREY: Actually, I was going to say it's a lot like *Going After Cacciato*, from a woman's perspective. The thing I liked about *The Healer's War* was that it drew me into some of the existential dilemmas we faced as nurses in a war.

WLA: Why are there not more Vietnam War memoirs by women?

FUREY: I really don't know why. When Lynda and I were compiling *Visions of War, Dreams of Peace*, we were surprised at all the poetry that became available. Most of the poetry had already been written, but the poets had not shared their work with very many people. They would share it with other women veterans, but that was all. When we decided to assemble the book, we were calling everybody, and since Lynda and I were part of this inner circle of poets, we were calling to say we wanted to create the book. We called to say, "We want to use your poems," and the poets would say, "Fine, just don't use my name." At one point Lynda and I thought we'd end up with a book of anonymous poems. We struggled with that, because we had struggled with owning our own work. I should say that none of us had the idea that we were writing great poetry. We just knew there was a tremendous catharsis and expression of pain we couldn't express any other way. And I think the emotions in the poems were so strong that they scared us. I believe we felt other people would just not accept our perspectives, would see us as being meek or not capable. This is why I think, early on, so many of our poets did not want to be associated publicly with their work. And this is 1989–1990 that we're putting together this book—not 1975. This is *after* the war.

WLA: Fifteen years had passed since the war had ended for most of the poets, twenty in some cases.

FUREY: Exactly. We spent hours on the phone with some of the contributors, encouraging them and sharing other poets' work so that the more timid would see that they really weren't alone in their feelings, in their experiences, in what they were trying to express. Our emphasis was that nothing was out there, and there needed to be something. Lynda and I had gone looking, and the only book we found was from World War I —*Testament to Youth*—by a nurse who'd served in that war.

WLA: How did you know who was writing poetry?

FUREY: Somehow or other we became part of this underground network. Lynda, of course, had published her memoir, *Home before Morning*, so she was a key figure. Lynda and I had served together in Vietnam, and we had kind of reconnected in 1982. I hadn't seen her since Vietnam. I had been writing poetry for some time, and I shared it with Lynda

WLA: But never published it?

FUREY: No. I didn't show it to anybody. I didn't even show it to my family.

WLA: These feelings you're talking about in Vietnam War women vets strike me as parallel to those of the men from World War II who, when they came home, refused to talk about war, their war. "Get on with life" seemed to be their slogan. Vietnam vets, in the eyes of WWII vets, are whiners. I've heard numbers of WWII vets say, "They talk too much." In the reticence of Vietnam women vets is there this parallel to the WWII male combat soldiers?

FUREY: I think that a big part of it was that the majority of women were nurses—nurses in the sense we were from a very traditional kind of nursing education background. Most of us were graduates of three-year hospital schools of nursing. People don't always appreciate what this means. We were indoctrinated with professionalism, the tradition of nursing, the honor, the self-sacrifice—all this stuff was part and parcel of what was engrained into us during those three years in hospital student nursing. One of the things that I think most of us believed was that if we were having any difficulty, it made us less of a nurse—somehow we weren't good enough, or that we somehow hadn't learned all that we should have. We couldn't own the very human emotions of being exposed to high levels of trauma. We couldn't get comfortable with feelings. They were very frightening to us, very confusing. We had expected we would have a degree of detachment and in no way were prepared for the experience of being a nurse in a war. It's not gall bladders and heart attacks. It's young men—your own age or younger. And again, I would like to point out, we're talking about *young* women. I was twenty-two years old, and I wasn't the exception. Most of us were twenty-one, twenty-two, twenty-three. We didn't have a lot of experience, and all of a sudden we were dealing with our peer group of young men who had devastating injuries—had been blown to bits! We were doing things we never thought we would have to do, seeing things we never thought we would have to see. In some ways the experience was incredibly empowering; in others, so incredibly destructive.

WLA: In Vietnam, as in all wars and especially in modern wars, a majority of soldiers never see the front line, yet nurses experienced the consequences of the front line all the time. So the Vietnam experience, considered proportionally, was far more traumatic for a nurse than for the average soldier.

FUREY: I think it took us a while to really understand that. I know now, having worked for many years in the field of PTSD [posttraumatic stress disorder], that one of the things we had to get nurses to understand (and I had to come to understand it first for myself) is that when you're exposed to a war environment, one thing becomes clear to you and that's your mission and your goal: to take care of injured soldiers, to get them better. What we understood was that our patients had given the ultimate sacrifice. When you've been dunked in that fact and believe it, you cannot own your own pain because it seems to diminish theirs. "Nothing wrong with me, look at this guy," you want to say. "Look what happened to him." To heal, you have to get to a point where you recognize and realize that owning your own experience diminishes no one else's. It's a big transition to make, because somehow or other you feel that you are not worthy of finding relief, because you constantly compare yourself to the patients you care for.

WLA: Survivor guilt?

FUREY: Exactly.

WLA: What was it like to come back to nursing in the United States?

FUREY: It was awful. Probably one of the most difficult things that I ever went through was to come back to nursing. All you thought about when you were in Vietnam was coming back to the world, real life. But as soon as you came back and went to work, you realized you were no longer *in* the real world. Vietnam was your *real* world. In spite of all the awful things in Vietnam and your incredibly negative feelings about that war, it was, nonetheless, the most meaningful work you had ever done. There was a real mission in Vietnam. There was a tremendous commitment to what we were doing in terms of care for young Americans and the Vietnamese, these victims of an awful catastrophe. *That* was real. You pulled out everything you had and you did things that you had never been able to do before. All of a sudden you come back to the States and people start putting limits on you, on your practice. In Vietnam, for instance, we would put in jugular catheters because there weren't always doctors available. They were in the operating room. Back home, I was about to start an IV and I was told, "You can't start the IV, you have to get the doctor." "Doctors to do this?" I said. It was people not responding when you made assessments that grated—this denigration of your skills and authority. In my first six months back, I kept having these kinds of experiences. I had a patient—I could laugh now!—she was younger than I am, probably in her forties, who had had her gall bladder removed. I had to get her up to walk. She was moaning and groaning, and my reaction was, "Get a life, lady, get real." In Vietnam, I got people up who had no arms. *They* walked. I got to the point where I couldn't tolerate patient complaints about what to me was minor. At the same time, I knew there was something really wrong about my feelings. I knew that on some level I'd become warped in terms of my measurement of pain and discomfort and a patient's right to not be well. I mean, in order for a patient to legitimately complain he had to lose two legs and an arm? On some level I knew that wasn't right, but I couldn't quite shake it, couldn't get things quite back into place.

WLA: Did it ever get closer for you?

FUREY: It did, but it took a long time. I left nursing for a time. I think a lot of people did that. What triggered it for me was, I was working in a community hospital and was called to ER because a bunch of teenagers had been in a car accident. I went to ER and they brought in these eight kids. It was Vietnam all over again.

WLA: It felt normal to you?

FUREY: I did what I had to do. There was blood everywhere; I was covered with it. We did what we had to do. And when we were done, I just collapsed behind this curtain. I didn't want to see it anymore. I didn't want to feel it. I didn't want to know what was out there. The night supervisor was a nurse who I knew had been a WWII nurse. She was working that night. She saw me. She said, "I just want to tell you one thing. When I came back from World War II, I thought I was going crazy. I thought I was going to have a breakdown. I didn't want to do it anymore. I just want you to know that you're going to be okay." I decided to quit right then. After my shift, I quit.

WLA: What did you do?

FUREY: I went to school. Again, this was at the time the whole world was dropping out and being hippies, but if you came from my background you didn't do that. I had the GI Bill, and I figured I could do that. I could go back to school. I wouldn't have to work in a hospital. I had the GI Bill.

WLA: Was your father in World War II?

FUREY: He was.

WLA: Have the two of you talked about this?

FUREY: It took a lot of years. We did talk about it a little bit. He's dead now. He died in 1989. He was never that forthcoming about his own experiences.

WLA: Where was he?

FUREY: He was in Germany and France.

WLA: During the bad years?

FUREY: Yes. In fact, I'm pretty sure he had PTSD. My mother always told the story about his being diagnosed, but this was before I knew anything about PTSD. When he came back, he couldn't hold a job.

WLA: Was he married before he went?

FUREY: Yes. It was in the eighties when he finally talked to me about his war. We ended up in the most intense conversation we ever had. I finally was talking about what I felt when I left Vietnam—how much I wanted to leave, yet how much I felt like I was letting others down, how difficult it was to make the adjustment. My father had been wounded and had to be evacuated from the front. And he talked —actually teared up—and started talking about how he felt that in being evacuated he was letting comrades down, because by then he was an experienced combat soldier. He'd been wounded and was leaving these war guys—he was choked up about that. That was the most we ever talked about it.

WLA: For the combat soldiers I've known personally who have been affected by war, dealing with authority remains very difficult, holding a job remains difficult, relationships remain difficult. I would think that would be true of most war nurses.

FUREY: I think we see that. I think the data are kind of interesting in terms of formal study, that women who served in Vietnam are much less likely to be married when compared to their peers. They have fewer children. They do tend to hold more jobs. It's all they have. They may stay in nursing, but not in direct nursing. Nurses from Vietnam are much better educated than their non-vet counterparts. They dropped out, like I did, and went to school.

WLA: Are there organizations for the nurse-veterans population?

FUREY: The biggest organization for women who served in Vietnam, and it's not really an organization per se, was the Vietnam Women's Memorial project. It was a project that brought a lot of people together, most for the first time. We dedicated the memorial in 1993, and the ceremony was overwhelming. We got to talk to other people. There was a recognition of the work we'd done. I think this was, and is, a need in general, for both men and women vets. In fact, I have come to see it as being a real key issue. Regardless of whether you feel pro-war, anti-war, or whatever, I think most of us—certainly those of us in the medical nursing profession—felt very good about what we did, about how hard we worked, about how we saved lives; that we were in Vietnam to help people and that we did that, beyond even what we thought was our capacity. When we left Vietnam, we could take pride in having done a good job. Except, you felt like you should feel guilty that you'd been there. One of the things we had to work through was that feeling good about what we did didn't mean that we felt good about the war. And yet, back then, it was, like, if I'm proud of what I did, that means that I'm proud of having been in this war. And there was so much confusion about the war and the purpose of the war that it just seemed like it wasn't okay to feel that way at all. So my heart goes out to a lot of veterans, men and women. I suppose most of us ended up feeling guilty about doing a good job.

WLA: It's very complicated.

FUREY: Very. It's less complicated now than when I was twenty-three and coming back and trying to work through all of this on top of having this really fresh and damaging experience. I was so against the war when I returned that I joined Vietnam Veterans Against the War. This was in New York, and they invited me to attend a rally at a local high school gymnasium. I was to be one of the speakers. As I got up to talk, I was overwhelmed with the sense that I was betraying soldiers.

WLA: But you see now that that's not true.

FUREY: I see that now. I got through my speech, and then I just felt bad. I couldn't take a stand one way or another because I couldn't get to peace with anything. It was a real struggle. I understand today how all those competing feelings can exist in one person, but it was a very difficult time, those first couple of years back—trying to work through your feelings about the war and your feelings about what you did in the war, the feelings about what the war did to you and to all these other people. I'm always amazed that any of us ever survived to go on. I think it does speak to the resilience of human beings, though, unfortunately, not everyone can rebound.

WLA: It seems to me that, given your experience, it would be pretty difficult for you to be other than anti-war. Did the war change your politics?

FUREY: Absolutely. I consider the Vietnam War for me a life-changing and life-defining experience. I became a very different person after the war than I was before. I think that the person who went to Vietnam would probably not be sitting here having this conversation with you if the war had not so readily changed my politics. And it changed me dramatically as a human being. I believe, and hope, that it made me a better person. I guess I believe I'm a better person because of the experience, although I wish my gains, whatever they are, had come in a less painful way.

WLA: I think for a thoughtful, thinking, feeling person, it would be impossible for it to be otherwise. What advice would you have now for yourself at twenty-two?

FUREY: One of the things that has happened to us vets is that we get stuck back there, and we judge *that* person by the values and ideals of *that* twenty-two-year-old. When I was working through my stuff in my thirties, I said to myself, "You have to get this thirty-five-year-old to look at what the twenty-two-year-old went through, to not be stuck in time, and also to realize that what you went through was in fact an aberrant, horrendous experience, that you were placed in a situation that few people ever are placed in. How to mediate the effects of war is the important issue for all individuals who have experienced war. Some people don't ever manage it. Simple as it sounds, we have to recognize that war is an incredibly dramatic and traumatic experience. What you see is extreme, what you're exposed to is extreme, what you feel is extreme, and what you do when you stop feeling is extreme. At some point, the experience has to be mediated. It probably can't happen while you're *in* the experience. It has to happen when you come back, but it can't wait too long. And it's not necessarily going to be short-term.

WLA: What was the most effective coping mechanism for you?

FUREY: I was a workaholic. Well, I probably still am. When things got really bad, I did self-medicate with alcohol, then realized that over the long haul that road would prove too destructive. The best coping mechanism for me came when I finally decided to sit down and talk with somebody about what my experiences had been.

WLA: Friend? Or professional?

FUREY: Professional. I went to see a therapist, a woman in her sixties. I remember walking into her office thinking, "Oh yeah, right, this woman'll understand me." But she was terrific. I would describe my experiences, and she would look at me and then say, "You really think you weren't supposed to be affected by that?"

WLA: Did such acceptance seem new to you?

FUREY: Yes, it did.

WLA: And how long was this after the fact?

FUREY: Twelve years.

WLA: That's a long time. Was it important that you were talking to a woman?

FUREY: For me at that time, I think it was. But I think even more important is that in 1982, I started to hook up with other women who had been beaten up by the war. Up until then, from the time I left Vietnam, got on the plane, and came home, I had never talked to another woman who'd served. People who knew me didn't know I had been in Vietnam. I was a head nurse—that's what I was. That I'd served in the war finally came out when I did an interview in a newspaper. I arrived at work the next day, and my colleagues just said, "Why didn't you tell us?" It was the publication of Lynda's book that had precipitated my interview and my "coming out of the closet," so to speak.

WLA: When was Lynda's book published?

FUREY: 1981, I think.

WLA: So in the meantime you'd been reading about Vietnam?

FUREY: I had started to read. I think I had read *A Rumor of War*, and I went to see *Apocalypse Now*. It was kind of out there, and I did have this obsession about Vietnam. I read Stanley Karnow's *Vietnam*. I was trying to get some mastery over my experience, so I was reading all this stuff.

WLA: Hemingway talked about that—the notion that when you come home from war, you start to read about it and look at the maps.

FUREY: Right. After I started to read, my ability to wall off memory weakened. And when that happened, I began to make contact with other women. That was key. When we sat down, just a group of vets—women vets, not male vets (because with the male vets it was always us and them, and they'd been *in* combat and we *hadn't!*)—we started talking and found we'd experienced so many similar things in our isolated worlds. By then, Lynda had become the central spoke, and we went up and spent a weekend in her house.

WLA: Where was this?

FUREY: In Virginia. We would get together at Lynda's house. Lynda had this big, hundred-year-old house. We would get together, but it wasn't like we knew each other. People had responded to Lynda's book.

WLA: Women mostly?

FUREY: Lynda became this focal point of bringing women together. And then the whole PTSD movement started. We started to go to PTSD conferences. There would be other women. I remember the first conference we attended—the International Society for the Study for Traumatic Stress. It was at King's Island, Ohio, and it was in 1982. Five of us went there. We didn't stop talking. I think I got about three hours of sleep that week. Everything felt so true. All of a sudden, our experiences felt valid.

WLA: I'm thinking of two books—first, Jonathan Shay's book, *Achilles in Vietnam.*

FUREY: I actually have that book. I haven't read it yet. I bought it when it first came out. The book that ran for me was *Healing from the War: Trauma and Transformation after Vietnam*, by Arthur Egendorf.

WLA: Is the author a vet?

FUREY: A vet psychologist who did a lot of work on Vietnam vets. The other book that helped me was *Out of the Night: The Spiritual Journey of Vietnam Veterans*, by Bill Mahedy, who was a Catholic chaplain with the U.S. Army in Vietnam. Have you ever heard of it?

WLA: No, but it's good to get them mentioned. Another book I think may speak to women is Kali Tal's *World of Hurt.*

FUREY: I'd like to talk some about PTSD. Prior to my present job, I actually was a driving force behind opening up the first PTSD treatment program for women.

WLA: Where was this?

FUREY: Palo Alto, California, at the VA. The *New York Times Magazine* made it a cover story in 1993. "How to Bandage a War" was the name of the piece. Laura Palmer wrote it. I'm one of the nurses mentioned in the essay. The essay captures the issue of healing in a way that the general media had not done before, at least to my mind. Let me say something about Lynda's and my book. When you're looking for validation, one of the places you go is to literature. Well, there was none. Because there was nowhere to go, we started searching out women vets who were writing. Although we were interested in literary quality, what was more important to us was that readers would see that women had served in Vietnam, bravely and honorably. Further, we wanted women-vet readers to know they were not alone in their ordeals. One of the more touching experiences Lynda and I had with the book was at the groundbreaking of the Vietnam Women's Memorial Project. General Colin Powell was the keynote speaker. In preparing for his speech, he'd read our book. He mentioned that; then he said, "And I was there. You cared for me." General Powell, as you may know, was awarded two Purple Hearts in Vietnam. In his speech he talked about war for the average soldier being calm, even boring, with episodes of fire and terror. He then talked about the relentless stream of casualties that nurses like us had faced and dealt with.

WLA: It was war every day.

FUREY: It was every day. Wherever the battle, the casualties were shipped to us. So if one soldier wasn't fighting, another one was. Most people probably can't imagine the incredible, incredible carnage that war creates. Even a big-city emergency room doesn't come close to what you face in a war triage area.

WLA: Big cities don't deal in napalm and cluster bombs.

FUREY: Or Bouncing Betties and B-52s. People have no clue. I look at the stuff going on in Yugoslavia, Bosnia, Africa. Whenever I give a public speech, I try to remind Americans that for the Vietnamese it was the "American War" and that the battle was on *their* soil.

WLA: Yes. And we buried some two million Vietnamese, as opposed to our fifty-eight thousand. Since 1941, our blue skies have been unmolested.

FUREY: The truth is, the people have no clue.

WLA: Final thoughts about female Vietnam veterans?

FUREY: When the Vietnam Veterans Memorial was first built, the original design called for only a wall. And the Wall represented many things to many people. It had the names of everybody who died in Vietnam, including women. There was great controversy over the design, although, I think, most everyone felt it was right. Then some folks decided we needed a conventional statue. When the statue was placed, it consisted of three men. I think most women had accepted the wall as an appropriate statement, but once the male-only statue was placed, it required a response.

WLA: The Vietnam Women's Memorial, like the men's statue and the Wall, was manufactured and erected by private funds?

FUREY: Yes.

WLA: Were you part of the fund-raising?

FUREY: I was. Diane Evans, who was the president and the driving force behind the Vietnam Women's Memorial, served at my hospital in Vietnam, as did Lynda Van Devanter. People have said, "What the hell was it in Pleiku—the water?" It wasn't the water. It was the level of activity. We had a very busy hospital.

A Civil War Memoir

When I was four years old, I was with my maternal grandparents visiting my great-uncle, Thomas Sherman, in Gorham, Maine. He was a telegrapher in Washington during the Civil War. He was in his nineties at the time. I sat on his knee, and he related his being in Ford's Theatre and witnessing the assassination of President Lincoln. At age four, this account meant little or nothing to me. Now, as I near eighty, I think back on those events and consider my paternal grandfather, Isaac N. Clements, who was wounded in the Battle of the Wilderness and then taken prisoner by the Confederates. As a consequence of his wound, my grandfather's leg was amputated in prison camp. Despite this loss of a limb and strenuous months as a prisoner of war, Isaac Clements went on to graduate from Wesleyan College, Phi Beta Kappa, and to serve for many years in higher education and administration.

Isaac N. Clements died before I was born. It is through my father, Theron Clements, and through my grandfather's memoir that I have come to know my proud heritage. My grandfather's decision to enter the Conflict between the States rather than enter college is evidence of his devotion to the Union cause. However, it is clear throughout his account that he felt empathy for the Confederate soldier. That he survived his wound and amputation is remarkable, considering the mortality rate for wounded soldiers and the medical care available. So many in my grandfather's circumstances perished. Without question, Isaac Clements's spiritual as well as physical strength played a role in his survival. His courage and perseverance have been an inspiration to me. Spelling, capitalization, and punctuation are rendered as they appear in the original document.

—Alvord White Clements

Preliminary

I was born in Draycutt, a little village near Wells, England, January 2, 1841, of George Clements and Harriet Richards Clements, his wife.

In the spring of 1842, when I was one year old, my parents came to the United States and settled in Sennett, a little hamlet near Auburn, New York.

When I was four years of age they removed to Skaneateles, at which village they remained until I was nine years old.

My first school days were spent in the Primary Department of the old academy building, which stood on the site of the present academy.

In the spring of 1850 my parents moved to a farm which my father had purchased in Tyler Hollow, a settlement in the town of Marcellus, about four miles south of the village of the same name. It was here that I passed my boyhood days—working on the farm in the summer and attending the District school about four months each winter. When I reached the age of seventeen I became desirous of securing a better education than the small District School afforded, and I made an arrangement with my father by which I was to allow him a certain amount each year for my time until I should become twenty-one years old. My father had planned to give each of his sons (of whom he had four) the sum of Nine hundred (900) Dollars when he reached the age of twenty-one years, and thus become by law the master of his own time.

By this agreement between my father and myself, I was to be allowed Four hundred (400) Dollars at the age of seventeen in place of Nine hundred (900) Dollars at the age of twenty-one, thereby allowing One hundred and twenty-five (125) Dollars per year for the four years involved.

I at once entered the Union School in Marcellus Village, walking the four miles morning and evening from my farm house. This I did for two years, scarcely missing a day. In the fall of 1859 I passed an examination for a license to teach school in which I was successful and engaged to teach a Normal district school in the town of Otisco, some four or five miles from my house. This maiden effort of mine in teaching was not a very great success but it gave me some valuable experience.

In the spring of 1860 I entered Cazenovia Seminary as a student. My father carried me with the few possessions that I had to Syracuse, at which place I took the stage for Cazenovia, a distance of nearly twenty miles. I secured a room in the dwelling on the corner of this Village Greene and Nickerson Street, now owned and occupied by Patrick Heffernan. I had as a roommate Edward S. Bowdish, brother of Dr. W. W. Bowdish, now of the New York East Conference. There were five of the Bowdish brothers and they all became Methodist Clergymen. We boarded ourselves for the sake of economy, but it did not prove to be very satisfactory and I soon joined a self boarding club. The term did not prove as profitable as I had anticipated, for after a few weeks I was taken sick with a slow fever from which it took me some time to rally. During this illness my mother came to see me and cared for me a few days. I remained in school, however, until the end of the term but my progress in studies was not much because of my enfeebled condition.

My stay upon the farm during the summer vacation restored me to my accustomed health and vigor, and in the fall I returned to the Seminary ready for hard work. I began to prepare for a college course which I had determined to take, and in two years I was ready for entrance to almost any college.

I thoroughly enjoyed my Seminary life. I formed some precious friendships that have lasted through all these years. I took a positive stand for the Christian life—a step for which I have never ceased to be grateful, for the peace and strength and optimism that this life has given me under burdensome circumstances has saved me from the fate that overtook many I knew.

I graduated in the College Preparatory course in June, 1862, with the full intention of entering college in the fall. During this summer vacation President Lincoln called for 300,000 volunteers to go to the front and shortly this call was followed by another for an additional 300,000. It was supposed, and with good reason, that so many thousands of new men thrown into the field would close the war within a few months. I determined to hold in abeyance my college course, and so offered myself as a volunteer to assist in restoring peace to the struggling nation, after which I should complete my college course as a preparation for life work in whatever line Providence should call me.

This sketch is preliminary to my experience as a soldier.

—I.N.C.

Epitome of the Army life of I. N. Clements, Jotted Down by Himself

Enlisted in the town of Marcellus, Onondaga Co., N.Y., July 29, 1862, in Co. F, 122nd N.Y. Volunteers. I was mustered into the United States Service August 28, 1862 at Syracuse, N.Y. after having been in camp two or three weeks in the southern suburbs of the City.

On the following Sabbath we broke camp, boarded the central cars and started for Washington via New York, Philadelphia, and Baltimore. I can't say that I had thus far enjoyed the life of a soldier. It was a new experience to me to have no will of my own, but I thought of the cause that required it and remembered that sacrifice had always been necessary to accomplish good, and thus came to make the best of it.

On the way we had no opportunity to see New York; took a short stroll in Philadelphia, but did not care to stray far from the regiments; in Baltimore, as we recalled the reception that one of the early Massachusetts regiments had met in this city, we had previously been ordered to load our rifles in readiness for any emergency.

In about three days we arrived in Washington and for the first time began to realize the effects of war in the appearance of the men who were just coming from the field of the second battle of Bull Run. While we were well dressed and tidy, having just come from home, they were worn, browned and soiled with campaign and battle life.

We spent a night and a day in Washington waiting for orders and then started for Chain Bridge a few miles above Georgetown, at which place we pitched our camp. Here began our field and camp life in earnest which did not cease until the regiment was mustered out of service in June 1865. All day the boys were busy selecting positions for tents, laying out the ground, choosing tenting companions, drawing rations, organizing the cooking department, scouting around the vicinity discussing the prospects of the war—in their eagerness to perform some exploit, hoping that peace might not come until they had seen at least one battle, writing letters home full of hope and enthusiasm, and in all things readily adapting themselves to their new mode of life; however, underneath this outward show of activity and cheer there was a feeling of seriousness and foreboding. The change was so great. Some had come from school, some from stores, some from the pursuit of professions, some from trades and the farm. Nearly all had left comfortable homes, and while they looked forward with courageous hearts, they looked backward with yearning thoughts.

That was the first night that we slept on the ground and for months afterward most of us did not pass a night in a house; no matter what the weather was we laid down where we were and slept as soundly as we would have done in a warm comfortable bed. The Ancients said, "Hunger makes the best sauce" so fatigue causes the sweetest and soundest slumber.

We were not allowed to remain and enjoy our quarters, for on the following day we received what were called "light marching orders" i.e., to march with no baggage so as to move quickly, a detail to guard the camp and baggage. We marched with nothing but our arms, ammunition and haversacks, expecting to return the same day or the next. We never came back to that camp and did not see anything for our clothing and such other things as we had brought from home for upwards of a month. We left behind us even our dress coats. I am inclined to think that the order was misunderstood, for after we had marched several miles a detail of men were sent back to bring our blankets to us. While in the darkness of the night we were marching under enforced silence through a piece of wood, a command was passed along in a whisper for us to load our muskets, which caused some to tremble; but a severer shock came to our nerves, when a few moments later as we were marching without a sound except the steady tramp of our feet, the colonel shouted, "Left face! Charge Bayonet." We almost stopped breathing so scared were we with the thought that the enemy was so near us, but it proved to be only a ruse to test us, and we were soon quietly moving on again. Wearied with our march late at night, we laid down beside the road for a few hours rest with not so much as a blanket over us. Being thinly clad and the dew heavy, we were obligated to rise and sit by a small fire that some one had kindled, or walk to and fro so as to keep ourselves comfortably warm. The next day our blankets were brought to us.

Thus we continued for three or four weeks to march in various directions, early and late, in sunshine and rain, through Maryland so as to prevent Lee and his army from passing into the northern states. In about two weeks we touched the Potomac River, opposite Bulls Bluff, where General Baker of California was killed. We encamped late at night, lying in the field pretty much as chance placed us, drenched by a rain that continued all night. Early in the morning, several of us went to a small creek which emptied into the Potomac, undressed, waded into the stream, washed our underclothing and put them on without drying as we expected to march every moment, as it will be remembered that we had no change of clothing with us, all having been left in camp at Chain Bridge. This was simply one of the inconveniences that soldier boys were obligated to undergo. We are getting used to hardship now so that we met almost anything with stoicism.

Our first view of a battle field was at South Mountain about the middle of September. We passed up the mountain side that day after the battle while the dead were still unburied. To us who had recently come from home the sight was sad indeed, and we marched by with averted faces. We afterwards became so familiar with such scenes that we could look on the dead with scarcely an emotion. We continued over into the valley beyond where we remained in line awaiting orders all day and night, and on the following morning we hastened towards Harpers Ferry to reinforce Colonel Miles, but he had surrendered before we arrived. We turned about at once and proceeded to Antietam where a heavy battle between the armies of McClellan and Lee was in progress. We reached the vicinity of the conflict after dark, and rested for the night with no opportunity to cook our supper. We ate a hard cracker and went to sleep not knowing what would occur on the morrow. In the morning we were ordered to take a position in line of battle but we suffered no loss as Lee's forces were re-crossing the river, protected by a flag of truce agreed upon for the purpose of burying the dead and no general assault was made. The next morning we advanced and found that the enemy had abandoned the field, leaving their dead unburied. We passed through Sharpsburg which had been battered by shot and shell, but after pursuing about a mile we turned about and retraced our steps, passed over the portion of the field which had been held by Lee and proceeded toward Williamsport. The field of battle presented a terrible appearance; the trees and fences were riddled with bullets and the dead were scattered over the ground like sheaves in a wheat field and behind the fence by the roadside they lay in rows just as they had fallen from the ranks. They had been lying there two or three days and their blackened appearance was terrible to look upon. We were very glad when we had left the field behind us. We marched to Williamsport, drew up in line of battle in the edge of a wood and for the first time were exposed to the fire of the enemies' guns. A battery was opened upon us unexpectedly and few were wounded by the explosion of shells. After a few minutes we were ordered back out of reach of the guns. The attack was so sudden and so short that the men exhibited considerable terror. We fell back some half a mile and encamped in a piece of woods where we remained a few days. This little skirmish was our first experience of actual battle and many, very many, longed for the peace and quiet of their homes.

After the battle of Antietam and the escape of Lee across the Potomac, our army went into camp for some four weeks for rest and recuperation. We were encamped in an open field and spent the time drilling as thus far we had had no opportunity to learn even the more ordinary movements of battalion drill. This soon became very tedious to us and we longed to be on the move so as to finish up the war and return home, little dreaming what was before us should we be privileged to greet home and friends again. While here my brother Ephraim, who had been with me up to this time, was taken sick and sent to the hospital camp near Alexandria, Va., at which place my brother John found him, apparently very near death's door, but succeeded in getting a discharge for him and carried him home just in time to save his life.

We soon became somewhat used to cooking our own food as the bill of fare was not very extensive (consisting of hard tack, salt pork and coffee), doing our own washing and mending. Somehow everyone looked pretty ragged and dirty. When off duty, the men passed their time sitting in groups, talking of home, criticizing the conduct of war, playing cards, or engaging in other amusements to relieve themselves of the tedium of having nothing to do for so great a part of the time. We spent nearly a month here getting ready to advance into Virginia. During the time southern cavalry passed around us and made a raid into Maryland. Our brigade went up the Potomac to guard one of the forts so as to intercept their return, but nothing came of it and we were soon ordered back to our camp. While here too we had an opportunity to see Abraham Lincoln who came up from Washington to review the army. He appeared about as the pictures represent him.

About a month after the battle of Antietam we were again moving south and crossed the Potomac at Berlin, a few miles southeast of Harper's Ferry. The Southern army fell back as we advanced. Little of importance occurred until we reached the vicinity of Fredericksburg on the Rappahannock. During this march General McClellan was relieved and General Burnside was appointed to succeed him. This did not please the older soldiers who had been with "Little Mac" as they called him, on the peninsula. The exposure, the water or the climate did not agree with me, for I was troubled with diarrhea, that disease so dreaded by and so fatal to soldiers. I drank tea made of cloves, which helped some. During these marches the men were accustomed to stray from the ranks, visit the houses along the way and procure whatever they could of food to supplement the regular rations of hard tack. Wheat flour, mixed in water and baked in pork grease, we considered a very good substitute for griddle cakes. Occasionally we helped ourselves to sheep, pigs or chickens as we could find them.

One or two such instances will serve as illustrations. One afternoon we encamped in a grove near New Market, Virginia for the night or longer, if necessary. Soon after pitching our shelter huts, word was brought to us that there was a herd of sheep in a field in the rear of the grove. My cousin and I started out to see what we could find. When we reached the open fields we saw a number of soldiers driving the sheep into a corner and we immediately joined them. When the sheep were cornered every man seized one, killed it and proceeded to dress it, but just at this time one of the Aids of the General appeared on the scene and ordered us to desist, leave the sheep and return at once to camp, which most of the men did. But I walked slowly along the fence until the Aid was out of sight, then I returned selected the plumpest sheep I could find and in company with another man dressed—divided it—and I returned to camp with my share. I found that a guard had been placed around the camp whom I eluded—and hid the mutton in my hut. As a result we lived on fresh mutton for some days.

On another occasion my mess mates and I had a dinner of chickens that were intended for the table of our Brigadier General. One day for some reason I had become separated from the regiment and was traveling along beside the supply train, when I observed three fowls tied together floundering under one of the wagons. After the wagon had passed over them and before the next wagon reached them, I darted into the middle of the road and seized them—slung them over my shoulder and trudged on. After an hour or two as I was passing the headquarters wagon that contained the equipment of the General—those in charge of the wagon called out to me. "Here, those chickens belong to General Shaler", to which I replied, "No they don't, they are mine, I found them in the road," and passed on, keeping the chickens. When I overtook the regiment my mess mates dressed and cooked the fowls, indulging in a meal fit for the gods. We subsequently learned that the chickens had been purchased at a farmhouse by the General's cook, tied together and placed in the wagon for safe keeping from which in their struggles they had flopped out. The General's loss was our gain.

In a few days the southern army had fallen back and taken a position on the south bank of the Rappahannock in the rear of Fredericksburg. The intention was to cross and attack immediately, but there was a delay in forwarding the necessary supply of boats for pontoon bridges, which gave the enemy an opportunity to fortify themselves. Hence, when on December 13th the battle of Fredericksburg was fought it was impossible to drive Lee from their strong position on the hills overlooking the city. After an ineffectual effort of two or three days our army retreated over the river, having suffered a loss of about fifteen thousand men. Though this was a hard fought battle, no advantage accrued from it to the Union Cause. Both armies now encamped on the heights of the river, facing each other for rest and recuperation. The soldiers of the Union Army laid out their camps in regular streets and made preparations to remain during the winter, but after a few days we were ordered to break camp and march up the river a few miles for the purpose of crossing and getting in the rear of Lee. On the day we started it began to rain and the roads soon became so soft that the artillery and supply trains could not be moved and after floundering in the mud for a day or two, we returned to camp.

The army was in a demoralized condition, but it had the satisfaction of knowing that the enemy could move no more easily than we. Each side was comparatively safe from attack. This attempt to move was known as the "Burnside's Stick-in-the-mud".

Now we settled down for the winter, though we had nothing to protect us but our shelter tents which we had carried on our backs during the marches thus far. Nothing unusual occurred during these winter months while we were encamped at Falmouth, opposite Fredericksburg. There was much sickness from exposure and lack of self care. Many died and by the Spring of 1863 our numbers were largely reduced. Many also deserted as there was great discouragement among the soldiers and they did not find the life that they were then leading the pleasant pastime that they had anticipated before leaving home.

At this time Gen. Burnside was relieved and Gen. Hooker succeeded him. Hooker was familiarly known as "Fighting Joe", and with him as leader the hopes of the men again revived. The winter seemed long but Spring came at last and with it preparations for an active campaign. About the first of May, the men "struck tents" and began a move against the enemy. The main part of the army, except the sixth corps to which my regiment belonged, proceeded about ten miles up the river, crossed and took up a position at Chancellorsville, which was in the rear of the main Southern army. The sixth corps, commanded by Gen. Sedgwick, remained behind to take the heights above Fredericksburg, and advance for the purpose of forming a junction with Hooker. The troops entered upon the campaign with high hopes, which, however, were doomed to disappointment. The sixth corps crossed on the morning of May 3rd, I think, and took possession of the city of Fredericksburg and its inclined plane in the rear of it. A charge was made up the plane where the Irish Brigade was so nearly destroyed at the battle of Fredericksburg. I had the privilege of standing with several others where we could witness the charge as it was made. The men advanced over a rising plane for some three quarters of a mile in the very face of constant fire from a line of men posted behind a stone wall and from a battery on the hill, but the men never wavered, notwithstanding the gaps that were made in the ranks by the horrible fire to which they were exposed. In a few moments they had scaled the wall, climbed the steps, captured the height and sent the enemy flying, but at the cost of many a precious life.

The corps pressed the enemy back four miles, but were then [met?] by the advance of a large force from Lee's main army. Sedgwick's men were in a perilous position, as they were in danger of being crushed by the overwhelming force of the enemy who had then concentrated nearly forty thousand men. The sixth corps of less than eighteen thousand men held the position against these fearful odds for some thirty hours and then retreated to the other side of the river under cover of the darkness, leaving this southern army in possession of the field. The loss on our side in this advance and retreat was more than a third of the whole number, the killed, wounded and prisoners being upwards of six thousand, five thousand.

During this battle I was detailed to assist in caring for the wounded and we turned some of the finest houses in Fredericksburg into hospitals for this purpose as the owners of these mansions had deserted them and fled. When we found that the army was to retreat we transferred the wounded back over the river [and?] made field hospitals for them on the northern side. In two or three days we moved back into camp again. This ended the battle of Chancellorsville—well planned but poorly executed and attended with heavy loss to the Union Side.

While in the City of Fredericksburg I took from a library of one of the houses which we turned into hospitals, a copy of the Complete Poetical Works of Sir Walter Scott. I afterwards sent it home as a momento of the Battle of Fredericksburg. I prized the book very highly, nevertheless I lost it by fire at the time the Boarding Hall of Chamberlain Institute, Randolph, N.Y. was burned. I was teaching there at the time.

We again had rest for several weeks while both armies were making plans for a vigorous summer campaign. After three or four weeks it became evident that General Lee was meditating an aggressive movement to the North and in the latter part of June we were ordered to break camp and move toward the Potomac. It was soon learned that Lee was invading the free states by way of the Shanendoah Valley with the intention of transferring the scene of active warfare. We proceeded North on a line nearer Washington so as to thus stand between it and the Rebel Army until we passed into the northern part of Maryland. These marches were long and severe and many men fell out of the way being unable to endure the strain. On the 1st of July, 1863, the Sixth Corps, footsore and very weary, was near Manchester, Carroll County, Maryland; we heard cannonading to the north of us in the direction of Gettysburg and to our experienced ears it foretold the deadly strife. As we were about to lie down to rest for the night, the bugler sounded the call to pack up and be ready for the march. At about nine o'clock in the evening we started on what proved to be the march to the battle of Gettysburg. Weary and lame with the long marches from Fredericksburg, Va., we proceeded all night and nearly all the next day, traveling about forty miles before we reached the field of battle, not even halting long enough to cook such provisions as were in our haversacks. It was almost the only march during my whole army life in which I was unable to keep up with the regiment. Marching continuously for so many days had blistered my feet so that I took off my boots, carried them in my hands and attempted to walk barefooted, but was unable to keep with the company. I found I could not travel without boots so I put them on again and limped along to the best of my ability, overtaking the company while the regiment was resting preparatory to taking position in the line of battle, where we were sorely needed.

About four in the afternoon the corps took the position assigned to it on the left of the army where the Union lines were gradually being pressed back. Being in the hospital service at this time I was attached to the field hospital just in the rear of our lines, which had been located near a running stream. We worked very hard during the third of July caring for the wounded as they came, or were brought to us. About noon of this day occurred one of the most memorable charges of the whole war. It was the Charge of Gen. Pickett's Brigade, of Longstreet's Corps, against the Center of Meade's army. A fierce cannonade of almost the entire artillery of the Rebel army had been concentrated on the point of attack for some time previous to the charge of the infantry under Pickett. It was vigorously replied to by the artillery of the Union Army. One can scarcely imagine the grandeur of this Artillery duel, just previous to the charge itself. The roar of the cannon—the whistle of the shells—the shouts of the men—the clouds of smoke—the carrying to the rear of the wounded—the hurrying forward of reinforcements, all conspired to produce a scene never to be forgotten. Then came the charge of Pickett's Division against the center of Meade's army. Thousands of men advanced in solid array, leaving the ground strewn with the fallen. Grape and shell thinned their ranks and when they neared the line of Union troops the fire of the infantry received them. The Southerners fought like heroes but it was to no avail; they could not break the Union line. Many were made prisoners and the reminant fled to their own lines in confusion. This charge practically ended the battle which had been raging for three days with a loss to each of nearly thirty thousand men.

During the night Lee withdrew his army and began his retreat into Virginia. The following morning, July 4th, as soon as it was ascertained that Lee was retreating, the Sixth Corps under Sedgwick, which had not suffered so severely as some of the other corps, was ordered in pursuit. The mountain passes which could not well be carried by assault were held by Lee, so we were obliged to pursue by a circuitous route, and near the close of the second day, July 6th, not far from Frederick we came to the Tetucton mountains, which we attempted to scale by a narrow foot path. Darkness came on, a heavy rain set in, the narrow path was almost impassible from large stones, the men were completely exhausted by continuous marching and the large share of them sitting down fell asleep by the side of the path. A few of us only reached the top of the mountain and then sat down beside a stone wall to pass the night as best we could until morning. It was a night to be remembered; the wind blew; the rain fell; the thunder roared; the lightning flashed and we were chilled through and through. Little sleep came to our eyes. About ten o'clock next day those who had fallen asleep on the side of the mountain came up and we continued our march down into the valley in which was situated the village of Middletown, but Gen. Lee and his army had passed by and we failed in our attempt to cut them off from their line of retreat.

Our corps pursued as far as Williamsport on the Potomac River and then finding that the Rebels had succeeded in recrossing the river the immediate pursuit was abandoned.

During the progress of the battle of Gettysburg, I was on a detail to care for the wounded, one circumstance especially is worthy to record, wounded from both sides were placed under our care, and while there two men died—a Union solider and a Rebel. A young man and myself volunteered to bury them. I proposed to lay them side by side in the same grave, to which no objection was made. I claimed that for them death had solved the question and they were no longer enemies to each other but brothers whom the hand of death made equally deserving as the last sad duties were performed. So we laid them away side by side as tenderly as we could to await the resurrection dawn, well knowing that loving hearts would long for their coming in vain. The Battle of Gettysburg made desolate thousands of homes. It was, however, the turning point in the war and has been called the "High water mark of the rebellion." Lee retreated south through the Shenandoah Valley with his army and Meade followed East of the mountains until he reached the vicinity of Culpepper where the two armies rested watching each other.

During this pursuit I was taken with typhoid fever and sent to the hospital in Washington City. I remained in the hospital, which was situated on the plains east of the capital building, about two months and was then returned to the regiment which was encamped in Virginia, not many miles from the Rappahannock River. One day while at the hospital I visited the City of Washington which I found very muddy and dilapidated in its appearance, very different from the same city of today.

On the 7th of November (1863) the fort at Rappahannock station, on the river of the same name, was taken by assault which allowed the army to cross the river and encamp at Brandy station and in the vicinity of Culpepper. Our regiment had a part in this move, having marched some eighteen miles in four hours and was immediately placed in support of a battery, in which dangerous position we lost several men by the explosion of shells fired from the fort at the battery, one of which came dangerously near myself. Nothing of importance occurred until the 26th of November when the army moved to Mine Run, in the vicinity of the wilderness south of Rapidan, with the intention of attacking Lee but after lying in line of battle for two or three days, during which time we suffered much as we were obliged to lie on the frozen earth, we retreated rapidly by night and returned to our old camp. It was found that Lee's army was too strongly intrenched to be attacked with any hope of success. We then settled down to what we supposed would be our winter quarters.

Early in January, 1864, however, our brigade under Gen. Alexander Shaler was detached from the army of the Potomac and sent to Sandusky, Ohio for the purpose of guarding the rebel prisoners on Johnson's Island, situated about three miles from the shore. It was rumored that as soon as the lake should be frozen over so as to bear the weight of men, a party would cross from Canada and rescue the prisoners. Our brigade was sent so as to prevent a rescue in case an attempt should be made. No attempt at rescue was made, however, but the brigade remained there on duty until the ice broke up in the spring.

During this stay of three months in Sandusky the 122nd Regiment had a restful time, as it remained in the city and simply took care of itself while the other regiments of the brigade were stationed on the island where the prisoners were confined. At times I was called to special duty in the care of the sick and one of my patients was a man who had been taken with the delirium tremens. He was very wild, being terrified by imaginary snakes, other animals and little devils that were after him. I tried to show him that they were not there but he insisted that they were and as they were after him they would not touch me. After a few days he escaped from the house unobserved and was seen no more. When the surgeon made his round that morning and learned the facts about the man's escape he wrote opposite his name "Gone to the devil" and we let him go.

In April we were ordered back to rejoin the army which was soon to make another move against Lee. Nothing important occurred during our return to Virginia, and we arrived at Brandy station, where the army was encamped, the latter part of the month. The army was making preparation for a move across the Rapidan into the region of the wilderness, behind which Lee was encamped with his army. I knew the nature of the work that we had to do, the great danger into which we must go, and presentment hung over me that something would happen to me. I could not shake this feeling off. Sometimes "coming events cast their shadows before". This seemed to be the case in this instance.

On the 5th of May everything was ready for the move and the army started across the Rapidan, the Cavalry taking the lead. The brigade to which my regiment belonged was detailed to guard the supply train as it crossed the river in the rear of the army. The train was well over by night and we encamped with it about one mile from the river and in the rear of the field in which the troops had been fighting during the day, as Lee had marched very promptly and attacked Grant in the flank as he was moving south and a severe engagement had followed in which neither side had apparently gained much advantage. We had heard the roar of the battle all day, but had not been near enough to observe it at all.

Soon after midnight we were quietly aroused from sleep and ordered to march to the field of battle which we reached about daylight, probably in the neighborhood of four o'clock in the morning. As we advanced to take our place in the front we passed over a portion of the field on which fighting had taken place the day before. The ground was strewn with the bodies of those who had been slain, their pale faces looking ghastly in the twilight of the morning and causing a chill to creep over us as we passed with the feeling that we might very soon lie among them. In a short time we turned to the right into the dense woods, and at the same time the artillery of the enemy opened sending the shells crashing through the branches of the trees, cutting off limbs larger than one's leg, causing a panic among the officers' servants and camp followers, most of whom disappeared through the bushes in the rear. We were marched some distance through the wood until we reached the entire right of our line, an extension to which we made, thereby forming the extreme right wing of our army. This was a mistake as there should have been a troop of cavalry pushed still farther into the woods so as to prevent a flank movement to our rear. We remained here, slightly changing our position a few times until about nine o'clock. Our arms were stretched a portion of the time and we were allowed to sit upon the ground and chat if we chose. Of course, our conversation was largely upon the progress of the battle and what might happen to us in the very near future. The thoughts of most instinctively turned to those at home whom many were destined never to see again, yet at this critical time there was no shrinking for you could see by the expression of the faces that all were determined to unflinchingly meet the responsibilities of the hour—let what would come. About nine o'clock, as nearly as I can remember, we were ordered to take and fix bayonets and advance. We at once knew that we were making a charge for we passed through the skirmish line, some of the men joining us and some remaining behind. It was difficult for us to keep anything like a correct formation on account of the logs, stumps, trees and underbrush, nor for the same reason could we see far ahead of us. As we were thus advancing suddenly a fierce fire poured upon us from the bushes in front of us, which checked our forward movement and the regiment 126th Ohio, joining our left was temporarily thrown into confusion and fell back a short distance, thereby causing the left of our regiment to retreat so as to prevent a gap being made in the line of battle. As the line was reformed every man sought shelter behind a tree, stump, log or other cover, so as to be protected as far as possible from the shower of leaden hail. I myself immediately sprang behind a tree somewhat larger than my body, and began to fire into the bushes in front of us, though I was unable to see any of the enemy. While thus engaged a ball grazed the bark of the tree just above my head, cutting a groove about the size of my finger. Shortly after dropping on my knee, so as to steady my musket in firing, a ball passed over my shoulder, bedding itself in my blanket which was strapped to the top of my knapsack, and protruded above my shoulder. This bullet would doubtless have entered my body and possibly have ended my life, had I not happened to kneel for the purpose of firing just in time to escape it. These incidents convinced me that some one could see me and was making a target of me. It was by the favor of Providence that I escaped. At this time looking forward from my position, I noticed Joseph Jones, one of the members of my company, lying on the ground about two rods in advance of the line as then formed. He had evidently fallen while we were falling back to take our new position. I could see his lips move as if calling to us, though I could hear no word on account of the noise of the musketry. I knew that he must be wounded and was calling for assistance, so I left my protected position and went out to him though becoming thereby doubly exposed between the two firing lines. I found that Joe, as he was familiarly called, had been shot through the thigh, shattering the bone, and desired to be carried to the rear out of danger and for medical treatment. His request could not be granted as we were forbidden to leave the ranks, even for the purpose of carrying back the wounded. I, therefore, returned to the line of battle, went to the head of the company where the captain was stationed, asked his permission to carry Mr. Jones to the rear. The captain sent me to the colonel. Proceeding along the line to the colonel I obtained his permission and returned to my company for the purpose of carrying it out. The firing was still incessant along both lines of battle.

I again stepped to the place where Mr. Jones was lying, unstrapped his blanket from his knapsack, spread it on the ground, rolled Mr. Jones up in it, obtained the assistance of three other men of our company and each of us taking a corner of the blanket, raised our load and proceeded to pass through our line of battle to the rear, but just at this moment the order came for the whole line to retreat and we carried Mr. Jones with us, thus saving him from falling into the hands of the enemy.

After withdrawing beyond the reach of the Confederates' fire, the regiment halted, drew up in line of battle again, and rested with arms ready for instant use.

Our little company of four continued to carry our wounded comrade to the rear for some distance until we came to a wagon track, by the side of which we laid him to wait for the arrival of the ambulance by which he was later taken to the field hospital where his leg was amputated and subsequently he was conveyed to the general hospital in Washington,

D.C., at which place he died a few days afterwards as the shock and the exposure was too much for his system to endure. The Joseph Jones Post of the Grand Army of the Republic at Marcellus is named in his honor.

The charge was disasterous to us, as our regiment lost some seventy in killed and wounded in the few minutes in which we were actually engaged.

After placing Mr. Jones by the side of the wagon road, we returned to the company which was resting on the ground in line of battle ready for any emergency that might arise. There was skirmishing in front of us, and fighting in some other parts of the battle line, which extended some five or six miles to the left of us but nothing of importance occurred to us until towards evening. Some of us snatched a little needed sleep even on the line of battle.

Perhaps it will be excusable in me to insert here an incident that oc-curred during this charge that indicates the character of some of our of-ficers, and how incompetent they were to lead men. When we were halted by the fire of the Confederates, as was perfectly proper every man sought to protect himself as best he could. In our part of the line Lieutenant Wooster one of the bravest men of the regiment who was afterwards killed at the Battle of Cold Harber, noticed a number of men huddled in a confused mass behind a large tree. He immediately approached them and commanded them to get into line, using force to carry out his com-mand. When he came to the man next to the tree, he found that it was the Lieutenant Colonel of the regiment who was clinging to the tree with both arms, trembling and in a frightened state of mind. It was not all surprising the men followed his example. After returning home this of-ficer became a worthless wretch through indulgence in intoxicating li-quors and died an inmate of some institution. Liquor was the curse of many of the officers and caused the sacrifice of many valuable lives. On the first day of January 1864 as I returned from picket-duty, I found one of our sergeants lying dead drunk in my tent which made me indignant and I immediately removed him to another tent. As a result I think he disliked me ever afterwards. This is a digression but it illustrates in too many instances the kind of officers under whom we served.

About six o'clock in the afternoon we were ordered to fall back and oc-cupy a line of breastworks that had been thrown up behind us during the day. We accordingly took possession of the temporary works, stacked our guns and laid aside our knapsacks, expecting to hold the works during the night. Permission was given to two or three men from each company to pass a few rods to the rear of the lines of battle for the purpose of making coffee, as we had been given no opportunity to do this for our company. We gathered the coffee and pails from the various members of the company, and passing back through the battle lines, of which there were three behind ours as I remember, selected a place near a small stream in which to build a fire for the boiling of coffee. We had kindled the fire and placed the pails of water on the coals and were about to put in the coffee, when there rang out on the evening air, a signal given on our right, and almost immediately this was followed by a yell from the same direction, mingled with the rattle of musketry. It was at once evident that a charge was being made upon our lines. The two friends with me ran to the regiment, one of whom I never saw, as he was soon lying among the slain.

I quickly snatched the pails from the fire so as to return them to the owners, but before I could do this and reach the company our line had given way and all were in a confused retreat. I turned in the direction of the retreating men as there was nothing else to do. All was confusion and no one knew what to do. Many seemed to lose their presence of mind, and while rushing to the rear loaded and fired their guns into the air or over their shoulders into the midst of their own men behind them. Many must have been killed or wounded by the men of their own side. Some threw away their guns and knapsacks so as not to be hindered in their flight. Finding that I could not rejoin my company I began to consider what I should do.

The bullets were flying thick and fast. One cut my canteen string and my canteen fell to the ground. It was lost as I was in too much of a hurry to stop and pick it up. My gun, my knapsack containing my clothing and my haversack with my rations were also lost as I had left them with the company when I volunteered to make the evening coffee. After a moment's thought I decided to throw away the pails and supply myself with such equipment as I could secure from those thrown upon the ground in a place of those of my own left with the company.

I accordingly threw down the pails, picked up a well filled knapsack and haversack, strapped them to my shoulders, and also a musket, so that I again had the large part of a soldier's regular equipment, though I was entirely unaware of what it consisted.

Passing along in the drift of the confused crowd, I came to a foot path down which I turned towards the left and soon reached a small clearing in the center of which stood an old log cabin. In this open space I observed that a line of battle was being formed under the direction of Colonel Hamlin, who was the Commander of one of the regiments in our brigade. I immediately took a position in this line which was intended to act as a check to the advance of the Confederates. Scarcely had I taken my stand when the enemy's line burst out of the undergrowth in front of us and our line broke and again retreated. Instead of keeping with our men as I should have done, I turned toward the log cabin, and just before reaching it a ball struck my left leg just above the ankle. Attempting to step upon it I found that the bones were shattered and that I was unable to rest my weight upon it at all. Not having fallen, and being near the door of the cabin, I hopped on my right foot to the door and beginning to feel faint, laid down upon the floor at which moment the Confederates reached us making prisoners of many men who had taken refuge within and behind this building. Observing that I was wounded they left me as I was and firing a volley after those of our men who were still fleeing, they themselves turned and disappeared in the underbrush of which they had shortly before rushed.

Being left alone in my wounded and disabled condition, I began to consider what I could do for myself. Observing that my leg was bleeding profusely, I took one of the straps that fastened the blanket to the knapsack and buckled it tightly around the wounded leg above the knee, so as to check, as far as possible, the flow of blood. Darkness coming on and lying as I was between the two armies I realized that no immediate assistance would be likely to come to me so I tried to make the best of my situation until the morning, trusting that then relief in some form might come. I was aware that another wounded man was somewhere in the cabin as I could hear his moaning but I could not learn who he was or how badly he was wounded; I never knew what his fate was.

The hours of the night dragged wearily along, as in my pain I could obtain no sleep and only one incident occurred to break the monotony. Sometime during the night the troops of Burnside's Corps, the ninth, marched by, having been ordered from the left of the army to reinforce our shattered line. I spoke with some of the men and asked for a surgeon to examine my leg. They replied that no surgeon was near but assured me that I was within our own lines, and would be cared for in the morning. The line soon passed by and I was again alone; but the coming of the men cheered me and helped me to wait patiently for the day for I believed that my leg would then be looked after and I myself taken to the field hospital. Day finally began to dawn and just as it was becoming light enough to distinguish objects, I saw a rebel skirmish line advance out of the brushwood and it soon passed the little cabin in which I was lying toward the ground occupied by the Union Troops. I then realized that I was within the Confederate lines and was a prisoner of war. The Confederates saw me as they passed the cabin and I heard them say, "There's a 'Yank' in there", but they did not molest me. As the hours passed occasionally one would look in at the door as they were passing to and fro. I sometimes asked them for water which they usually gave me if they had any and once or twice they kindly filled a little pail which was standing on the floor beside me, so that I could drink whenever I desired for I suffered somewhat from thirst, from the fact that I had bled profusely from my wounded leg. The hours of the morning dragged wearily away without special incident until about midday, when an Aide of one of the Confederate Generals came into the cabin and remained a while. He was apparently waiting for someone. While there he asked me some questions as to whether General Grant was in command of our army, how many men we had, etc., etc., to which I replied indefinitely as my knowledge of those things was not very accurate.

I asked him as to the probability of my being picked up and cared for, to which he replied that their surgeons and ambulance men were gathering up and looking after their own wounded and after this had been done they would gather up and look after the wounded of the Union Army. I admitted that it was to be expected that they would [take?] care of their own wounded first. After he had waited some time, a man, who appeared to be a scout, came into the hut and reported to him that he had been into the woods beyond their lines and had ascertained the position of the Union forces, who were strongly posted and throwing up breastworks. The Aide-de-camp inquired about the scout's companion who had gone out with him. The scout replied that in taking their observations they had crept near to the Union lines and had been discovered by some of the northern soldiers at which they both ran, but a volley was fired at them. He saw the friend who went out with him fall and he supposed that he must have been killed. These two men then went away to report to their superior officers what they had ascertained.

Some time after the middle of the afternoon four Confederate soldiers came in bringing a stretcher upon which to carry me back to the place where the wounded were being gathered. These men were very considerate in their treatment of me. I asked them to cut the boot off the foot of the wounded leg. One of them suggested that they take it off without cutting as it would be a pity to spoil so good a boot, but I replied that the condition of my leg would not allow the boot to be drawn off, so it was cut off and the leg thereby relieved of the painful pressure.

The bullet which shattered my leg was found in my boot and I carefully placed it in one of my pockets and so preserved it, and brought it home with me to be laid away and kept.

I was then laid upon a stretcher which the men placed upon their shoulders and proceeded to carry me toward the rear of their lines, so that an ambulance could take me to the spot where the wounded were being gathered. Having carried me some half a mile they came to a heavy line of battle strongly posted behind breastworks. In front of these works I was laid on the ground in company with a number of others as it was expected that an ambulance would take us farther back. Two or three Confederate surgeons came and looked at us, and I requested them to examine my leg to see if anything could be done for me, to which they replied that they did not have their instruments with them and consequently could do nothing for me.

While lying here a rapid musketry fire was begun in our front and it seemed that an assault was about to be made upon that position by the Union men, and in that event there would be no hope to escape from death for those who were lying in front of the breastworks, but fortunately for us the advance was checked before it reached us and thus our lives were saved. The men who held the line, seeing our exposure when a lull came in the firing, lifted us over the breastworks and placed us a short distance in the rear in much less exposed position. Here we had an opportunity of talking with some of the Confederates, and one of the first questions asked us was, "Why do you'uns come down here to fight we'uns?" One man told us that Grant had been beaten and was retreating to the other side of the Rapidan, and that if he ever crossed again with his army they would not take a prisoner, meaning of course, that

every one falling into their hands would be put to death, which predic-
tion, however, would not have been fulfilled, but General Grant was not
beaten and was not retreating as the sequel proved, so that the truth of
his words was not tested.

A Confederate noticed that I had a watch cord and desired to purchase
my watch, which I sold to him for about fifteen dollars in Confederate
script, but the money proved to be counterfeit and was of no use to me. I
hope that my watch was of service to him.

About ten o'clock at night some ambulances came in to remove us to
the rear of the field of battle, where the wounded were being gathered.
Two of us were laid on the floor of one of the ambulances as we could
not sit up, and in this way we were carried one or two miles through the
woods, pouncing over stones and roots and logs, so that we were nearly dead when we reached the field hospital, as we had then been lying
over twenty-four hours uncared for and our wounds had become greatly
inflamed so that the slightest motion was very painful; but all things
have an end so our slow torturing ride was finally finished. I was laid on
the ground and my knapsack, which had been placed in the front with
the driver, was placed beside me, but not until most of its contents had
been taken out. Perhaps they thought that I should have no use for the
clothing and such other articles as it contained. I certainly never missed
them, as I did not know what the knapsack held as it was one I picked
up on the field while retreating, but that did not excuse the men who
took the articles but I suppose that some consider everything fair in
war. When I had been laid upon the ground several Confederate soldiers
crowded around me and offered to give me opium to relieve the pain but
I declined to take it as I preferred to endure the suffering rather than become stupefied. Thus I passed the night, getting no sleep and wondering
what the coming days and weeks would bring me. Frequently, during the
night I observed men with torches moving about among the wounded,
apparently caring for them, and occasionally they passed where I was lying. As they did so I would look at them and usually ask them to render
some little service for me, such as changing the position of my leg so as
to ease it somewhat, which they willingly did.

When morning came and the wounded awoke they found that they
had been robbed of money, clothing and almost everything they possessed. The Confederates, under the pretense of relieving suffering had

given opium to the wounded the night before, thereby putting them to sleep and during the night had robbed them of their possessions. My refusing to take the opium and my consequent wakefulness saved me from being robbed.

It was now the 8th, the second day after I was wounded and the two armies had moved toward the south and was battling for the mastery at Spottsylvania. As a consequence the surgeons and the nurses had been ordered to follow, and we wounded were practically left to care for ourselves. There were several hundred of us and so far as I remember only one or two surgeons for the whole number, and that too not withstanding many were severely wounded and needed immediate attention. As a result many died who would have lived had they received proper care. The less severely wounded brought water and did what they could to relieve the worst cases.

I was lying on the ground unable to move and my limb was becoming worse every hour, in being more swollen and inflamed; yet, I could do nothing. Thus another day and night passed. The third day brought no relief and no attention from the surgeon, who however, was doing all in his power to meet the demands upon him. On this day however, one of the slightly wounded men undertook to care for the wound and spent about an hour endeavoring to remove the exudation that had dried on the limb, and the worms that had already been produced in the wound by the action of the flies which were very busy whenever opportunity offered. Nothing, however, of lasting benefit could be done for the wound in the absence of the surgeon to either cleanse the leg and set it or take it off as the need should require. Thus the third day passed and the fourth day came when it became evident that something must be done or my life would be the penalty, as my strength was rapidly diminishing and in a short time I should be unable to endure the necessary operation. One of the men able to walk informed the surgeon of my critical situation and he came, examined the leg and ordered me taken to the operating table which was a few rods distant. When placed upon the table the surgeon asked me whether I would be willing the leg should be taken off in case he decided that it could not be saved. I replied that I was willing. I was well aware that the mortified condition of the leg would not permit its being saved. Upon this chloriform was administrated and I became unconscious. When I regained consciousness, I observed a man standing at my head who remarked that I had become conscious and asked the doctor whether he should administer more chloriform, to which the doctor replied that I was too weak to endure it. I then became aware that the leg had been severed and they were about to tie the arteries. I heard the surgeon remark to those assisting him that there was an unusual feature connected with the arteries in that there were five in a cluster. After the arteries had been taken up and the necessary stitches taken—processes which were exceedingly painful—I was carried back and placed upon the ground where I had lain before. I was very sick and weak from the effect of the operation and chloriform, from which it took me a long time to rally.

Three days passed without my limb being dressed or even examined, and it was becoming very painful. I then induced one of our own wounded men to remove the bandage and see in what condition the end of the limb was. It was found to be swollen, badly inflamed and filled with worms. He kindly spent a long time in removing the worms and cleansing it, after which it felt easier. Thereafter I cared for the limb myself. A small tin pail of water was kept standing by my side with which I kept the end of the leg moist, so as to keep down the inflammation. I had just two bandages, one of which was washed and dried while the other was bound over the end of the leg. The exchange was made each morning at which time the limb was bathed and cleansed as well as I was able to do it. I was fortunate in having in my pocket at the time of my capture a small pocket mirror which I still retained, and with this I could examine the end of my leg and thereby know its condition and progress day by day. During all these days we continued to lie on the ground under small shelter tents, which served as a protection against the rays of the sun, but did not keep us dry when the rain was heavy which frequently happened. At such times we simply remained until we dried out as we had no change of clothing.

Lying next to me and using the same blanket for a cover, was a soldier of the 126th Regiment from Ohio. He had been wounded in the ankle, yet such was the condition of his leg when he was cared for that it was found necessary to amputate his limb above the knee. He gradually grew weaker and died after a few days. Before dying he gave me the name and address of his wife and requested me to write her the circumstances of his death should I live to be exchanged and return home. A promise which I fulfilled and gave the wife the first definite information as to the circumstances connected with her husband's death while a prisoner of war.

The days here dragged wearily along. We had very little to eat, and that not at all suitable for persons so severely wounded. What little was furnished us consisted of coarse, unsifted cornmeal, mixed in water and baked in a dutch oven in the ashes and coals of a fire built on the ground. The mixture was not more than half cooked and so we could eat only from the outside which would frequently be burned while the inside would be raw. As a consequence it produced diarrhea in the case of many of us which aided in rapidly thinning our numbers, while discouragement and homesickness caused many to give up hope and they were soon laid away in unmarked graves. I induced one of the men who could be around to procure me some white oak bark and steep it for me over the fire. I drank the solution and it was of some benefit to me. Having a small amount of money, I sent to a farm house, distant about a mile and procured a quart of sweet milk for which I paid the sum of one dollar. This I had boiled and I drank it while very hot. This had the desired effect and the trouble was checked for the time being, though it returned again later. While I remained in these woods I wrote three short letters home. We were allowed to write one face of a half sheet of note paper, and the envelope was to be left unsealed so that the letter could be examined by the proper authorities before being passed through the lines to make sure that nothing objectionable should be told. Of course I wrote very briefly—simply that I had been wounded in battle, captured and had lost my left leg by amputation; that I hoped to live to be exchanged, etc., but nothing as to my treatment and lack of proper care and nourishment, lest the letter should not be allowed to pass. The three letters were all received at home at the same time some two months after they were written.

About two weeks after we were captured, some thirty of the prisoners who had been less severely wounded and had partially recovered so that they could walk somewhat comfortably, left in the night with the intention of escaping to the Union lines and thence to Washington, a thing which they accomplished after various hardships. Among the number was Sereno Smith, a member of my own company, and from the same town. During the day previous to their departure, he told what was to be done and I gave him a message to my father and mother in case he should reach home in safety, which he delivered to them. This was the first reliable information that they had received as to what had happened to me as in one report of the battle I had been reported as "killed," and in another as "missing". No definite information could be given as I had been separated from my company at the time I was wounded and was drawn up in line among entire strangers.

One man, Uriah Moore, of my company was near me at the time, but he was captured and died in prison but no one knew when or how as little was heard of him save that he was captured and never returned home.

During these days it was difficult for us to keep clean and some had little ambition to do so. "Eternal vigilance" was the price of cleanliness and comparative freedom from being overrun by the parasites called lice. Every day I turned my clothing inside out and carefully examined every seam so as to be sure that none were being harbored there. All were not so careful and suffered accordingly. I also had in my pocket a fine comb which I used faithfully every day and thereby I kept myself comparatively free from vermin which preyed upon the strength of life of so many of the men in their sickness and weakness. We were somewhat buoyed up with the thought that possibly some scouting Union cavalry might find us and see that we were taken to our lines, but the days and nights dragged their weary hours along one after another and many became discouraged with hope delayed and every day and every night made our number less. Out of some three hundred wounded men gathered together at the close of the battle, about one hundred fifty only remained alive at the end of four weeks, on account of exposure, lack of care, and insufficient and unsuitable food; yet, amid it all there was scarcely any complaining, every one enduring the inevitable with courage and fortitude. What was in the hearts of those heroes, who thus wasted away amid strange scenes away from home and loved ones, only the Book of Life when opened will reveal.

The end of our stay here came at last. On the third of June, nearly a month after I was wounded, some ambulances under Confederate drivers came from Orange Court House for the purpose of taking away such as could be moved. A few of the worst cases were left, but these were taken to Alexandria a few days later by some Union men with ambulances. However, even this did not save all of them. On June 3rd, 1864, nearly all of those still living were loaded into Confederate ambulances and we started toward Orange Court House, Va., some twenty miles distant. We were not reluctant to leave this place in the woods when we had passed nearly a month with so much suffering.

It consumed a good part of two days in traveling this twenty miles to Orange Court House, spending the night by the roadside on the way. As we were very hungry and had little to eat, we helped ourselves to corn on the ear which the teamsters were carrying along [for] the mules. Though this corn was hard and dry it seemed as if nothing had ever tasted so good, so we cracked it between our teeth.

Nothing eventful happened on this trip to Orange Court House and we arrived at our destination sometime during the 5th of June, and we were unloaded at the railroad station where we were to take the train for Gordonsville, a few miles distant, which we reached a little before evening; and we were taken from the cars and placed in long buildings lined on either side with rude wooden bedsteads on which were coarse ticking filled with straw for beds. Being placed on these we tried to make ourselves as comfortable as possible under the circumstances. We remained here for some two weeks. We fared somewhat better here than in the wilderness, but that which was given us to eat even here was not calculated to give much strength to our weekened frames. While in this place I was told that some two miles in the country, milk could be purchased at one dollar per quart. Though I had but very little money I sent a dollar for a quart of milk for I was very anxious to boil it and use it as a medicine to check another attack of diarrhea, but imagine my disappointment to discover when it came that it was only buttermilk and I dared not use it at all. I could have cried, if I had allowed myself to do it, I was so disappointed and so discouraged. One day as we were lying on our so-called beds, some ladies came into the building and began to talk to the men. When they came to where I was lying something in my appearance caused one of them to ask me whether I was a Yankee, and upon my saying that "we were all Yankees," they ran out as if they were fleeing from contagion. They had entered supposing that we were wounded Confederate soldiers and as soon as the mistake was discovered they fled.

In about two weeks we were again placed on board the cars and carried to Lynchburg. Arriving at Lynchburg we were transferred to buildings formerly used as tobacco warehouses. There being so many men to be provided for, and the buildings assigned to the use of the prisoners not being sufficiently large to accommodate all, a few of us were placed temporarily in one of the buildings occupied by the Confederate wounded. Here we were fairly well cared for during the few days we remained. The southern ladies came into this building every day to bring delicacies to their own soldiers, but they paid no attention to the Yankee prisoners. It was a very hard thing to lie and see others near you eating delicacies, which you yourself could not touch, though you stood in ever so great need of such to nourish you: But such is war. In a very few days there was room for all of us in the buildings assigned to the prisoners, as every day some gave up the struggle and were laid away under the green sod, to await the final roll call and we were transferred and placed with the rest of the Union prisoners. We were placed upon straw beds placed in rows lengthwise of the room, there being four rows, if I remember correctly. We continued our struggle for existence and our members diminished daily, for there was nothing to encourage one, as we could not learn that there was any prospects at all of our being paroled or exchanged. No agreement could be made as a basis of exchange, because of the negro soldier, while the National government at Washington would not agree to an exchange of prisoners unless the negro were placed on an equality with white men.

As a consequence thousands wasted away and died, that would have lived and recovered, if they could have been nursed in the northern hospital or in their own homes. The room in which I was placed was on the second floor, and scarcely anything occurred to vary the monotonous routine as the days went by. We could stand a distance from the windows and look out, but we could not put our heads out of the windows to look about, under penalty of being shot by the guards who were posted around the buildings. One of the prisoners, a young Irishman, looking out of the window, saw a young lady in a window across the street and attracted her attention. In some mysterious way they became interested in each other. After some days the young lady sent a slave girl over to the prison with a note for the young man. The father of the young woman discovering what was going on, shut the girl up and flogged the slave, and so the clandestine correspondence was suddenly brought to an end.

Our living while here consisted of coarse corn meal made into what we northerners call "Johnnie Cake", but without baking powder, without shortening and without salt, and of course, it was about as hard as a brick bat. Occasionally a small piece of meat was served, but it only made us long for more. This kind of diet did not give us much strength, nor very buoyant spirits. We relieved the tedium somewhat by making light of it, and telling of the excellent dishes our mothers used to make. In adverse circumstances, recalling the past and hopefully talking about the future, are certainly great gloom dispellers.

About this time many of the wounds became infected with gangrene either from lack of proper care or on account of the exceedingly hot weather, and mine was one of them. I have always thought that my limb became infected on account of lack of sanitary care, as the attendants were careless about cleansing the dishes and wash cloths. At any rate, at a time when my limb was almost healed, the stump became infected with gangrene, and in a short time it was in a worse condition than when first amputated. The operation of cauterizing, or burning out the wound was very severe and I was held on the floor by the attendants while the surgeon did it. I begged him to amputate the limb higher up, so as the remove the affected part, but he said that I in my weakened condition could not endure the operation and I now believe that he was right. Thanks to a kind Providence the progress of the disease was checked and after the end of my stump had sloughed off, uncovering the bone, the wound began again to heal, but the progress was very slow and it took weeks to recover the ground lost by this attack of gangrene. Almost every attack of this kind proved fatal, and I cannot account for my own recovery in a way short of God's goodness in making effectual the means employed, and I have always been exceedingly grateful. Diarrhea again set in on account of the corn meal diet, and although opium was prescribed in large doses as a remedy it became chronic and never ceased until long after I reached home. During these weeks of prison life, no news of the outside world came to us, only as it came through Confederate sources, and, of course, the facts were much distorted. We knew nothing of the progress of the war except such as the attendants would give us, and that would always be in favor of the Confederates. Once only a gleam of hope came to us. When we heard cannonading in the vicinity of the city and learned that some Union troops were attacking the place, but our hopes of release were soon dashed to the ground as the Union forces retreated without gaining an entrance. It was Hunter's troops that made the attack, but Hunter proved an incompetent General and his expedition failed. Many, many lives were sacrificed during the war because of incompetent Generals. In midsummer, a few of the stronger prisoners were selected and sent to Richmond for exchange. To one of these I gave the name and address of my father, with the request that he write my father in case he got through the lines, as to my condition, surroundings and hope of living to get home.

He wrote as requested and my parents thus learned of my whereabouts and circumstances. At times during the imprisonment plug tobacco was issued to the prisoners. I took mine and gave it to some person that was a user of the weed, as I had never learned to use it in any form. I looked at it sometimes and wondered whether it would satisfy the cravings of my stomach, but I never tried it.

As the summer wore away many of the men grew weaker and weaker and our numbers became fewer and fewer as death took this one and that one, until all could be accommodated on the first floor and those of us on the second floor were moved down to the first. Here some of the conditions to which we were subjected were very unwholesome. There were no closets in the building. During the day the men were allowed to pass out and around the building inside the line of guards to attend to calls of nature, but during the night the doors were locked; a large tub made of one end of a hogshead was moved into the room and the inmates were obliged to use this whenever necessity required. The stench during the whole night was enough to make one sick, and yet there was no escape from it.

The early part of September an order came from the Confederate authorities in Richmond to send to that place for parole all that could endure the journey. The surgeon in charge passed around the room examining the men to ascertain who were strong enough to be sent; when he came to me he told that he did not think that I could endure the removal and so had better remain for the present. I replied that I was constantly growing weaker and the sooner I could get away the better it would be for me. He said that the weather would soon be cooler and that with the ending of the hot season I would begin to grow stronger and I could then be sent forward. So he marked me as one to remain; but after he had examined two or three others I called him back and begged him to allow me to be taken. He yielded to my entreaty and placed me among the number to go. This gave us all new courage and hope. We could scarcely wait for the dawn of the next day when we were to start. The time came at last and we were placed in ambulances and taken to the depot, to await the arrival of the train. The train, however, did not come during the day nor during the night and we endured the suspense and anxiety of those twenty-four hours of waiting as best we could, with nothing but the hard floor in which to lie. During the night, several, among whom I was one, were taken worse, produced, I presume, by the tension of the situation. As a result the surgeon made a reexamination of the men and selected a few to be returned to the prison. I was one of them, and as I was being carried back I felt as if all hope of life had gone out. The future looked all black without a single ray of light for my last chance had failed. This feeling influenced me to such an extent that for some time I could not recuperate from the recent attack, but in a few days I began to regain my wonted courage.

In about a week another order came from the authorities in Richmond to forward for exchange all that could be moved from their beds. The surgeon in his rounds of examination to select those who should go, placed my name among those who were to be taken, and you may well imagine that the hope of exchange gave me strength for the journey. In the morning of the day on which we were to start for Richmond, we were carried to the railroad station to wait for the coming of the train. We were not obliged to wait a long time. We were lying around on a station platform in a nervous condition, fearful that something might happen to interfere with our getting off. Of course, in our weak condition every little thing disturbed us. After a time, which seemed long to us the train came, we were placed on board, and so began our journey to Richmond. The seats in these cars were the usual upholstered ones and were comfortable. Nothing special occurred on the trip to Dansville, Va., which place we reached somewhat after noon, though I have no recollection of the exact time. At Dansville we were obliged to be changed to another train, and as I could not walk I was carried on the back of a large stout Confederate, and placed on board the new train. My only baggage was an army blanket.

This new train was a poor one, consisting of box cars with only boards for seats, which made the ride a very hard one for such as were not strong enough to sit up. I shall never forget the journey. Not being able to sit on the seats, and there being no opportunity to lie down, I supported myself as best I could between two seats, partly resting on a side of bacon that had been thrown on the floor, resting my elbows on the seats on either side of me, holding my limb in my hands to prevent its being jolted against the floor. Though nearly five months had passed since amputation the leg had not yet healed, making it necessary to keep the end from coming in contact with anything. The bed of the railroad had become much worn and badly out of repair so that the cars swayed and jolted as we passed along, keeping one constantly on the quivive lest he should lose his equilibrium. On the way the Confederate guard on the car desired to exchange blankets with me, which I very foolishly did without looking to see how they compared in quality, and as a result when I was taken to the prison hospital in Richmond a blanket was brought to me literally full of holes, which I repudiated with fervor and insisted that mine was a better one and to pacify me, I suppose a better one was brought to me. However, it would have made no difference to me for a few days afterwards, when paroled, everything I had was burned and new issued to me. Well like everything else in this world, this hard, nerve-wearing journey finally came to an end and at about ten o'clock at night we pulled into Richmond. We were laid out on the station platform to wait for conveyances to take us to the prison hospital. The platform which was exposed was wet from a recent rain, and the night air was damp and chilly which made our stay at the station very uncomfortable. In attempting to crawl a few feet I was rounded up by one of the guards and I told him that I should not attempt to escape.

In time we were taken in vehicles to the hospital where we were to remain until the steamer called the "Flag of Truce" should be ready to take us to the Union lines on parole. We were all grievously disappointed because we were not able to be placed on the "Flag of Truce" at once as we had been told that we were being taken to Richmond for that purpose; but for some reason the steamer "Flag of Truce" had left that morning not waiting for us, so there was nothing for us to do but wait for the return of the boat and no one knew just when that would be.

The room in which I was placed was on the second floor and would hold about fifty cot beds. The cot on which I was placed was in one of the interior rows, overlooking the James River and on which the steamer "Flag of Truce" made its trips, and from my position I could see the dock to which this boat was moored while taking on its cargo. Every morning as soon as daylight appeared, I looked anxiously toward the river and every morning for two weeks I was disappointed as no boat with a white flag flying at its masthead appeared; but I must not anticipate, for I must tell of my life for the time I was confined here.

In the morning after our arrival, a physician with an attendant passed around, taking the names and regiments of the new comers, making an examination so as to ascertain the physical condition of each one and when necessary prescribing medicine. There was not much variety in the rations issued. Soup was sometimes brought to us but I did not dare take it, as it was evidently only the water in which the meat had been boiled, with scarcely any seasoning. My appetite was gone so that I could eat very little, though I was very much in need of nourishment. The physician prescribed some medicine for me which I regularly took, but I do not remember what the prescription was. It did not seem to help me as I was continually growing weaker.

From four to eight daily gave up the struggle and their places were immediately filled by the sick who were brought from Belle Isle in the Potomac River where so many Union prisoners were confined.

The physician made his round every morning to ascertain how the men were faring and one morning after I had been there four or five days, he stopped at the foot of my cot, and looking at me intently asked the attendant what my prescription was. Upon being told he said, "Give him iron." I know that that was simply to give strength, and usually was one of the last things prescribed, all of which did not add to my courage.

About the first of October an attack was made on Fort Harrison by the Federal forces in an effort to break through the Confederate lines. The attempt failed. Many were killed and wounded on the side of the Union. The wounded were made prisoners and carried into Richmond. A wounded man, a sargeant from a Maine regiment I think, was placed on a cot next to mine. He was severely injured. The spinal cord in the small of his back was severed and his body was completely paralized. He knew that his case was hopeless; that he could live only a short time, but he did not repine, he simply expressed a desire to live until he could be paroled and so have the satisfaction of dying under the "Stars and Stripes." I believe that Providence often times grants the earnest wishes of his children, and so in this case the solider lived to be carried on the steamer,

"New York," which was the "Flag of Truce" boat on the Union Side, and just as he was on the steamer under the floating folds of the "Starry Banner" his spirit took its flight. The soldier's prayer was answered.

On the morning of the sixth of October, about two weeks from the time I had been taken to Richmond, as I awoke and looked toward the river, I saw a white flag flying at a steamer's masthead and I knew that the boat for which I had longed had come. Immediately all were in excitement and you cannot imagine the joy that was in the faces of those men as they realized that the hour of deliverance had come. Everyone began to pack his little belongings for the trip. Soon the physician came in to take the names of such as he decided should go. I was exceedingly nervous fearing that there might be some slip in my case. When the surgeon had examined me, had consented to my going and had put down my name, I was so eager that I could not wait for the nurses to take me out as my time came, but excitement adding strength, I managed to get myself to the door, and sliding from step to step on the outside stairs reached the ground where the ambulances were gathered to take us to the wharf when the boat was moored. I was like a child and had no control of my feeling. In due time we reached the river and were carried on board. When all were loaded the boat began its course down the stream to the point at which we were to disembark and be conveyed in ambulances about three miles to the place below where the Union boat was lying. The boats could not meet because a large number of torpedoes had been placed in the river to prevent the Union gunboats from passing up near enough to shell the city of Richmond. Though on the boat and actually passing down for parole, my nervousness did not leave me as I was constantly haunted with the fear that something would happen to prevent my getting through. It now seems so foolish for me to have been so but I certainly could not help it then. At the time of disembarkation I had the same restlessness to get off that I had to get on, and I was among the early ones to land and be placed in the ambulances that would take us to our own boat. The ride of about three miles to effect the transfer was made without any delay and we were carried on the steamer that would convey us to Annapolis, Maryland. The difference in the appearance of the two boats was very striking. The Confederate boat was unkept and the men were laid around on the desks, in many instances with nothing under them, while the Federal boat was clean and tidy, the decks were covered with cots on which were mattresses and white spreads, bespeaking care and comfort. When I was placed on one of these there came to me such a feeling of peace and rest, impossible to describe, for the gloom of five months of prison life was ended and we should soon be in our well furnished hospitals, looked after by experienced surgeons and nurses, and in communication with our own homes from which no word had come since the day of capture.

After becoming adjusted to my cot, looking around the deck I observed attendants passing around ministering to any that needed attention and here and there a surgeon giving directions. Attracting the attention of one of the attendants, I told him I wished to speak to one of the surgeons. When one came to my side I asked him for some brandy as a stimulant for I felt very weak and exhausted, and he very kindly ordered some sent to me which was the very thing needed after such a day of exertion and nervous tension.

The attendants [then?] passed hard tack to the men but I said that I could not eat them, and inquired whether a piece of soft bread (for that was the name we used to distinguish common bread from hard tack) could be found for me, and as you can well imagine, nothing that I had ever eaten in my life seemed so good as that. After this I soon sank into a quiet slumber and when I awoke I found that it was morning and we were anchored off Annapolis, Maryland, the place of our destination.

During the early part of the day we were taken ashore and carried in ambulances to St. John's College buildings, which were then being used as a hospital for paroled prisoners, as buildings used for that purpose were overcrowded. Immediately after our arrival at the hospital, every person was given a thorough bath, all clothing of whatever nature was taken away and burned and new clothes were distributed, as the medical authorities would allow nothing that had been used in the Confederate prisons to be retained, less some contagion should arise, and it was certainly a very wise precaution. After the bathing and the putting on of new garments we felt like new men, and we really were new men on the outside.

It is scarcely possible to imagine the relief and rest that came to me after the long months of imprisonment with its deprivations and anxieties to find myself among friends and sympathizers, and able to get in communication with my home. Not a word from home had come to me in five months and, though I was exceedingly anxious to hear the joy was not unmixed with sadness from the thought of the changes that might have come to pass in that time. Yet, as you might as well suppose, I at once wrote a letter home and I did it with my own hand so as to avoid conveying the impression that I was too sick and weak to do it. Lying on my side, I wrote a few lines with a lead pencil, telling of my arrival and how I was situated. Most of the letters sent home by the paroled men were written for them by the hospital attendants, but I could not bear that any hand but my own should pen the glad news that I was out of prison and hoped to see them before many weeks.

We were all regularly examined by the surgeon to ascertain our condition and the kind of diet that would be best for each one, for it was necessary to keep a strict watch over the appetite of all. It was not safe to leave men under such circumstances to follow their own desires or inclinations, and in fact, the authorities were obliged to put a guard over the refuse or "swill" barrels, as they were commonly called, to keep the men from devouring the contents for such was their ravenous hunger that they could not refrain from helping themselves to what would have been injurious, and often times fatal. Every precaution was taken to prevent men from doing themselves harm, as they would not hesitate to do in their weakened condition, both physical and mental.

One case coming within my own observation will show the condition in which many were found. On the cot next to mine was placed a man belonging to some regiment from Maine. When in health he must have been a man of good size and frame over six feet tall, but the hardship and neglect to which he had been exposed had made him so emaciated and weak that he could do scarcely anything for himself. His long hair was full of lice which were taking the very life out of him. His hair was cut, his head was cleansed and he was properly cared for, but even under treatment he was too weak to rally, and after one or two days of suffering the end came and he added one to the thousands and thousands who had yielded up their lives under similar conditions. I was placed on a diet of oyster soup and that constituted the bulk of the nourishment given while I remained.

After three or four days, my brother Ephriam from home came to see me to ascertain what could be done for me. He remained a few days, but as I could not be taken home on account of my weakened condition, and as I was well cared for to which he could not add anything of material advantage, he returned home. I was to follow as soon as I was strong enough and could get a furlough which I hoped would be in a few weeks. I gradually improved for a few days, when a new batch of paroled men came from Richmond, and to make room for the new arrivals a number of those already there were taken from the room in which we were and placed in a hall which was not properly heated. As a result I caught cold and became worse so that I was in a serious condition. Writing a letter home to this effect caused my mother, in company with my brother Thomas, to come to Annapolis to see what could be done, but before they arrived I had been returned to the room from which I have been taken, and consequently was more comfortable again. My brother Thomas returned home leaving my mother with me until she could take me with her. Having my mother with me was a great boon, and kept me from discouragement. She was admitted to a home established for the benefit of mothers and wives who should come to look after the interests of those who were dear to them. This home was free of expense to those who were entitled to be admitted. There were many women there who had come on the same errand and not a few arrived too late to be of any assistance except to soothe and cheer. Many a touching scene occurred between mother and son, wife and husband as a son or husband was taken.

My mother remained several weeks spending most of the days at my side, but I did not gain very rapidly; I longed to be home, for somehow I had conceived the idea that only home life would cure me. I could not shake it off. We tried to get a furlough but the authorities said that I could not endure so long a journey and refused to grant it. In order to accomplish my purpose I demanded my discharge which could not well be refused as I was absolutely disqualified for further service. My discharge having been procured about the 29th of November, 1864, my mother and I started on our homeward journey. Soon after taking the train I became exceedingly sick and we were obligated to remain over night in Baltimore. With others in like circumstances we were provided for at the Christian Commission House which had been established for just such emergencies as this. Being in great distress I was given a hot sling which in time gave me relief and I fell into a deep sleep from which I did not awaken until morning. I have heard my mother say that several times during the night she came to my cot to see if I were still breathing, for she was alarmed at my lying so quietly.

I was somewhat better in the morning and after resting during the day, we took a sleeper in the evening for Elmira, which place we reached next day without special incident. We remained in the depot at Elmira several hours waiting for the train to Watkins (then called Jefferson, I think) as my transportation ticket was by way of Seneca Lake. Only one incident do I recall while we were waiting at Elmira. An old man who was selling home made molasses candy offered to give me some, which I felt obliged to refuse as I dared not to eat it. However, this little act gave evidence of a kind heart. My mother procured a cup of tea for me while here from a neighboring restaurant and she was required to deposit a small sum of money for the safe returning of the cup and saucer which was given back to her on the return of the dishes. This requirement was a proper safeguard.

About four o'clock in the afternoon, as near as I can remember, we took the train for Watkins, which was a very slow train for it took a long time, some two hours I think to go twenty miles. Arriving at Watkins we took a steamer for Geneva at the foot of the Lake. On our way down the lake, being somewhat overcome by the trip, my mother procured a hot gin sling which gave me strength for the remainder of the journey. At Geneva it was necessary to transfer by omnibus from the boat landing to the railroad station. We found a sister of charity on the pier waiting to receive us as we landed. As she saw me she exclaimed, "You are the one I am looking for." She immediately placed me in a hack with my mother and we were driven directly to the railroad station. She reached the station soon after we and she proceeded at once to make me comfortable. She brought me a piece of pie which I was unable to eat and when she learned of my condition she brought me a bottle of blackberry cordial, gave me a dose and insisted that I keep the rest for future use. No mother could have been more interested in my welfare or have done more for my comfort than this sister. In some way she had learned that a wounded solider was on board the steamer and she was at the wharf at its arrival to see what was needed. She was a type of a multitude of women who gave their time and service to the welfare of the soldiers in hospitals and elsewhere during the latter part of the war thereby saving the lives of hundreds.

In due time the train from the west arrived and we were placed on board. My mother and I expected to spend the night in Syracuse and complete the journey home the next morning, but when we came to consider that we were to pass through the station at Marcellus to reach Syracuse, we decided that we would stop at Marcellus station and endeavor to get someone to take us to the village which was distant about two miles. The public stage did not meet the night train for Rochester and we had no way of getting to the village at that time, except by securing some private conveyance. We reached the station between ten and eleven P.M. We were disappointed in our hope that some conveyance might be at the station on the arrival of the train. Being unable to secure anyone to take us to the village, we were obliged to remain in the waiting room of the depot all night. My mother sat looking after my welfare as best she could, while I passed the hours getting what rest I could on the hard wooden benches, which was very little indeed. In the morning at the hour for the first train from Syracuse my brother Ephraim came with a horse and carriage as he had done for several trains before that had come from Syracuse, but he did not meet the trains from the west as they did not expect us to come from that direction. Our friends at home had been expecting us for one or two days but they could not tell upon what train we might arrive, and as a consequence, had been driving for one or two days to meet the train.

Home at last after an absence of two years and three months, filled with labor, fatigue and suffering. No one can imagine the feeling of relief and comfort that came to me when I was again under my father's roof; the very consciousness of it gave me new vigor and life.

As I anticipated, home was just what I needed to enable me to improve. I was in want of no physician but simply the home atmosphere with all that it implied. Though extremely weak and emaciated I soon began to grow stronger and put on flesh, I had been without sufficient food for so many months that no amount of food would satisfy me and seemingly I was just as hungry after a meal as before, consequently it was necessary for me to exercise a great deal of self control in refraining from eating more than I might, as suffering was sure to follow any indiscretion in this respect.

Reaching home about the first of December in the fall of 1864 it was nearly spring before I was able to get out of the house very much. However, when physical strength began to return, courage and cheer came back for long bodily weakness had depressed my spirits. The coming of spring with its mild pleasant weather gave me an opportunity to be much in the open air and as a result I began to grow stronger more rapidly. The summer months were spent partly in the village of Marcellus and partly on the farms of my two older brothers who resided about four miles south of the village, doing light work which increased my strength and improved my health.

I then began to consider what I should do for my life work, as I had practically given up a college course. I thought of fitting myself as a bookkeeper in some business concern, of teaching school, of becoming a musician, etc., but none of these callings appealed to me without more education. My brother Ephraim had learned photography and had brought a gallery in Syracuse. He invited me to enter the business with him which I agreed to do as he was very confident that it would be profitable. However, after a few months I concluded that there was not enough in this enterprise for two and my brother took the entire business for himself. This ended my first business adventure.

While still unsettled as to my future, I made a short visit to my school friend M. P. Blakeslee who was then on his father's farm in Perryville and he carried me to Cazenovia, where I remained two or three days visiting among former acquaintances. This return to the village where I spent two pleasant and profitable years in the Seminary revived my old desire to go to college and I went back home with that purpose in my heart. I immediately hunted up the Latin and Greek textbooks that I had used in my preparatory work and began a review of the requirements for entrance to college. My years of demoralizing army and prison life had unfitted me for mental effort, and I found my self-imposed task decidedly up hill work, but persisted, even against the advice of friends, and in September of 1866, in company with a young Irishman, John Welch by name, I turned my steps toward Middletown, Conn., to enter the freshman class of Wesleyan University. Perhaps I ought to say in this connection that I had become so strong in my determination to take a college course, that I refused the proffer of the nomination for School Commissioner on the Republican Ticket, which was equivalent to an election in that district, and I have never had cause to regret the choice I then made.

We went to Middletown, via New York going from Albany to New York on the night boat and from New York to Middletown, Conn., the next night on the boat running between New York, and Hartford, thus giving us the privilege of spending one day in New York which we improved in looking around. The city was then small compared to its present size. We reached Middletown about three o'clock in the morning, and, as I remember, as we were walking through the main street in this city wondering what we should do, we found a meat market open which we entered, sat down and waited for the morning light. When day had fully dawned we went to the waiting room of one of the hotels and remained until a suitable time to proceed to the college grounds. In due time we made our way to the office of Dr. Cummings, the President of the University, and were shown our rooms which had been previously assigned to us.

The entrance examinations which all were obliged to undergo were held that day. They were oral in charge of the teachers of the various departments, the candidates entering one department after another until he had made the round. As four years had passed since I had finished my preparatory work in the Seminary, I suffered in comparison with those who were fresh from Seminary life, but I managed to pass the ordeal without any condition except the requirement in plain geometry for which I was profoundly grateful.

I was obliged to work very hard on account of the long period that had elapsed since my Seminary days and my record for the first term was not very high, my standing putting me about the middle of the class, but then having gained better control of my mental faculties, I began to do better work and gradually gained in my class standing so that at graduation I stood ninth in rank among the thirty-eight who completed the course, which I regarded as very creditable.

I became a member of the "Mystical Seven", which, during my freshman year was transformed into a chapter of the Delta Kappa Epsilon fraternity and it is now one of the leading fraternities in the University.

I was Principal of the High School in Plantsville, Conn., during the winter of my Junior year and during the winter of my Senior year I taught three weeks as Principal in the High School in Cromwell, Conn., in place of John Welch, a classmate, who returned to college to review with his class the work of the term so as not to fail of graduation with the other members of the class.

During the spring of that year I made an arrangement with Dr. James T. Edwards, Principal of Chamberlain Institute at Randolph, Cattaraugus Co., N.Y. to teach Mathematics and German in that institution the next year, the duties of which I began in the fall. I remained in this institution three years and then accepted the position of Professor of Greek and Latin in the Cazenovia Seminary. I entered my duties in Cazenovia in August, 1873 and remained in the institution in various capacities until 1896, as Professor of Latin and Greek until 1884, at which time I was elected President, which position I held until 1896.

During this academic Year, 1877–8 there was an epidemic of Typhoid in the Seminary, which came very near closing the doors of the institution. Though this was not done the number in attendance became so few that the Seminary became greatly embarrassed financially. On account of an accumulated indebtedness of over $40,000 and to save the institution from seizure of its property under judgments, the Trustees in the spring of 1879 leased the Seminary to me as far as the current receipts and expenditures were concerned, which continued until the creditors were satisfied under a compromise settlement by payment of forty cents on the dollar, after which the institution took on new life.

In the fall of 1879, James D. Phelps was elected President, but the financial management was left in my hands during his administration which duties were performed by me in addition to my work as Professor of Latin and Greek.

During Professor Phelps' term of office as Principal, the foundation was laid for a permanent endowment by the subscription of $25,000 by Mrs. Livia Guernsey Griffin of Troy, N.Y. to be paid in equal annual increments of $5,000, and by the raising of a fund of $5,000 by the residents of the village. In the spring of 1884 Professor Phelps resigned to become the pastor of a church in Utica, N.Y. and at the annual meeting of the Trustees in June I was chosen to succeed him. I held the position for twelve years, resigning in the summer of 1896 on account of ill health and was chosen President emeritus on account of my long service. The cottage was built during my administration—water was brought to the institution from a spring about one mile east of the village and many other improvements made. The endowment was increased to about $40,000.

Dr. C. C. Wilbor was chosen to be my successor, and he held the position for four years. During his administration the gymnasium was erected which filled a long felt need. In the summer of 1900 Dr. F. D. Blakeslee was made President, holding the position until 1908 at which time Dr. C. D. Skinner was chosen President.

Soon after my election as President, the health of G. L. Rouse the Seminary Treasurer, failed and I was chosen Treasurer, which position I am still holding after a period of twenty-five years. In the fall of 1902 I was elected School Commissioner of the Second School Commissioner, District of Madison County, and held the position for six years, usually visiting the rural schools twice each year.

In the summer of 1872 I was married to Abbie Smith of east Bridgewater, Mass., sister of Richard W. Smith, one of my college classmates. She died in July 1876 and in March 1881 I was married to Harriet C. Alvord of Cazenovia. We have one son, Theron A. Clements, now practicing Law in New York City.

The preceding is a brief epitome of my life experiences, written solely for my son, who has frequently expressed a wish for such a record.

Now, in conclusion I would simply add that my life has been a strenuous one, handicapped as I have always been by the loss of my limb, with the suffering incident thereto and a constitution broken by months of prison life; but notwithstanding all this I have never regretted that I had a share in the preservation of the Union for I have always felt that it would have been a world of disaster if the government of the United States had been broken into fragments, and if this government "of the people, by the people, for the people" shall fulfill the high mission, the sacrifice will not have been made in vain.

I BELIEVE IN GOD, IN HIS SON, JESUS CHRIST, IN THE SIMPLE CHRISTIAN LIFE, IN DOING JUSTICE, IN LOVING MERCY, IN WALKING HUMBLY WITH GOD, IN LIVING IN A HOUSE BY THE SIDE OF THE ROAD, AND BEING A FRIEND TO MAN.

Isaac N. Clements
Cazenovia, N.Y. September, 1913.

JAMES H. MEREDITH

My Chickamauga

In 1863, northwest Georgia was desolate country—the westward expansion of the 1800s largely sidestepping this part of eastern America. In fact, even today its values are more similar to those of America's old frontier than to those of the rest of the postmodern South. Although the metropolitan reach of Chattanooga from the north and Atlanta from the south is swiftly maneuvering throughout north Georgia, and while this encroachment is quickly bringing the accoutrements of modernity—fast-food eateries and strip malls—it is not bringing a sudden change in values and beliefs. This area is more anxious about the present and future than about the past. Despite the pockets of wealth made from the tufted-carpet industry—in this, the carpet capital of the world—northwest Georgians defiantly refuse to change; they like who they are and for good reason—they are good people. I know this because I am one of them.

On the eighteenth and nineteenth of September 1863, Union Major General William S. Rosecrans's Army of the Cumberland lumbered into Confederate General Braxton Bragg's pensive, bickering Army of Tennessee at Chickamauga Creek, exactly on the line between Catoosa and Walker counties in Northwest Georgia. The result of this maneuver—a clumsy dance between two forces of immense destructive power—was 34,633 total casualties, the most devastating two-day battle of the Civil War—not far behind the three-day carnage at Gettysburg.

I know the Chickamauga battlefield less as a historical event than as an actual place where too many good Americans suffered and died. As a young boy, I not only covered the Chickamauga National Battlefield Park, I traversed all the other places both armies traveled before and after the main battle—places like Alpine, Ressaca, Kennesaw. In fact, my hometown of Summerville almost became the epicenter of the battle, missing its place in history and the horrors of unimaginable misery by some quirk of military expediency and luck. Evacuating the dead and wounded must have been a nightmare for the few locals at Chickamauga, equal to the fighting itself. The total casualties of that battle are roughly equal to the present populations of Rome, Georgia; Gadsden, Alabama; Fort Dodge, Iowa; or Elk Grove Village, Illinois.

I feel a personal connection to this Civil War battlefield. I did not have a relative who fought there (at least not that I know of; my family never kept track of such things), but it is a place where my mother took me to satisfy my hunger to understand this conflict. It was one of those times she was able to take time off from her busy adult life (time that I now can appreciate the value of) to take me to a place she had no particular interest in. She did it just for me. Recently, I found the 35 mm slides I took on that trip. Among those slides was one that I had "wasted" on my mother. She was standing next to one of the blue-green bronze cannons that festoon the park; she was wearing clothes that she had made herself, smiling, distracted, but satisfied that she was doing her duty for her son. I'm so glad now that I took that photo of her then because it is the last full image of her that I can now muster twenty-nine years later. Soon after that photo was taken, my mother began her own dance with death, eventually succumbing to the onslaught of cancer.

I don't mean to be sentimental here; my point is that history— especially military history that records suffering and death—can be extremely personal. I connect emotionally to this historical event that occurred ninety-one years before I was born not just because it happened in my backyard but also because my backyard metaphorically took place in it. While learning about the mortality of soldiers, I have learned about my mother's mortality, as well as about the importance of time and memory. Chickamauga demonstrates to me that history lives in the mind, imagination, and heart, and unlike others from northwest Georgia, that I seem to have a lot more anxiety about the past than about the future.

PAUL WEST

My Father at War

One

Having been taught in school about ancient alchemists who changed base metals into gold, or "mufkuzt," or were supposed to have, I naturally thought of my father as an alchemist too. Part of his working day, he dealt in white-hot iron in white-hot ladles, but sometimes he also had to deal with brass. The iron, once cold, was dumped outside as "pig iron," awaiting collection, but whatever he did with brass remained unknown, maybe on its way to transmutation into gold. Filing a piece of brass one day, he got some brass filings on the skin of his legs, and so began a saga of skin trouble in which the outer layer kept peeling and he had to stay at home, fuming, with special wet bandages arrayed around his calves. He itched and squirmed just like, as he said, someone from the trenches with dermatitis hidden within the puttees they wound around their calves. Sometimes, I could tell, he was in a special state, not quite knowing where he was and whence his trouble had come, from the trenches or from brass. Imagine, having been spared trench-rot only to undergo the caress of filed brass. Doctor Crawford, an affable, garrulous Scot, visited him almost daily, and they invariably settled down together for a straight Scotch after the daily dressing with penicillin. I shall never forget my father's characteristic semi-crouch from those days, when he reached forward almost like a water diviner (minus twig) and groped for some part of his leg that was itching and perhaps paining him as well. Pain he could assimilate, having become a past master at that dreadful tryst, but the itch subdued and vexed him, requiring more and more Scotch, especially when Crawford was present. In fact they were cordial drinking buddies, and our Gaelic doctor was one of my father's newfound friends. With him, my father became more voluble than with me, his child, or with my mother, and from a distance I attuned myself to the rhythm, the give and take of their exchanges, punctuated by what I supposed was bawdy laughter (at that stage, I thought most laughter was bawdy). Crawford had been in the army too, but had not seen action, so it was likely that my father was airing for the second time stories of mud and glory that had kept me countless times from my sleep.

My father's leg never healed, although the physical sensations diminished, and I had the impression that Crawford's visits would go on forever, and my mother sniffing the Scotch-laden air with mild censoriousness. Clearly, the things my father and I did together, pretending or embellishing, would not figure in his recitals for the good doctor; I felt like their jealous protector, unable at that time to do much about preserving them, but already beginning to regard my father as a man of mystery who told different listeners different pieces of his epic, and possibly none of them all of it. Did the pieces hang together, as if in the mind of some sublime, omnivorous overseer? To an extent they did, but I never conferred with Crawford, not about my father anyway, but only enough for him to wash out my ears or diagnose spondylitis in my neck. Some people, I thought, came into the world to baffle others, who tended to think of their fellow-creatures in clichés or archetypes, allowing little scope for chronic idiosyncrasy. We were surrounded by enigmas of weather and chemistry, so why not enigmas that were people, even people you knew well and, knowing them well, credited with predictability? Whether my father had set out to puzzle us, I never knew, but I always assumed he thought of himself as a minefield grafted into a sweet-smelling garden in which place-names and names of battles sat uncouthly beside the names of women or even lost friends, that remained permanently under the surface as the property of a man whose vocation was to keep the most volatile parts of himself under lock and key.

Sleep is tyrannical with even the meekest of us, subduing and enslaving until we can stand no more. My father, however, after retiring at eleven, would often be up again by four, downstairs, poring over erudite histories of his war or relaxing with a racing story by Nat Gould: Linklater's *Impregnable Women*, or some harmless drivel put out in orange binding by a publisher called Herbert Jenkins. He would read until dawn, or so my mother told me, she who had now and then crept downstairs to see what he was up to. Yet to ask my father what else was in his mind while reading was like bear-hunting with a piano. What seemed to appeal to him was the indecorous availability of life, as found elsewhere in the licentious prose of André Gide. I myself had read somewhere about how the ancient Egyptians used to think of the Nile as one thing, something they could lift up bodily in their arms, from end to end, and hug, not as a series of waterways and canals, but a huge breathing baby river. My father would have understood this, and when I told him about it I suspected he began thinking of the war in much the same way, more in a flowing, intact sweep than did Captain Liddell Hart, one of his favorite historians. He did not sleep much, no doubt waiting for the next opportunity to—do what? I never quite knew, but sensed in him a blithe expectancy.

Was that it? I discovered that the reasons for someone's secretiveness had nothing to do with logic, as with my own. There were parts of human beings, even to a boy in his early teens that remained unquantifiable or were quiddities of a special stamp. Their presence in the human gamut enlivened the stuff on the surface, providing what etymologists trying to pin down the source of the word, "absurd," identified as a twisted or irrational root. Absurd, they said, means irrational root in Arabic. That was enough to feed me for ages, culled from the least visited appended pages of an obsolete dictionary that came as a free gift with a subscription to some war magazine. I myself was finding gold among the ruins of language. I told my father no such thing, but was tempted to, having noted in his blithest performances a certain skill with words culled not from his beloved history books but whipped into an agitated, teasing froth deep inside him that remained mostly for his own delectation but sometimes edged out just for the fun of it. "Imagine," he said once in boisterous tones, "Oxford and Cambridge decide to stage a boat race between the millionaires and the billionaires, with skiffs and coxes or coxswains, all the rest. Now, what's the difference between the millionaires and the billionaires?" How would I ever know something like that? His answer was brief: "Millionaires row." A double pun? In my father's darkest depths, neither blood nor brass, neither rusting pig iron nor flukey penicillin held sway, but only some unrecognized word-hoard gleaned from years of solitude, a gift given back to himself in the midst of disaster. A man floundering in several quicksands, ocular, vocational, and parental, my father chose to see the sludge as protective coating for his vital spark.

Two

Wartime as I write this. I am an old boy restaging an old war while remembrancing an even earlier war's warrior. How the wars pile up, an-
nihilating so many people in the interests of some politico's rabid whim.
The imagery remains much the same, though the weaponry mutates.
The bloodletting does not alter much, except for getting easier, and one
wonders if the hypothetical observer on Planet X finally dismisses us as
suffering from some form of lethal St. Vitus's dance: helpless killers of
themselves, he notes in his cylindrical spacetome. On the increase, there
are even those who do not covet life itself; if not their own, what reck they
of the lives of others? We will never get taken up, adopted, turned into
pets, which I recall was the comedian Johnny Carson's abiding cosmic
fear. Life is frail, which is why we quell it with such abandon; if it were
almost impossible to wipe out, would we take the trouble? I doubt it.

My father, sometimes reducing his glance to a pair of shoes he had
decided to repair, saw nothing beyond them, but only the rim of the
sole, the tiny heads of nails driven in. He did this with shoes to achieve
a certain invulnerable calm, and I envied him his indolent laissez-faire.
There he would crouch, legs splayed wide to accommodate the last and
his clutter, at ease by the spluttering fire, putting those neat, Byronic
hands to work on something pacific. He would almost vanish into a cob-
bler's trance, firm in his belief that, if you gave someone something firm
to tread on, their life improved. It was very much a manual workman's
point, but it ranged far and wide beyond him, from the explorer to the
drill sergeant, from the ballerina to the sentry. He had learned this kind
of thing in his teens and was unlikely to forget it, even as he remembered
that long walk to his dinner in Market Street, a walk he could roll up into
a ball and hold close to his chest, like the Nile. It was what he had been
allowed to keep at the cost of an eye, and it never wore out. He would
have walked it barefoot, if required to, such was his sense of reprieve;
indeed, he was the saint of any humble chore, having at his command a
host of savage comparisons.drawn, say, from the salient at Ypres, or the
London hospitals. Reconstructed as a jack of all trades, he was a homemade man, as certain American poets have been, and was in some ways
a match for John Clare, who walked in search of the horizon, except that
my father knew what lay beyond it.

In a photographer's studio I saw an imposing display of corners for decorative frames, the rest of the frames cut away so as to draw attention to the corners. In fact the corners were so mounted, in tall tiers, that I had a fleeting impression of being next to an immortal sergeant whose good-conduct stripes reached far out beyond him. All those chevrons made me almost hallucinate, wondering if any NCO could have served so long and distinguished himself so much. It was quite moving. Then I regained my bearings and the sergeant faded from view.

"You're far away," my father said, or something like that.

"I am dreaming," I answered, "a dream of soldier's stripes."

"Never mind those," he said, "just a bauble. The real good conduct's in how you manage to control your breathing when the game is up."

"Like taking an examination."

"No, never. Blood on the moon, my boy, and no questions asked."

Was he being literal? It usually took a chat such as this to expose how far we had wandered away from one another, each from the other's suppositions about life and death, and it took some effort to manage to overlap with him again. The English are a sentimental people, and very much ashamed of it, but the Irish and Scottish strains in his make-up steadied him no end, as did his profoundly irreligious outlook. One day, apropos of nothing, he said, "Human beings, trapped in the playground of life, are like children at a birthday party, wanting magic tricks, from no matter who." Of all the devout forces afflicting soldiers, only one, the Salvation Army, earned his praise, ever on hand during the worst bombardment, he claimed, always toiling with the worst of the wounded when the rest of them, chaplains and other godbotherers, had fled for the rear. Talk of the Salvation Army, and a catch would form in his throat, a tear in that omnivorous eye. He held very little holy beyond the memory of his father, smashed up in a mining accident and restricted thenceforth to rolling and plaiting bellropes for the local church, and of his incessantly busy mother beating her offspring with a short cane, then plying them with food to make up for the onslaught. There was an old wartime friend who had gone on postwar to Iran to work in the oilfields, and to whom my father wrote regularly, in reply receiving photos of the oilfields and derricks. This fellow, at least as long as the correspondence endured (until his marriage), seemed to give my father a leaning post, a serious confidant who had been through the same ordeals, as had the two local men, with whom his relationship was less earnest. Somewhere in my father's spiritual background, if that is not too overblown a way of putting it, there were saints and lairds, to whom he extended a perfunctory, haphazard nod for at least providing a dimension of sorts, but he never lingered on his heritage. His new standing, not so much *mutilé de guerre* as grandee of survivorship, depended on doctors he had known, including the American from Pittsburgh, of whom he spoke glowingly, and locally Dr. Crawford, one of the many Scotsmen who figured in my father's life, whether in the firing squad at the Tower of London or as authors, whether as army officers or as doctors, the last of these a visible echo of the local myth that saw England overrun with the brilliant sons of poor Scottish crofters who sent them south to make a living Scotland denied them (there were no doctors in Scotland; so said the myth). Indeed, even at Oxford there was an offshoot of the same myth, claiming that Balliol College, where Scots roosted, was the intellectual powerhouse of the university—was that why a recent Master of Balliol turned out, on his death, to have been a Russian spy?

There was a pagan dependency in my father that squared little with my mother's sketchy piety (she took flowers to the altar in the local church but refused to do anything else, including playing the church organ, which, since she was an outstanding pianist, she was often begged to do).

Concerning the afterlife, if any, he stamped out all rumors. There was nothing there, he just knew it, except perhaps his father rolling bellropes and his mother doing endless washing, or himself at last using the scholarship he had won long ago to attend grammar school. Flowers he adored, but not the standard pieties of everyday, or the lip-service accorded men in dog collars, whom he saw as frauds. This time around, he was not going to miss the main chance. In other words, he was a disappointed man who made the best of what he had.

Other times, between four and dawn, he would finish one of my mother's crossword puzzles, or pretend to, screwing up the result into a mangled twist of paper to hide his doubts. Or, with peeping tongue and a good deal of sighing, he would inscribe in copperplate hand his football coupon, on which he gambled against next Saturday's scores. When his weekly coupon arrived, the envelope addressed him as Esq. for Esquire, thus installing him among the nobility, barristers, and members of the universities of Oxford and Cambridge. This arrant promotion pleased him in a minor way, much more than the rank of sergeant had, and I think it summed up the pretensions of the Crusader figure who crouched in red beside the *Daily Express's* headline. He was certainly fastidious enough to be a man of quality, with a shield bearer (me) at his side; indeed, Esquire itself descended etymologically from "shield bearer," from Latin *escutarius* and French *escuier*. He knew nothing of any such word story, and was better off without it. The mild and noble greeting on his weekly coupon was more than enough for him to linger on, and he might have been tempted into adding the title to his friends' names on greeting them each day. Would any etymology have helped him to polish off those crosswords? I doubted it, and words like "bane" and "saw" were best left to my mother to tinker with. Had I been awake when he was, I might have been able to read aloud to him when his eye wearied, though he would probably have protested that such reading was unfit for somebody young. He was exaggerating; there was worse in Shakespeare and Dickens than he would ever have found in his middlebrow reading.

In another sense, however, each was the other's child. Having had little enough of childhood, he was having a second one, and certainly we were having an adolescence together, he mine, and I his. We learned together how to cope with the industrial strength yahoos we ran into: his officers, my freshmen. Yet he was ambivalent about both, sometimes commending the good breeding of the first, the earnest ignorance of the second. He did not feel obliged to give final verdicts on anyone or anything, contending that everything was in flux, though he didn't use that word. If he was a born survivor, then he had escaped only by the skin of his teeth, an expression he disliked for its inaccurate melodrama. He was always waiting for life to improve but reluctant to give it a helping hand; he had done his best for life, he felt, and now it was up to the Herbert Jenkinses, the Nat Goulds, the Eric Linklaters, and other men of letters to see things through. If he was a meliorist, he was a lazy one; with more sleep he might have been busier, less inclined to say live and let die. His joke, that a one-eyed man needed only half the usual amount of sleep, was a poignant excuse for a bad habit, but I do declare, after all this time thinking about him, he got out of bed when he did because he wanted extra time to be left alone in. He had suffered a lifetime's bother in his teens, and wanted no more of it, which is to say he treated almost all he met or who came to see him with the same cordial condescension, excepting only his wartime pals and Doctor Crawford, just possibly Constable Swain. For a man with a huge memory, he was oddly absent-minded. You might call him altruistically indifferent if that made any sense at all, but he was also mercurial beyond any of Elgar's enigmas and, minus his mustache, bizarrely juvenile, as if his face had decided to follow his mind back into the teens he'd missed. Trying to follow him as he zig-zagged amid the phenomena of a new century already ancient to him, I sometimes became blurred with protean sympathy as I felt my natural personality beginning to shear away from his, less and less able to empathize as I almost casually discovered the self I wanted to have, growing gradually away not from him but from where he had situated his remaining life, and feeling guilty about it, as it were abandoning him in his durable routine.

We would have been more useful to each other marooned on Elba.

We would have been more father and son had I been more of an engineer.

We would have shared more experiences had he been more open and I a better listener.

In one sense, he held himself captive, no doubt in the company of certain ecstatic events, but these were epiphanies wrapped inside abstractions torn away from primitive phenomena. Asking him why, why, I kept running into Liddell Hart, whose elegant military trajectories he had more or less memorized as if he were going to be tested. Somewhere in those elegant summaries stood my young father wishing he'd stayed at home for the beef and mustard sandwiches his mother plied all of us with. A lover of maps, he was an oddly homeless man, polite but like certain zones of war unoccupied.

Three

My father did not live long enough to discover how grains of sand, fiercely spun by the rubbery throb of a helicopter's seething blades, turn into sparks like prim iotas in the early visions of philosopher Democritus. Nor did he ever hear, as the voice of the laptop was heard in the land (*vox laparae*), the anemic, subdued cry of the machine's voice: "Not my fault." But, thousands of times, he heard the sounds of one of those infiltrating, note-taking rains as he squatted unsheltered amid mother nature's indiscriminate husbandry, wondering if he would survive until tomorrow. I often think of him thus, cornered in his shrunken, fatal world, in the end arriving at his own accommodation to the facts of life and death: You live not for the moment, but for the nanosecond, whose resident dwarf, *nanos* in Greek, he had never encountered in his schooling for war, though maybe some of his officers had. He remained interested in words, however, as did my mother, in his case regarding them as some parallel frieze to the world of violent things, much as my mother saw them as failed adjuncts to the joys of theory and harmony evinced on her piano. *Sporadic* and *shrapnel* interested him no end, as did *hosiery* and *fedora*, and there I was, the maven, explaining Ali Baba's etymological cave to him as if I were ripping off the lid of the placid world, along with *muscular* (which had a Roman mouse scuttling through it) and *cape* (which in escape gave us the escapist's vital motion).

"You mean shrapnel," he said, "comes from the name of a British army officer? I wouldn't have believed it. He must have had some special interest in bits of flying metal. Like me. Do you think the likes of me could give his name to the cartridge cases as they fell, emptied out?" *Sporadic*, merely from the Greek, he found a little bit lacking, inferior even; why *spor*, he wondered. How did *its* sound, rather than all others, come to reflect intermittence? *Hosiery*, from a maker of stockings, socks, also seemed to him insufficiently theatrical whereas *fedora* amazed him, commemorating the play *Fedora* by Victorien Sardou. I could tell he liked the wild notion of wearing a fedora among flying shrapnel, in other words impersonating an army officer in a soft felt trilby with a crease along its top. Indeed, words, with some disappointments, came to seem to my father a street of gaudy brothels, all striped awnings and lolloping bosoms, and who was I to deny him his latter-day revels? They merely matched my own, that had a more donnish aspect.

All through the war he had kept in his silver-tinted booklet his favorite or most stunning words, to which in the long run I added my own before running out of space and eventually devoting an entire thick book, *The Secret Lives of Words*, that I think he might have enjoyed dipping into.

To these parochial allusions he would add squibs drawn from practical affairs. "The forsythia is up. The towel rail in the bathroom has snapped. The letter-holder you made with your fretwork saw has come unglued.

The letter box needs oil. They have begun serving cold beer at the Duke."
I could fathom most of this. If you have gone down with the Lusitania,
you know the names of the fish. I tried to respond in kind, aping his
staccato clicks to attention, but unequal to the task because my own tendency has always been to unveil the full envelope of the phenomenon,
while he reduced all to chevrons. In the end, though, more for my own
convenience than for reciprocity with him, I amassed a word-hoard of
things I would have loved to tell him: new football players with such unusual names as Trésor Lua Lua, Macaroni, Sommeil (*slumber* in French),
and Henry, whom they pronounce Awnree. One team, full of foreigners,
had become known as Sam Allardyce's Continental Chocolate Box. Was
that a tribute or a rebuke? Language was still being mangled: Cockney
for Heathrow was *Yfra* and for the pianist Angela Hewitt *Anjlaooit*. Had
he ever seen a rocking horse with jaws of glass? If he ever in the trenches
played poker, what was a Montana Banana? Was a trombone burner really a kind of stove? A diploma was a paper folded in two, Da-Di. Did he
remember, at Manchester Airport, his one and only round trip by air,
the men who parked the Viscounts with their pink pistoleros? What on
earth was Bartholomitis? A disease of mapmakers? Who were Turnbull
and Asser? And Steiner, Dalby, and Brown? Did he know them? How did
astronomers know that the Boomerang Nebula was the coldest place in
the universe, at minus 272 degrees Celsius, just one degree above abso-
lute zero? And what about the wasted degree? Had he noticed how one
TV presenter's top pocket had a rearward panther in it, a crumpled gray
hankie achieving stupendous bestiality? Did he know yet that a sponge
left stranded in the body after surgery had been named a *gossypiboma*,
from *Gossypium* (cotton) and the Swahili word *boma* for place of conceal-
ment? It had happened so often. There was a whole universe to tell him
about, an avalanche of particulars fit to justify anyone eyeing unemploy-
ment as the way to go. I would get back to him.

   I would not, but, true to the style of our lives together, I mean their almost Luddite primitivism, I renumbered pages by daubing liquid paper
on the old number and held the corner up to the hot bulb of 150 watts
to dry it out, almost like roasting lice alive in a tin can in the trenches.
None of this linguistic fascination appeared in his letters, most often
cryptic appendices to my mother's cursive, pianistic runs of tender eu-
phoria. "Fine day, but dull so far" was one of his runes, unfitting you

for whatever followed, as if you had run into a bit of Beckett while read-ing Jane Austen. There would, often, follow a string of allusions, exact and hunched, about village life as he had seen it. "Sharman going soft on the brilliantine these days. Race got a cough. Colin was here, beg-ging, with his sheaf of knives wrapped in brown paper, just like Jack the Ripper. Raymond is repairing motor mowers. Mabel is back from Blackpool, worrying about that young lad of hers with the undescended testicle. Only the other day, Raymond told me, driving a jeep in Italy, he fell asleep along the edge of a ravine. Not heard from Culver, I think the oil derricks in Persia have swallowed him up. In the hotels, make them change the blankets too. You never know who's been sweating into them or been sick. Love, Pa." This was weird, embedded stuff, requiring me not only to read between the lines, but to animate present faces he himself recalled with censorious economy. Most of them I knew, includ-ing the uncle whose mustache was too thin, the only redhead daughter among his sisters, and the cabinet-maker who had actually built himself a coffin with a mail-slot.

ALFRED KERN

Hang the Enola Gay

General Tibbets, the man who flew the airplane, surely is right. Exhibit the Enola Gay and say nothing. But then I'm a writer (mere crewman to Tibbets's authentic moment) and argue that saying something constitutes duty. As one version of the recent story got played, the people arranging the Smithsonian's exhibit of the Enola Gay had made some perfectly reasonable comments about the war in the Pacific. These historians and archivists wanted to bring us the truth that a fifty-year perspective could now allow us to accept: the American war in the Pacific was one of vengeance and cruelty against the Japanese, who fought only to protect their culture and way of life. Furthermore, the United States did not drop the bomb out of any strategic necessity but to impress the Soviet Union with both the might and willingness of American power. The dropping of the second bomb (about which some question might be asked) is proof of American perfidy, a perfidy made all the more emphatic if only because the American Legion rose up in its predictable chauvinism to deny it. And so the Enola Gay's last mission—its own hanging—would reveal the truth of America's evil intentions.

To argue against this premise risks endowing it with a respect it doesn't deserve. Still, a sentence or two might be helpful. The decision to drop the bomb was not made easily; neither was it a callous message to impress the Soviet Union. From Port Moresby—only a long spit from Australia itself—we had come all the way to Okinawa and Ie Shima. While the Japanese still put airplanes into the air, including the suicide missions that attacked American naval vessels off the harbor at Naha, we prevailed in the air war. Our B-29 raids were producing the kind of damage that should by then have persuaded the Japanese, and so—yes—by early 1945, the question remaining was just how and when we would win the war. Still, the Japanese had not surrendered, and if you had come the whole way or a fair hunk of it (I began at Nadzab, New Guinea, a few miles inland from Lae), you were not all that certain if or when the Japanese would ever surrender. The argument that we justified the dropping of the bomb by deliberately overestimating the number of American casualties to be suffered by an invasion of the Japanese home islands is worse than specious. As measured by the number of American casualties in the island wars, Japanese resistance against an invasion of the home islands certainly could not be expected to diminish. Does anybody need to be reminded that the Japanese were fierce fighters? Ask the Marine veterans who recently marked the sixtieth anniversary of Iwo Jima.

Then, too, how many American casualties were to be suffered in order to justify the use of the bomb? At a cocktail party a year ago, I heard an acquaintance condemn our dropping the bomb as having been cynically unnecessary. Speaking about an American invasion of Japan, he said something like the following: "The estimate of one million American casualties was never even close to the truth. At worst, there might have been fifty thousand casualties. Less than fifty thousand. Maybe thirty to thirty-five thousand." My unit was scheduled to go in D+2 [D day plus two days]; with respect to what would have been suffered by the first waves, those two days would have been like a century later. But I'm still impressed enough with D+2 not to have said anything at all to the man at the cocktail party. Anyhow, what are you supposed to say to somebody arguing that at worst we would have lost only fifty thousand American lives?

In agreeing with the calm and measured tones of the American Legion—far softer than I would have spoken—I say first that I am not a member of the Legion or of the VFW. Back in civies after World War II, I joined the American Veterans Committee, the veterans association founded by people like Bill Mauldin, Gilbert Harrison (then publishing the *New Republic*), and Chet Bolté. Just as the far left despised anti-Communist socialism more than it feared the right wing, so, too, did it live easier with the American Legion than with us AVC liberals. In fact, the left did its best to destroy the AVC, whose motto was "Citizens first; Veterans second." Nearly fifty years later, I haven't much changed my political stripes and am among those who have not grown more conservative with age. Whether you think of my brand of politics as wisdom or senility depends on your own politics, but let's get one notion straight from the start. The revisionism that makes the United States the bad guys in the Pacific war is in no way a premise of American liberalism. Neither is the view of the Smithsonian historians an argument between liberal Democrats and conservative Republicans. I remind you that it was Harry Truman who gave the order for the mission of the Enola Gay. If you need your memory refreshed, David McCullough's work on Truman will provide the historical perspective.

For my generation, this foolishness about the Enola Gay flying an evil mission has refreshed memories. I remember the day. I'd been working on the strip we ran on the Motobu Peninsula on Okinawa. Somebody came into the engineering shack and said that this enormous bomb had been dropped. *So how enormous is enormous? They got it into an airplane, didn't they?* No, not enormous in size. Small in size—enormous in the power to destroy. One bomb knocked out most of a city. *Tokyo?* No, not Tokyo. Some other city with a funny name. *And one bomb did all that?* One bomb. The guy said this bomb implodes. Ask the armorers what that means. *Our armorers? Our armorers don't know shit from shinola about anything.* What the guy really said was that troops stationed on Okinawa had better keep a tight asshole cause there's no telling how the Japanese will react to whatever-that-thing-was. *You say it implodes itself? And that's why it blew up a whole city? Cause it implodes? Was this implosion supposed to happen or just some kind of lucky screwup?*

That flight of the Enola Gay has got to be the most impressive single mission ever flown. Nothing can compete with its awesomeness. Unlike a routine mission, the Enola Gay was History from the start, and those involved knew it. But for those of us who served in the Pacific, the A-bomb mission was an ending that in some ways seemed to have little to do with the Pacific war as we had fought it. For example, during the New Guinea campaign, I worked at the strip where still only Captain Richard Bong's P-38 squadron returned from missions. By the time Bong had knocked down eleven or twelve enemy planes, GIs from all over the base began to line that strip like cheerleaders at their high school football game. We waited for that P-38 to come in hot, level out flat what seemed only a dozen feet above the strip, and then climb to its victory roll. And on numbers of those days, Bong flew back around for a second victory roll. We would look at each other, nodding and smiling and holding up two fingers. "Two. He scored two."

For me, a Dick Bong victory roll remains in memory as a thing of beauty, and those moments were an enormous lift to morale in what was a difficult war. Look at a map of the Pacific. Find Port Moresby on the southern New Guinea coast and then calculate the distance in miles to the Japanese islands. And while you're at it, calculate that distance in time. I mean the amount of time it took for us to get there. We had already used up *Never More in '44* and were hoping for *Back Alive in '45*, though the squadron pessimists predicted *Home or Heaven by '47* or even *Golden Gate in '48*. We were ready for the miracle we didn't begin to comprehend, a miracle involving something called atomic fission. For Fifth Air Force veterans, the years of scrounging to get airplanes into the air, the awesome distances to be traveled, the ersatz food, names never before heard—like Buna and Pelelieu and Samar—the holding on to a civilization from which we have been removed: all of these represent the war in the Pacific more than the flight of the Enola Gay, and I have a hunch that nobody knows that better than General Tibbets himself.

Our pilots flew the requisite number of missions (and more), but GIs didn't get rotated home. Most of us had been at if for a long time when The Bomb was dropped. Not yet twenty-one, I'd already been in territories designated as combat zones for nearly two consecutive years. If some old infantry veteran is reading this, let me say here and now that us air corps types aren't making any claims. At least in your presence we aren't making any claims. Being in a combat zone usually meant only that you were close enough to understand what being closer could mean. My squadron did get a bit closer, stupidly a time or two, but that was because I served in something called an airdrome squadron.

The idea for such a unit was borrowed from the British, and, like a British aircraft engine, was more to be admired in design than lived with. An airdrome squadron was to arrive the moment an airstrip was taken or completed for use by our engineers. We were staffed and equipped to run the strip for a month, after which—in theory anyway—bomb and fighter groups would move in safely with their own personnel and heavier equipment. Until then, we did everything: control tower, crash crews, weather, communications, armament, and aircraft maintenance far beyond minor repairs and preflight once-overs. We took our squadron's assignments and the general mission of the Fifth Air Force as being perfectly sensible; fifty years later the wonder is how we did it. I understand more keenly now than I had time to understand then that our airdrome squadron was to move itself up to the next airstrip and function. Instantly. Snap a finger. Just like that. And we did it, did it before a tent got pitched or a latrine got dug. We also learned what could be the real meaning of "a moment too soon." The airdrome squadron that had been on the boat with us arrived at Hollandia more than a moment too soon and got shot up. We disembarked at Lae and went inland to Nadzab. In addition to running a strip there, we were assigned to do the maintenance for the Fifth Bomber Command's flight section. A bit more about that later.

I always figured that somebody at the command level had fought against the very idea of these airdrome squadrons. Having lost the argument, he figured out another way to make his point. My impression of that unit—unchanged more than fifty years later—was that you were assigned duty there only if you had impressed someone in charge of you—fairly or unfairly—that you were, or could become, a square peg. Surely, we had more people who had done prison or guardhouse time than the typical Fifth Air Force unit. Others of our people had flunked out of air corps training schools, or to put it as kindly as possible, had not been among the class leaders. Anyone who had told us to our faces that we were at best a collection of shanghais would have committed a grave diplomatic error; he would not, however, have been entirely inaccurate.

I had done nothing terrible, yet I see now that from the very start of service I was destined for assignment to the 92nd. My first summons to a CO's office occurred as early as basic training; I was told that in Ohio a warrant had been issued for my arrest because I had not registered for the draft. Why had I not done so? I explained that I had volunteered after my eighteenth birthday, which fell months before my age group was supposed to register. Rightfully unimpressed, the CO grunted and said that he'd do his best to keep me out of jail. Next, having taken the battery of tests, I was sent to the Buick motor division in Flint, Michigan, where after eleven weeks of instruction I would become a specialist in Pratt-Whitney aircraft engines. The Flint assignment was wonderful. Our nightly retreat ceremonies were held on a public street and watched by girls working in GM war plants. These young women not only produced the equipment and weapons we would soon be using but respected our future bravery with a patriotism that could inspire from toe to head.

About a month after I arrived, I was again summoned to the CO's office. I still remember his name—Lieutenant Balch. In appearance and mildness of manner, Lieutenant Balch looked as if he had taught general science at some midwestern high school. After about thirty seconds of sighing, he explained to me that I had made one of the highest scores of any soldier ever to be sent to his school. He then said that my performance also placed me among the most inept students ever assigned there, and that he might well have to get rid of me. How had I done so well on the test only to do so wretchedly in his school? I tried to explain that the test had been simple. For example, you might be given an illustration of interlocking gears. You were told the direction of the first gear and asked whether the last of the gears was moving to the right or left. I explained that such a test had nothing to do with fixing an airplane engine. On the line, your hands seemed to be more important than your head. And the tools had funny names. Somebody kept asking for his ratchet or Phillips head. Who was this Phillips anyway? By the end of the eleven weeks, I did know the difference between a ratchet and a hatchet, but anybody who flew an airplane I had worked on would have flown more easily if he did not know that I had done the safety wiring.

My final move to the 92nd Airdrome Squadron occurred at Hunter Field, Georgia, still an army airfield. In a replacement squadron there, waiting to be assigned, I was once again summoned to the CO's office. He was Major Robinson, a West Pointer, called out of retirement to what for him had to be an unfulfilling assignment. Little did either of us know that indifferent gods had destined each of us to find the other. The first sergeant advised me to be scrubbed and starched, and like most GIs, I wondered what I had done wrong. In posture and bearing, Major Robinson impressed me as never once in his entire life having been at ease. I stood at attention and did my best not to breathe. The major first explained that he himself was a graduate of West Point. He then said that the army has issued a new directive. Any GI who met the requirements—age, IQ, physical condition, educational background, score on the GCT, and whatever else—could qualify for West Point. He had ordered his clerks to go through the entire roster, and I was the only man currently assigned to him who met the requirements. He was proud to have a man in his outfit who qualified for the Point, and he was going to back me all the way. That's when he said, "And, soldier, I'm going to back you all the way."

The requirements weren't all that steep; there were just a number of them, including a year of college. I had graduated from high school at sixteen (a bad idea) and so had been a college sophomore when I entered the service. At that moment anyway, Major Robinson was unlucky enough to find only one person assigned to his outfit who qualified. But I didn't want to spend those years in school. Stupid as it may sound to most current presidential candidates in both political parties, I didn't want to miss the war. But what I said then to Major Robinson came out wrong—wrong for both of us. "But, sir," I said, "I don't want to be at West Point." Only four hours later, I threw my duffle bag into the back of a 6x6 and headed for the other side of the base. That's how I came to spend the war with the 92nd Airdrome Squadron, surely the only GI in the outfit who got there not by robbing a bank but by declining a chance to attend West Point. My friend, Brigadier General Jesse Gatlin, retired head of the English department at USAFA [the U.S. Air Force Academy] and himself a West Point graduate, thinks what Major Robinson did was terrible. Had I said yes, Jesse and I would have been classmates. About a year and a half later, by then in the Philippines, my orders for OCS came through. But I didn't want to go to school in Australia then because my squadron was about to leave for Okinawa. No, Major Robinson may have been right about me. And then, you never know about a shift in assignments. The old major may have saved my life.

Those first few weeks in New Guinea, we experienced what surely was the typical shakedown of any initial combat duty. Some people cracked up, not one of those being somebody I would have figured to do so. The people I thought were loony-bin candidates all did fine. Our squadron physician, a Cleveland Heights obstetrician-gynecologist and thus a typical assignee to my airdrome squadron, lasted a bit longer—three or four months. Wisely, I was taken off the line and assigned to the engineering shack. Soon after, the NCO in charge was moved up to command headquarters, and I was given his duties. Then, over the next few weeks, I discovered about our squadron what is hopefully typical of any organization, military or civilian. We had the dozen necessary people who knew what they were doing and also how to make do. In a month, we were functioning adequately. A month after that, we were good.

The planes we serviced regularly were those of the Fifth Bomber Command Headquarters. The tactical aircraft flown on missions was the B-25D2, a medium bomber and marvelous airplane. But bomber command headquarters was also a sort of WWII menagerie, and so at one time or another we also worked on the B-26, B-24, A-20, and one stripped-down fat-cat B-17. We also had a couple of those wonderful little two-seater Taylorcrafts. When one of the pilots discovered that I was still a kiwi, he took me up in a Taylorcraft and, once off the ground, immediately initiated me by demonstrating stalls and loops; that flight was not a gentle initiation, but I enjoyed it. No, it's more than sixty years later, and I no longer have to say that I enjoyed it. I did not, however, get sick.

A few of our pilots had been rotated out of their combat groups. While waiting for transportation home, they continued to fly missions. More of our pilots had been detached from their squadrons for a variety of other reasons. I had a bit of airtime with them, and I can attest to their having been first-rate fliers. They were also—how to put this politely?—apt to prefer their own war plans to those of the Fifth Bomber Command, and a time or two they saw something on their way to a target that appealed to them more than the object of the briefing. Perhaps these days they might be court-martialed, but remember that we are talking about a bunch of civilians fighting the war in the Pacific. In retrospect, I think they were handled just right, but then, for us, they fit perfectly with the Ninety-Second Airdrome Squadron. Put all the nonconformists in the same outfit and don't bother to kick butts about minor infractions, and you just might get yourself an outfit that can be called upon for bigger stuff.

The only two regular army people in our squadron were the first sergeant and the line chief. I suspect each had been chosen with us in mind. The first sergeant was tough and unyielding. At Hunter Field, before leaving for embarking at San Francisco, we had played tackle football wearing only fatigues and had broken his collarbone. (Do I dare say by now that I never regretted having been in on that tackle?) The first sergeant could be one unpleasant SOB, but when the war ended and he had more points than anybody else in the squadron, he stood in the mess hall, tears streaming down his face, and said good-bye by telling us that he loved us. The first sergeant was an archetypal career soldier, and I'll tell you how much I respected him. When I saw him standing there and weeping, I believed that he meant what he said but still thought he was an SOB.

The line chief, Master Sergeant Morris Jones (Sarge Mo), a big and handsome Georgian, was quiet and self-possessed. Although we had an engineering officer, Mo and I became good friends and, with others, shared quarters. Mo was determined that we would always put planes in the air, and we never failed to do so. Meeting such assignments wasn't easy, but we were superbly staffed for it. The 92nd Airdrome Squadron excelled in its use of the moonlight requisition. While he could not be represented on the table of organization, we came to employ a full-time scrounge-spy. At a midnight meeting in the engineering shack, attended only by enlisted men, the scrounge might say, "The 101st Bomb Group just received a dozen new 1830-radials. They've been sitting there for a week, still crated and pickled." We never stole just to steal, and we never stole a whole engine—just the parts needed to get our own planes in the air. In that sense, the Pacific war belonged to us civilian enlisted types. I assume our officers knew what we were doing, but not even Mo Jones came to a requisition session. Mo could call for a meeting, however; all he had to do was raise an eyebrow.

After a few months in Nadzab, we moved north to Owi, an island just across a strait from Biak and maybe an hour off the New Guinea coast from Hollandia. Biak is another of those places, long forgotten, that saw intense fighting. We were told that the airstrip on Biak changed hands two or three times, so that before the island was secure, we and the Japanese had actually taken turns flying off it. Owi was a barren hunk of coral, desolate and sun drenched. With nightfall, the moon merely replaced the sun for more hours of white on white. Such constant light can be as depressing as darkness. Owi is the only place I know where the phrase "like pissing on a flat rock" is not a figure of speech.

Mo Jones did not care for the Owi assignment either. He told me that the Fifth Bomber Command was to send a detachment of three B-25s, including flight crews and ground support, to Anguar in the central Pacific and that he had volunteered our services. When one of the pilots overheard me say, "I hope to God they won't fly up there in formation," that is exactly what they did. But by then I knew what to worry about.

I assigned myself to the lead plane, climbed into the bombardier's forward station in the nose, and enjoyed the flight. One does learn. And as it turned out, that is why we were being sent to Anguar; the Seventh Air Force, fresh from Hawaii and new to combat, had use for a few of us nineteen- to twenty-five-year-old veterans.

We were assigned to a b-24 group that had too often failed to reach target, and we were going to fly pathfinder missions for them. I remember how healthy they all looked, in contrast to us. Despite our hours in the tropical sun, we wore those Atabrine yellow faces. But by then we were also different in other ways. Landing at Anguar, one of our b-25s needed a bit of work done; I went to the tech supply tent for some parts, only to discover that nobody was there. I found the squadron technical supply sergeant and told him what was needed, only to learn that tech supply was closed on Sunday. For me, duty at places like Nadzab and Owi in wartime pretty much did away with any sense of calendar time, and so my question to the supply sergeant was in no way sarcastic. "Today is Sunday?"

I then found my way to the squadron's engineering officer, told him what we needed, and politely asked if he would request his tech supply noncom to be open for business. I must have managed to say it in the proper tone of voice, because no captain ever responded quicker to the request of a three-striper. In speaking to that captain, I mixed the appropriate enlisted man's umbrage with the right seasoning of disrespectful battle weariness. But so, too, did everybody else in our Fifth Air Force detachment play that same role. After all, we had been dispatched there to bring just such experience. By then, we were no longer impressed that we had such experience to bring. We kept those three b-25s in the air, flew the pathfinder missions, and got the b-24s to their targets. A month later—maybe less, maybe three weeks—they didn't need us.

From Anguar we flew to San Jose on the Philippine island of Mindoro. The mission now was to fly China coast reconnaissance missions, a far piece of flying for a b-25. I've still no idea how they managed to rig it, but our mechanics put an extra gas tank in the crawl space between the front and midsection of the airplanes. While I still was not to be trusted with either a ratchet or hatchet, I had long before begun to read the tech orders rather than just file them away. Typically American perhaps, I had kept all sorts of unreported data on these planes and knew their individual eccentricities. Along with our crew chiefs, I was possessively jealous; as far as we were concerned, these were our planes, which we consented to lend to the pilots who flew them. I suspect that sense of ownership hasn't changed to this day.

The pilots to whom we lent our airplanes accepted our ownership. For months, we had been advising them about the best settings for any particular flight, and they were now especially interested in asking our help for these China coast missions. Even more than on previous assignments, we waited nervously at the strip for the return of the mission. On some days, only one plane was designated to fly, and it was one of those days that the plane did not return from its mission. I hung around the operations shack most of that night. In the morning we were told that someone had seen the plane go down, not all that far offshore but nearer to a small island than to Mindoro. The problem was that these were still contested waters, and if the crew did manage to get itself to the smaller island, we could not be sure they wouldn't be captured.

Next day—sing for joy—they returned, rescued by a navy patrol boat. The pilot stared at me not quite menacingly and said, "We ran out of gas, Sergeant." But his radioman stopped by later. "We were maybe fifteen minutes from base," he said, "and he saw some Japanese shipping and went down after it. We made three or four passes and then had to climb back up." I was immensely grateful for his honesty, but that's how closely we had figured the safe completion of those missions. You simply could not vary the course without risk. Well, maybe we allowed for some manageable two-minute finagle. This pilot not only had the customary individualistic derring-do of a Fifth Bomber Command pilot, but he was also—if you don't mind my saying it, sirs—a stupid jerk. I was thankful for his return, but now that he and the crew had returned safely, I wanted to tell him that he had lost one of my B-25D2s, an airplane we had been flying since the Nadzab, New Guinea, days.

From Mindoro, we went to Luzon, where we ran the strip at Clark Field. Some brilliant army tactician located our quarters just behind the infantry but in front of the artillery. That was not the first occasion for our involvement in ground alerts, but we did—for us—have a fairly extensive go of it. Luzon was the first place we'd been stationed that had a large and fluent civilian population, and in that sense we'd returned to civilization. But we also saw some of the horrifying consequences of

Japanese occupation. A friend, the master sergeant in charge of communications, had an aunt, a Roman Catholic nun, who had been a nurse in a Manila hospital. He had promised his mother that he would try to find his aunt and asked me if I'd go to Manila with him. We found the hospital where Sister had worked but could not find her or anybody who had known her. We had only an overnight but did see the extent to which the city had been devastated. The Intramuros—the old walled inner city—had been hit particularly hard and was still smoldering; even in its ruins, we could tell how beautiful it had been.

And so we were running this strip on Okinawa the morning the Enola Gay lifted off with this enormous thing that imploded. We were still scrounging for supplies, and we were weary of the whole business, including each other. Our campsite sat on a high bluff from which you could look down on Ie Shima, another tough fight and the place where Ernie Pyle, the GIs' war correspondent, got killed. My college roommate was also on Okinawa, and we managed an afternoon's reunion. We had entered the service and gone through basic together, but we had not seen each other for more than two years. My old roomie was a second lieutenant in the infantry, and while Okinawa had been taken, there was still fighting. Some of you may remember how MacArthur handled that sort of thing. The press release would read, "General MacArthur has stated that the island is now secure except for minor mop-up operations." We were getting weary with that nonsense as well. My roommate observed that day, "If this is the mop-up, I'm glad I wasn't here for the battle."

We were ready for that miracle. And then the Enola Gay made its flight. And then the second bomb. And it was over. Traffic was very heavy the next couple of weeks with the flights to and from Japan. Many of the American POWs flown from Japan to Okinawa landed on our strip. I watched General Skinny Wainwright being helped from the airplane. He managed to stand tall and erect even as he accepted the needed help. Shortly after, the first sergeant wept his I-love-you valedictory in the mess hall and departed. Most of the squadron went on to Japan, but those of us who had been in the detachment that served on Anguar and later in Mindoro were credited with time in additional battle areas and had extra points. We stayed in Okinawa and waited for a ship. On the way home, I edited the ship's paper to get an early chow pass. The ship received a news service, which I used for the paper. The war being over, the United Automobile Workers Union had gone on strike, and I wrote an editorial assuring the GIs that the UAW was just getting us a raise before we got discharged. The ship's captain sent his exec to bawl the hell out of me and tell me not to write that sort of unpatriotic drivel again. I toned it down, but to honor the captain and the ship's speed, I changed the name of the paper to the *Daily Creeper*. We disembarked January 1, 1946, in Seattle, where German POWs were working in the mess hall. Unlike Skinny Wainwright, they looked both healthy and at ease. Ain't the United States terrible?

Now then, there's one thing I haven't talked about, and it's what motivated my writing this in the first place. Without making a big psychological deal out of it, I may well have been putting it off for years. But the nonsense about the Enola Gay compels me. So here goes.

After I read that in the Pacific war the United States was motivated by vengeance and cruelty, I began again to see the faces of friends who did not return. Any war veteran knows what I'm talking about. From my freshmen dormitory alone, I count seven people. I'm going to list a few names. You won't know them, and by now their parents are also gone. But indulge me. I just want to put some names in print. There was Pat Murphy, our class president, a bright and athletic kid who led us in the annual pants fight against the sophomore class. And Emmett Corrigan, who had prepped at some fancy private eastern school and had a surer sense of who he was at age eighteen than I have now; I never thought anything could happen to Emmet Corrigan. And Don Turk, the upperclassman who lived in our section of the dorm and who gave me some help for a course I shouldn't have taken; I couldn't believe it when I heard that he'd been killed in a navy training mission—not Don Turk. And from my hometown, Billy Kline, with whom I double-dated in high school, a B-24 pilot who didn't return from a mission. When I got back home, I went into his father's small clothing store to say how sorry I was about Billy, but his father saw me coming and went into a back room and couldn't talk to me.

There is one other incident though. In Nadzab, New Guinea, our first overseas assignment, I met a kid exactly my age who had also graduated from high school early and gone on to college. We'd managed to put together a kind of dayroom there, and this kid and I had a series of late night Ping-Pong games. We were both good players, and we kept ongoing statistics from night to night about wins and losses and scores. After a session, we also talked. We even discussed the possibility of going back to college together after the war. The kid was a radioman/gunner, and he was especially eager to play for hours any night before he had a morning mission. Well, by now you know where I'm going. On one of those missions, he didn't return. I've been referring to him as that kid because I cannot remember his name. I kept thinking that when I got to this point in the writing, the fingers would simply type out the letters. He was killed in early 1944, and I've been telling myself that it's perfectly sensible if I cannot remember a name from sixty years ago. Maybe I'll remember later, just sit up one night and say it.

I could tell a number of these stories about each of those stopping points on the way from New Guinea to Okinawa. For example, on Anguar, December 31, 1944, the detachment celebrated New Year's Eve. Somebody had managed to bring some liquor from Australia. Inspired, I removed the astrodome from a B-25 and used it as a mixing bowl. What the hell, why not? But the CO of that B-24 group heard about what we were doing and came down himself to put a stop to it. He confiscated the booze and told me to replace the astrodome immediately. We cursed him out pretty good later and did not wish him a happy new year. And the colonel did not return from the next mission.

On that same island, we also had a series of ground alerts. Not far from the hospital tent in which we were all sleeping, a half-dozen sailors—also detached—were running a navy weather station. As our ground troops pulled out for other places, the Japanese intensified their forays. Sixty thousand of them were still on the island of Yap, skillfully bypassed but hungrier by the day. One of those nights I had taken the jeep and driven somewhere to see a movie. I even remember that it was *Porgy and Bess*. (If I can remember the name of that movie, why can't I think of the Ping-Pong player's name?) When the signal for a ground alert lit the sky—red puff, red puff—I drove back to our campsite. Mo Jones told me that he'd had to set up the perimeter and had given my carbine to somebody serving on it. I said okay then, I'd take his Thompson sub, but he'd also lent it to somebody on the perimeter. Just then we heard gunfire and decided we'd relieve the people who had our weapons. Well, these air corps stories about ground war are surely both inane and amusing to anybody who served in the infantry. I'm telling this particular story because that night the little navy weather station got wiped out. They were stationed a bit closer to the shore, and from the looks of it, the Japanese had simply walked up to the door and tossed in grenades. Not one of the navy guys survived.

Enough of these stories. Most everybody has them to tell. And I haven't mentioned that many names. Maybe a dozen is all. Now what I want you to do is take any one of those names—just one. Or choose a name of your own, a name from one of your wars. I'm going to go with the radio-man/gunner Ping-Pong player from Nadzab. When you're sure that you see the face and hear the voice as if he's in the very same room, multiply it by fifty thousand. Or as my acquaintance at the cocktail party said, *only* fifty thousand.

I prefer to end on another note. Almost thirty years ago, I spent a year teaching at the Air Force Academy. For one of the formal occasions, an officer friend there got all my campaign ribbons, replete with battle stars, and explained that civilians might wear them on a tuxedo for formal occasions. Most of those ribbons and battle stars were awarded to types like me not for any bravery but for survival. Still, they looked pretty impressive even to me. During the evening, and standing with the USAFA brass, I was presented to an older man in dress uniform who lived in Colorado Springs. He was General Crabbe, none other than the CO of the Fifth Bomber Command. We shook hands, and I said to him, "The General has no reason to remember me, but I once crew-chiefed for you out of Nadzab, New Guinea." Eyes bright and alert, as I remembered him years ago, he gave me a quick inspection including the campaign ribbons. "Well then," he said, even better than David Niven could have said it, "I take it the mission was successful." He was smiling.

"Well, sir, it wasn't exactly a mission. It was in the fat-cat B-17 to Australia. I don't know what you were doing there, sir, but we were getting booze." There was the slightest ripple of movement among my USAFA hosts. Had the civilian professor gone too far with the general? General Crabbe stared a few seconds more. Then the smile grew broader. "92nd Airdrome Squadron?" he asked.

"Yes, sir," I said. And we both burst into laughter that neither bothered to explain to our colleagues. When we said good night, we held the handshake an extra second. If General Crabbe was astonished that anybody from the 92nd Airdrome Squadron could have become a distinguished visiting professor at his own United States Air Force Academy, he didn't seem to be displeased.

What else? In Pittsburgh we live in an apartment complex that houses mostly older types like us and young Japanese professionals and their families. Unlike us older folks, the Japanese move in and out of the building. Numbers of them are physicians who are specializing or doing a residency in one of the hospitals or taking courses at Pitt's medical school. Others are computer types studying at Carnegie Mellon University, and there's also a batch working toward MBAs at both schools. Those with small children send them to American schools. There is also a group of little Japanese toddlers, and I'm on special hugging terms with a number of them. These families are, of course, a very bright and special group of people, and I am very glad they are here with us and willing to be part of America's evil intentions.

And a last word to General Tibbets. Sir, I agree. If they choose to do so, just hang it up there at the Smithsonian for a few weeks and say nothing. We don't owe the Japanese an apology. Neither do they owe us one. It's over. So let the Enola Gay fly its last mission, and people can make of it what they will. With no disrespect intended, sir, I do not myself need to give it a gander. But I do heartily agree that it would be better if everybody kept his mouth shut. Even me.

PAUL WEST

A Boy's Blitz

There in the archaic light of a late fall afternoon, the field of dead search-lights glinted a little and awaited the switch. At midnight, or soon after, Nazi bombers that had flown the forty-five minutes from their bases in northern France would arrive en route for the city and drop their so-called eggs. Huge lenses would eye the night, even the fog, and catch them, moths in the quiet flame. Or so we thought, eyeing the glass ar-rayed at regular intervals throughout the field, once a pasture or the big juicy bed of hay or barley. We had faith in the anti-aircraft devices of our country, little as we respected the anything of anybody. A little bit of each of us was Nazi to be sure, much as a little bit of each Nazi boy was pseudo-English. War was between adults, wasn't it, and boys just approaching puberty were entitled to smaller wars of their own making, in which no one took much interest or offered to help. Whether or not the searchlights, flicked on in a big thunder of the lamp, spotted and trapped a bomber was beyond us. Somehow, we felt, being young and cocky, we would survive, our heads and hearts full of the vainglorious cheer of greenhorns.

After all, so far we had survived, even the landmine that landed a half-mile from our village and converted an entire field into a quarry with deep sides and enough water to drown in at its bottom, thirty feet down. This Nazi toy had floated down on a parachute, intended to do something more monstrous than shred a rural postbox, an ancient plow, and one decrepit outhouse in which women laborers from the nearby farm took hot tea from thermos flasks and told one another obscene sto-ries about their Friday nights. Surely the Nazis were poor aimers, this far from the city that made famous steel, a good ten miles to the north. What had they got against us? Had they somehow divined our futures, recognizing the terrors both civil and martial, we were going to be, and decided to wipe us out before our time: gutsy little guttersnipes with less

than Aryan blood, yet boldly inheriting our guts from Lord Nelson, the
Duke of Wellington, even Sir Francis Drake, and more recent heroes,
especially of the air war, already gone to an early grave, in the parlance
of those times "buying the farm" or "going for a Burton," which we knew
meant going down in the drink (the Channel). The expression meant,
really, going for a bottle of beer.

We were staring at those big glass eyes, seen sideways on and therefore
lopsided, deciding what *we* would do with them if the switch was within
our grasp. The guns were nowhere near, of course, because anyone shooting down the long cylinders of white light would hit the gunners as well;
so the anti-aircraft guns were a mile away, trigonometrically arranged to
fire when the lights touched a target. We understood only too well.

What possessed us next I have no idea. It was surely no whim of paci-
fism, or even envy of the full-blown role of grown-ups in all this massacre. Playing marbles along the gutters, with glass alleys or steel ball bearings filched from the war effort, we knew what it meant to eye what shone
or gleamed, almost like a model version of the big show. So too with our
little war—bows and arrows in the bluebell woods, bows of yew and arrows of thin cane—in which we either imitated or parodied, whooping
and yelping as Indians or the U.S. Cavalry, who perhaps did not whoop
or yelp at all. Indian women had captured the dead Captain Custer and
shoved their knitting needles into his ears, through his brain, to make
him listen better in whatever happy hunting ground he had gone to.
We were, I see it now, little infidels: we had lost our loyalty, our faith,
neither targets nor conquerors, but weirdly shoved aside so that adults
could get on with their killing. Yet the war, certainly in those years of the
Blitz, had readied us, we who were supposed to be marginal, restricted to
the world of our school reading (*As You Like It*, the campaigns of Caesar
in easy Latin) or adventure books we read by flashlight under the bed-
clothes: John Buchan, Eric Ambler, Leslie Charteris. The war had singed
us after all, at least on the night of the landmine, when six other bombs
had landed too, killing nobody but wrecking the uncanny cross-plan
of the village, an old Roman settlement with a Northgate, a Westgate,
and a Southgate, these three being the old routes in and out of chariots.
There was no Eastgate, for reasons unknown, it having been suggested
that the Romans quit England before they had a chance to build it, not
having gone clockwise, which was to say (to us) they had derivatively

timed themselves by King Alfred's old candles, on which he had scored the hours. He invented this. So: the Romans went away eastward, fed-up, not north, west, or south, before the English occupation struck them as too costly, too locally unpopular. What slowed our minds as much as the crescendo whistle of bombs, driving us to shelter under the kitchen table, or deep in the cellar down sweating concrete steps, was perhaps the clean retreat of the Romans, the little we were told in history lessons about their invasion and evacuation. The truth, I mean, not some easily memorized outline convenient for examiners. Did they itch? Had they scabs? Were they drunkards? What happened between them and local women? Did the Ella, Bella, and Della of those ancient times incite them amid the muck of urine and manure in the Gates? These were three streamlined, bosomy sisters who swung in step down the village street, farting behind them a brackish aroma of beer nobody could resist. I remember wanting to know. We all wanted to know, but we were no doubt going to be killed before we found out. War, like peace, kept so much of what really mattered away from us. We were growing up on rumor and soft soap, buttered up by genial parents and austere teachers, never having our noses rammed in what mattered, what had driven the Germans to occupy France and Belgium, and God knew what else. All I had to ballast my juvenile imagination was a picture of some poor slob of a German wheeling a barrow full of paper money, *pfennigs* (their word for penny, I'd thought), and this was what he needed to buy a loaf of bread. In such a world, where a loaf cost us tuppence, not a thousand million, wasn't something missing, some explanatory flash of light, or recognition, as in aircraft recognition (a "subject" already being taught at school to boys over fifteen, callow members of the Air Training Corps, which I had tried to join at twelve—the number of the Apostles, I said, and of scintillating noon). I was turned away, too much of a kid, though my mind, early suckled on simple Caesar, vainly hunted Marcus Aurelius and kept busy arranging belts on my brown blazer to mimic the military belt called a Sam Browne (which supported your revolver holster by spreading the weight up over your opposite shoulder). Holster, I later found out, was a word for darkness, so the holster was where you nestled your gun in darkness like a baby kangaroo. A joey.

I am coming to it now, the moment of shame, brought into being by ignorance, lack of knowledge, and general impatience with a war that, too much with us, wasn't with us enough. I had seen the wounded and battered from the Dunkirk evacuation sipping soup in the street and having their bandages changed, and heard them talking, grandly, about shoving impaled Nazis with their booted foot off their bayonets. They had escaped, but they had also lost, and so had we, excluded from the bloodshed and the infamous betrayal of the French, left to cope with the Nazi horde as best they could.

What, out of spite, we did, was to pelt the array of lamps or lights in that field with fist-sized rocks, pitching perhaps fifty in among the glass and doing some damage, though not as much as bombs. Could we be shot for this? Disgraced, certainly, and stripped of our medals, if any we had. Why did we do it? What did we gain? Was it an act of pure scorn, saying a pox on both houses, to hell with your war, down with all your flags? Include us in, to help, or expect only the worst from us, patriots nipped in the bud and cankered with Nazi caterpillars. What did the local crooners sing about? Ann Shelton and Vera Lynn? "When the lights go on again all over the world." Left to us, they would never go on again, and Churchill would condemn us to be bound in barbed wire and kept in the slop of a pig farm. We sabotaged the often-mentioned war effort, not from afar but on the spot, eager to be doing something crucial.

Sufficient unto shame is the occasion thereof. Or so we had been taught. Or had we read it in Shakespeare and was this the garbled version? The Romans were gone, wrapping their togas around them against the dank northern winds, but we were stabbing Caesar all over again. No, it was worse. What I came at last to understand, many years later, was that the glassy optics in that field were not searchlights at all, but a cunning device to foul up German radar beams conducting bombers to the city. A clever man called Jones, a boffin or "backroom boy," certainly no boy, had come up with a way of conning Nazi bombers with a false beam that led them several miles astray, and they were none the wiser, expecting a beam and following it almost blindly. The counter-beam was the stronger of the two, aimed up at the advancing bombers by a one-eyed king. So, we had not sabotaged the local artillery in its role of "ack-ack" or anti-aircraft, but, by destroying the exquisite symmetry and coordination of the apparatus in the field, exposed the neighbor city to appalling punishment night after night until repairs were made, and repairs were never made at speed in those days. Who would ever have predicted that a bunch of boys would mess up a clever spoof that saved thousands of lives, throughout the breadth and length of the land so often invoked in hymns? We were never found out. We never confessed, not having done much amiss, as we thought. The night when the landmine and the other bombs fell near our village had been proof that Jones's decoy beam was working well. The navigator and bomb-aimer were off by ten miles or more. We lived on in a blaze of indolent glory as the war erupted, then slowed, and victory began to be talked of, colloquial standby long deferred. I winced only later, when the desire to get it out all in one lethal word took over, ousting any desire for precise, cogent explanation, so that I wanted to ram the *oh* of dismay into the *but* of shame, and the *if* of evasion: *ohbutif*, no more meaningful to me at that point than *Stuka*, *Zersplitterung*, or *shaduf*. It was as if we had left poor old clever Jonesy's magnificent Erector set, all ten shiny boxes of it, from Beginner to Advanced, along with its batteries and neat electric motors, out in the rain, hoping he would blame the cows.

Notes from Ban Me Thuot

At 0910, I wandered into the operations section where Jess, Major With-erspoon, and assorted operations staff were silently listening through the static on the tactical radio. Over the buzz, a voice cracked, "Oscar six alpha, how many were on board, four or five? Hell, we've got enough parts here for six body bags, over." The big Okie radio operator replied, "Romeo Zulu, according to our manifest there were only four, over."

Major Witherspoon spat on the dirt floor and wiped his sweaty face with a dusty rag. Sergeant Stevenson, a muscular redhead, whistled, "Damn, I just saw ole' Captain Ray and the el tee at coffee." Jess just stared at the radio hard, his blue eyes never blinked.

Jess and I had been scheduled to make the flight north to the industrial site named Waite-Davis but gave up our seats on that morning's aircraft to the group surgeon and our refrigerator repair man, a favor granted as casually as one of Colonel Buckton's insults. With the colonel's final threat that if the refrigerators were not up by noon, he would have Chief Lopes's "spic ass," the junior officers left the morning briefing and ad-journed to the mess tent for coffee and a parody of the good colonel's morning performance.

The only West Pointer, other than Colonel Buckton himself, Jess had commanded a remote, land-clearing company for six months, during which his wounds earned him Purple Hearts and authenticity, estimable stock in a combat zone. Much to his chagrin, he was finishing his tour in the relatively safe Engineer Group Operations TOC (Tactical Operations Center). Jess was the longest in country, the biggest soldier on the com-pound, and our acknowledged and undisputed moral authority. If Jess thought something was wrong, we paused to reassess our position. Of course, Jess hardly ever questioned the most hare-brained scheme, thus his unchallenged supremacy in the unspoken hierarchy of the informal bureaucracy.

In fact, about a month earlier, it was Jess's idea to pitch rocks on the tin roof of the field grade bunker and scream, "Incoming!" In the dark mad scramble, the fat major broke his arm trying to get to the fighting position. Major Witherspoon, who hated the fat major as much as we did, had to use Jess's West Point credential to argue the colonel out of pressing charges against us all.

I looked to him to see me through this crisis, too. Jess would be able to make sense out of our very close call. His silence and distant stare unnerved me, and I felt a chill in the crowded heat of the TOC. In the dark of the sleeping bunker, I lay on my poncho, my mouth full of ashes, morning coffee acid boiling in the back of my throat, fumbling to pull the flip top on a warm Falstaff beer.

Ray, Dan, Doc, and Mr. Lopes had tried to fly below the highland clouds but had slammed into a mountainside. "Romeo Zulu, according to our manifest there were only four, over."

Drinking the second warm beer, I stared through the dust particles that rose in the slivers of sunlight and listened to roaches scurry across sandbags, the buzz of a fly, the distant crackling refrain of a tactical radio, and the steady stroke of my heartbeat, louder and louder. Jess found me around noon and asked me to help him get the dead guys' kits in order.

We didn't say a word as we inventoried the footlockers. I yearned for a wise-ass comment that would make small sense of second lives. I thought back to the morning coffee and how in his best Buckton voice Jess had lampooned the 0600 briefing, "Lopez, you better have that refrigerator perturbation under control by lunch, or I'll *find* someone with half a brain who *can* do the job right."

Lopes stirred his coffee and muttered in his cup, "Can you believe dat asshole. I've only been working for the shithead for seven months, and he doesn't even know my damn name."

Captain Gage, the Intelligence officer who was always sweating added, "I couldn't believe how he reacted to that shit about the kid at Whiskey Mountain. The one who got his leg caught in the rock crusher."

Jess pointed out, "You could see wheels in his head turning. His first question was, 'How long did you say the plant was down?' He never asked if the kid was alive, did he lose his leg? No, 'How many hours did you say the plant was down?' He was trying to figure out how hard the battalion was working before the accident. He had to make up his mind if they were using the accident to cover up their poor statistics, if he had to go down there and kick some ass."

Gage added, "What a cold-blooded bastard! Lopes, just cut the ass-hole's heart out and carry it with you up to Waite and stick it in the fridge—permafrost!"

"Did we ever find out what happened to the kid? Did he lose his leg?"

"Everything is numbers. People are numbers. Production is numbers. It's a war of attrition, and Buckton's a cold-blooded, heartless computer. Every stretch of pavement is one more step on his path to a star, and he knows that the higher-ups have their calculators out measuring his leadership just like he's measuring us."

Tired of what he considered work talk, Ray Lanning, a stringy Texan with an exaggerated drawl, adjusted his aviator sunglasses and theatrically drew out what he hoped to be the last word on our esteemed leader, "Hey, it's the only goddamn war we have. What do you all fuggin' expect? Ghandi, Martin Luther King, or somebody who gives a rat's ass about some numb-nut, pot-smoking private who slips and falls in a rock crusher? Shit, as long as the kid didn't loose his nuts, he'll be back home in a month and collecting full disability!"

In what seemed to be his natural state, Ray was nursing a serious hangover. As an Engineer Group aviation detachment commander, he felt he was missing the shooting war of gunship pilots but made up for his deep and bitter disappointment by sitting in a lawn chair on top of the O'Club bunker raising beers every time incoming rockets randomly tore up the airfield.

Dan Dougherty, Ray's copilot, on the other hand, didn't drink and carried a Bible. He quietly stirred his coffee, shook his head at Ray's exaggerated cynicism, and knew what was coming next. As usual, in part because of Dan's squeamishness, and in part because Ray's imagination never strayed far from the mostly fictitious world of his sex life, Ray quickly turned to a conversation you might hear if dogs could talk.

Dan tried to look bored as he sipped his coffee, but Ray smiled his gat-toothed smile and continued, until Jess added the last word to the morning coffee klatch, "Ray, I sure am tired of your disgusting bullshit! Let's get to work."

Following Jess's benediction, Ray and Dan picked up their hats, swatted at the flies, and raised the tent flap. Ray adjusted his aviator glasses, breathed in the heavy air, and exhaled, "Awh-he-yauh! The fresh smell of burning shit! Lovely Vietnam, the civilization that took two thousand years to learn to carry two piles of shit with one stick and eat a pile of shit with two." We answered Ray's host-country cultural synopsis with our wishes that he go screw himself and have a safe flight.

"Romeo Zulu, according to our manifest there were only four, over."

That day I had my fill of haphazard, senseless destruction. Almost a year of booby traps, mines, casual rockets, unseen snipers. The desultory violence and the random waste of lives. American and Vietnamese. Soldier and civilian. The very young and the very old. Victims of accidents in the air, accidents on the roads, ambushes, and, always, a pervasive and wanton disregard for life and decency that characterized this war.

The teenage woman on the back of a moped hit by a speeding GI truck lying face down in sticky, fly-covered blood. Her hips shattered, body twisted so that her small feet pointed up. Her dark, flitting eye the only sign of life.

The dead, dismembered Vietcong's torso and limbs planted in Montagnard earthenware pots and left, fly-covered, on the hairpin turn of a mountain road as a warning, a sign.

The two soldiers who feigned engine trouble to stay behind the convoy for the wet of warm beer and sex, ambushed a few miles from the work site. When I got to the bullet-riddled vehicle, stepped up and opened the door, the driver's pooled guts and blood splashed over my legs and feet and soaked the red dust of the road. The dead driver's partner sobbing a half mile back, where he had jumped and hid in the open sewer that ran next to the road.

For weeks after that ambush, every time I walked by the bullet-ripped truck, clouds of flies would rise from the cab where remnants of viscera rotted in the still, hot air.

It was the same stumbling hum of flies I heard every time I went into the latrine to take a dump. The same murmur that rose in a cloud over the woman dying in the road and from the swarm that feasted on body parts in Montagnard crockery. It was the zoom that greeted those who found an airplane disintegrated on a mountainside, its human freight smashed, sliced, and scattered in the elephant grass.

"Romeo Zulu, according to our manifest there were only four, over."

Imagine those who found the wreck, bent over like farmers planting rice in the valley below. A rescue party harvesting bone and body parts from among shattered airplane pieces, solving the puzzle of mangled flesh, trying to make whole a scene of senseless mutilation. Did they ever sort out the gore? Does Ray's family know that perhaps it is Dan's mutilated hand folded on their son's torn chest, or what is left of Mr. Lopes's shattered leg stuffed alongside Doc's torso in the cheap tin coffin. All as one making its way home on slow cargo planes.

Buried in small towns, different body's body parts stacked as are the names on the granite wall. What do we carry from that wreck? Memory and monument. Time and death fold in on themselves.

And that night in Ban Me Thuot, in the old French hotel with the high ceilings and empty bar, after we spent the afternoon inventorying their footlockers and in the process lifted a bottle of Ray's Jack, Jess and I sat silently drinking neat whiskey like cowboys in a bad movie. Perhaps it was a dream, or is a dream now, but it happened, and that night in Ban Me Thuot is with me still. As is the piano up against the dark wall and Jess picking notes carefully, trying to play Mozart, through a drunken haze to the rhythm of the distant echo of B-52 strikes just over the Cambodian border.

The big, balding, dirty soldier, playing beautiful music deliberately on a dusty, untuned piano. Two of us alone, as headache drunk and silent as that night after Jess helped me get the truck and the dead boy back to the compound, and I tried to wash the blood off my legs and boots but could never get rid of the smell. The smell, the dust, the dry headache, and Jess's sweet notes leaving the big room for the night air and beyond—his big, filthy fingers picking just the right small notes.

JOHN WOLFE

A Different Species of Time

The paratroopers of the Second Battalion, 327th Infantry, sometimes fought in lowland areas; however, most of our time was spent stalking North Vietnamese on the ancient game trails that weave through the jungles of the Anamese Cordillera. Geographically, these mountains lie on the Laotian border; psychologically, they seem to exist in some mystical realm. In the midst of their cloud-hidden summits, one senses the restoration of something primal. Reason, sanity, and order seem remote peculiarities of a civilization from which you have been isolated, banished, and your Christian God seems a deity out of His jurisdiction.

In a way it seems appropriate that such a surreal landscape should host an event in which humans hunted other humans. It is as if, when the world was created, allowances were made for special zones, nonhomogeneous with the rest of the world, redolent with supernatural mystery, where human beings could experience the full expression of their darker side. On trails that seemed to come from nowhere and to go nowhere, we moved through the fog-shrouded forests of this reverse Shangri-la.

Weighed down with sixty pounds of equipment, we would pass days of tortuous climbing with no sign of the North Vietnamese. The heat was suffocating and the terrain difficult to nearly impossible to traverse. Torrential rain fell for days, turning feet to sponge; under every leaf, leeches waited to attach themselves. Dysentery was frequent and parasite infestation certain.

The sudden appearance of sandal tracks, bloody bandages, log-reinforced trails, or other signs of human presence would send adrenaline rushing into the blood of the point man and his slack. The possible meaning of hesitation at the front of a moving unit was clear to all behind, and hearts would pound all down the line.

Sometimes the fighting started and ended with a single burst from the point man's M-16, but on other occasions the forest erupted in horizon-

tal firestorms of terminal rain; red and green tracers filled the air, and
RPG rounds whooshing and exploding were answered by the thud of
M-79 rounds. Squalls of deadly fire moving through claustrophobic open
areas hacked at vegetation and flesh, splintering trees and bone; death
danced through the forest among the nominated of both parties.

Anyone familiar with the "flight or fight" choices offered by the survival instinct knows both can exert a compelling and irresistible force
over a soldier's actions, one primal urge sending him into shameless,
panicked flight and the other launching him on an equally shameless
attack, the ferocity of which often startles the attacker more than the attacked. Training, discipline, and comradeship help ensure that the latter
response occurs and not the former.

It is later, nauseous and shaking, that one actually comes to conscious
grips with the full awfulness of combat events. The same atmosphere of
quiet sacredness that inspires silent monks to choose the mountains as
sights for their temples added, I think, an extra and malignant dimension to the carnage committed there.

Few things in this world are as unforgiving, pitiless, ungovernable,
and irrecoverable as lead and steel loosed from a weapon. The transfigu-
rations they effect on the bodies of friend and foe alike form a permanent backdrop to all of a soldier's future visions. While others experience
intervals of silence between thoughts, a combat veteran's intervals will
be filled with rubbery Halloween mask heads housing skulls shattered
into tiny shards, schemeless mutilations, and shocked, pained expressions that violent and premature death casts on a dead face. These images are war's graffiti. They are scrawled across the veteran's mind, de-
facing the silence and peace that others enjoy. At times the images may
seem to fade, but an unguarded glance into the gloom is sufficient to
exhume them.

The possibility of being overwhelmed by such events was always one
small horror away. In other wars, at such times, men probably called in
desperation to their God to sustain and deliver them. In the 101st Division, we employed a secular technique of emotional first aid handed
down from short-timer to cherry. If we felt ourselves at that point of sat-
uration, we chanted the mantra, *it don't mean nothing, it don't mean nothing!* If chanted defiantly enough, the phrase took on the feeling of an
affirmation, almost a doctrine.

Some individuals seemed to acquire additional stamina by nurturing a hatred for the "gooks," by creating a dehumanized image of the enemy at which to direct rage. I could never see the North Vietnamese Army as other than our companions in misfortune. I would have liked to hate them, but the scanty personal bric-a-brac found in the pockets and packs of the dead dramatized not their difference from us but their essential sameness. We found family pictures (theirs black and white, ours color), a few small bills, a comb, and maybe even a bag of marijuana. Assuming the role of nemesis to poor, rice-eating, subproletariats yanked from their lives of subsistence farming seemed ridiculous. The NVA themselves had a slogan that best summed up their plight: "Born in the North to die in the South!"

A great sense of displacement existed in my unit as well. This sense of displacement was exacerbated by the constant turbulence and changes in our membership. The social structure of my platoon and company seemed inspired by the Hydra. Members killed or seriously wounded were physically and emotionally amputated from the whole. New members would eventually appear to replace them in a process of constant regeneration. Though discarded by the communal will of the unit that remained, these amputated parts of us forced us to consider what new trail the less fortunate now took and what the likelihood was that we'd follow them at some point.

My own process of introversion began on the morning of March 18, 1969. Hue had been rocketed the night before from a mountain to its west. As the closest unit to the suspected location, we were ordered to proceed in that direction. It was my turn to walk point, and I was amazed to arrive at the launch site without enemy contact. In deference to the harrowing walk I had just led, I was allowed to remain on top of the mountain, to serve as a rallying point for other soldiers if contact was made, while the rest of my company split up and pushed down the sides of the hill in search of caves. When the squads had pushed a good distance down the sides, the NVA struck my position with a brief, furious barrage. An RPG round threw me several feet. I felt tumbled inside a churning wave of hot dry vapor. And then I went blank.

My blackout must have lasted but seconds, because twigs, leaves, and dirt were still showering down around me as I regained consciousness.

Lying face down, I felt the lower half of my body engulfed by a nauseating numbness, and I was initially convinced I had been blown in half.

Wanting to spare myself the sight of my own bisection, I decided to confirm or dispel this suspicion by trying to kneel. Finding my right leg and pulling it up underneath me filled me with relief and emboldened me to roll over to assess the damage. Blood drenched my uniform; my left leg was shredded and my right one badly mauled. Blood bubbles were sudsing from a hole on the left side of my chest, and breathing was painful. Yet, things were better and left more room for hope than I had at first envisioned.

Finding myself largely intact, I became optimistic, almost joyous. Oddly, I next found myself singularly concerned with a sense of propriety, with responding to the situation as a soldier should. My M-16 found its way into my hands, and although I could see no target, I emptied the magazine into the face of the forest. This seemed the correct, reasonable response, a familiar and comforting bit of behavior rooted in the rational, orderly world from which I now seemed to be inexorably slipping.

Other paratroopers started to arrive at my side. Hugging the forest floor, some moved in front of my position to shield me from further harm. The top sergeant and medic began working, furiously wrapping gauze and plugging holes while I drank blood and swallowed their reassuring lies. The captain, our company commander, was on the radio, employing emasculating insults and threats to coax a timid chopper pilot into hovering over our position long enough to lower a rigid litter and effect my evacuation. His final menacing transmission—"Do it now, or I'll drop you out of the fucking sky myself!"—ended the debate.

A cable hoisted me through the jungle canopy and into the aluminum belly of the chopper. A full-length portrait of Wily Coyote greeted me from the back of the pilot's helmet with the words "Slicks are for Kids" painted beneath it. Halfway through the flight, some impulse caused the pilot to turn his visored face around to stare at me. Perhaps he wanted to see if I was still alive; maybe he just felt my eyes on the back of his helmet, wanting the Roadrunner cartoon to begin. He made nothing like an attempt at communication, but I smiled him a red smile and formed a peace sign with two bloodsticky fingers. After touching down near the sea, I was jerked out into a marvelous blast of heat from the glaring

Asian sun. It felt liquid on my arms, face, and chest, like being basted with warm butter.

In the Quonset-hut hospital I became frigid again. Shivering, I was placed on a table. People started to surround me. To a clerk who asked me if I wanted a priest I screamed, "I don't want a fucking priest! I want a doctor!"

Surgeons started to probe my legs with a needle. "Do you feel this? How about this?" Suddenly my heart started to convulse, as if some rabbit-sized animal was struggling to escape, to break free from my rib cage. "Forget the goddamn legs," I screamed. "My chest—something's happening!" My heart had stopped. I fell back and then . . . silence—more of a stillness, really, a stillness that made me feel that my heart had been, since birth, pounding thunderously.

I was not unconscious. As a matter of fact, never had my thoughts seemed so palpable and lucid as in that stillness: "Oh, fucking great!" I thought. "I'm dead! Shit! Now what?"

I realized all the terror and pain were gone, and that although I wasn't breathing, it didn't bother me in the least. A most pleasant sensation came over me. I felt as if I were grass waving in a slight summer breeze. It was a delicious sensation, and I felt as if I were actually overlooking such a scene: a hill covered with tall, swaying grass.

Perhaps at the moment of death the mind searches the sum of one's experiences, and then the most soothing all-is-well-in-the-world sensation detaches itself and rises to the surface of consciousness. I say this because I seem to recognize my death sensation as an experience I had as a child while searching for arrowheads on the grassy hills behind my grandfather's farm in Indiana. It was just before sundown when the combination of warmth, breeze, grass, and color coalesced to create such a sense of well-being in me that I had to interrupt my search to more fully surrender to the sensation.

From what I've been able to piece together from my records, memory, and a recent meeting with the doctor who saved me that day, I suffered three cardiac arrests. After performing two open-heart massages to restart my heart and expending thirty-nine pints of blood, the two senior surgeons gave up when the third arrest occurred. The junior surgeon, Captain Barton Nissoson, convinced the anesthetist to remain behind, and together they postponed my death.

The rigorous leg of my inward journey was just about to commence. Like a traveler coming upon the last oasis, the last outpost before setting out across the bleak immensity of desert, I regained a final and brief conscious contact with what I accepted as reality.

Dr. Nissoson was sitting next to me. After reminding me that I had lost a limb, he joked about how I had frightened him the day before, and I joked with him about my concerns that he might be Polish.

Lieutenant Colonel Dyke, who had recently replaced Charlie Beckwith as my battalion commander, also visited me during that brief respite. He leaned over me, gave me a fatherly embrace, a kiss, pressed a 101st Airborne Medallion into my hand, and placed a dagger emblazoned with the division's Screaming Eagle on my stomach. He whispered words in my ear that I did not hear, but his warmth and that of Dr. Nissoson were vital provisions that went far to sustain me on the lonely journey I was about to embark on.

The life-support equipment I needed to survive was several miles out at sea aboard the USS *Repose*. Cruising the South China Sea, this hospital ship steered a course parallel to the hostilities, drawing close at points to pick up the results of flare-ups and inland carnage. Its cargo of broken bodies was eventually delivered to Subic Bay in the Philippines. For the short hop out to the *Repose*, Dr. Nissoson huddled next to me in the chopper, rhythmically squeezing a football-shaped bag to keep my lungs inflated. After we landed on the ship, my life was officially a navy responsibility. Nissoson, his duty accomplished above and beyond the call, stole a self-indulgent moment in the galley, snacking on popcorn and chocolate milk before flying back to the war.

Liquids had begun to fill my punctured lung; the result was pneumonia and high fever. What little physical strength I may have had quickly dissipated, and I slipped into unconsciousness. When I awoke I was disoriented. I was only semiconscious and under the heavy influence of narcotics. Slowly, bits and pieces started to come to me: the ambush, the medevac, the cardiac arrests, Dr. Nissoson. I grasped that I had been hurt badly and that I was now on a hospital ship. That's when the first devils appeared, climbing brazenly up onto the foot of my bed.

The troupe consisted of a female and two males; the males dragged a grass hut with them. They were probably ten inches tall, gray in color, with a peculiar, semitransparent, mother-of-pearl quality to their skins.

They were hairless and completely human in shape and proportion, except for doglike snouts and pointed ears.

Using the hut like a stage backdrop, the males lit it on fire and proceeded to pummel and rape the female with exaggerated theatrical gestures. She reacted in a similar manner to the assault, employing exaggerated and stylized theatrics like those seen in traditional Chinese opera. The skit completed, all three disappeared over the side of the bed.

Having grown up on the edge of the East Village, I was aware of the mind's capacity to hallucinate, especially under the influence of the drugs I knew I must have been given. This rationalization helped me to dismiss the event, but as the devils' visits persisted, several things began to bother me. First, they always looked the same; I came to realize this as I repeatedly ogled them, studied their bodies, and watched their muscles flex and relax as they moved. Secondly, they used the real environment, obeying the laws of gravity and physics as all real objects must. They walked on horizontal surfaces and climbed when they reached a vertical structure. When negotiating thin pipes overhead, they walked like acrobats, tightrope performers, visibly struggling to maintain their balance.

In addition, I noticed that they responded to me and other humans emotionally. Catching me staring at them, they would become angry and threatening. One male mocked my efforts to free myself from my wrist restraints. They seemed to possess heightened senses of perception and active nervous systems—they were easily startled by loud noises and would scatter when nurses or doctors approached. At times they were exhibitionists and showoffs. A lone female, wearing nothing but the faded, worn bottom half of a ballerina dress, once climbed up on my bed carrying an early-model phonograph. After starting the music, she performed a short ballet for me.

A psychiatrist aboard ship started paying me visits. Perhaps he sensed unusual psychological activity, and his professional curiosity was aroused. Whatever his motivation, he seemed to take a personal interest in my plight. I was in dire need of communion myself. I'd have preferred a shaman, a Dantesque chaperone to help me navigate this dimension now intruding into my consciousness, someone who could posit me, sanity intact, back in my own milieu. Lacking such a person, I thought the psychiatrist seemed my best and only bet. On those occasions, therefore, when a small part of my mind would rise up out of the underworld-like altered state to consciousness, I anxiously scanned the space for his presence. My small gray play pals had, in my mind, achieved the recognition, the status of reality, and I desperately wanted to share the fact of their presence with him.

In response to my entreaties for an opportunity to portray my secret visitors, the psychiatrist provided me with a pencil and legal pad. I worked on the task without real cognizance; as I handed the pad back to him, I saw that I had drawn not devils, as I had intended, but scores of tiny Indians and cowboys shooting it out. As a young child I had filled many hours drawing such scenarios, miniature battlefields with opposing armies forming up and facing off. I had vicariously experienced their mutual slaughter as they exchanged volleys of lethal scribbles until one side was obliterated.

Despite the difficulty I had communicating my impressions of reality to others during this period, I did, I believe, achieve perfect communion with one person aboard the *Repose*. Semiconscious and strapped into a wheelchair, I was wheeled down to a physical therapy room with various exercise bars, tables, and gym equipment around. Weights about the size of baby rattles were placed in my hands. Just a few feet away, a physical therapist was busy balancing something on a table that at first looked like a sack of potatoes. When I focused, I saw that it was a young Asian man, probably Korean, who had lost both arms and both legs close to the torso. No sooner would the therapist balance the torso on its buttocks than it would topple over on its face with a painful-looking impact, and then the process would be repeated.

The Korean's eyes met mine, and for a long moment the presence of everything and everybody else in the room blurred, faded out, dematerialized, leaving only his mind and mine on that spatial plane in an uninterrupted convergence. And then we both started to laugh hysterically. Neither of us expected to meet another human in the private dream to which we had been transported. So remote was the place we inhabited that Neil Armstrong could not have been more surprised had he bumped into someone taking those first giant steps for mankind on the moon.

The nature of my visions eventually underwent a drastic change for the worse. Space itself was now becoming unstable, and the environment as a whole started to undergo kaleidoscopic transformations. Space became elastic, stretching and shrinking around me. At one point, I gazed over the side of my bed, and I felt high up in the stands of a stadium. It was dark, and the playing field almost too far away to see. On another occasion, every object in the room revealed its design as being sexually inspired. Anything longer than wide became a penis, and anything with an enclosure or opening became a vagina. Occasionally, the walls would open up. Once, the entrance to a long jungle trail appeared in the wall. I could see the backs of soldiers moving away from me. I wanted to go with them, but a huge black spider crawled out from the opening, straddled my bed, and began to gnaw away at my legs.

Under the propulsion of some malignant force, the pace of these kaleidoscopic changes quickened, and for what must have been a week I lived in a cubist maze of shifting agonies and disorienting absurdities. The space around me churned, forming and reforming itself into a living torment of dark permutations, a fluid gestalt that shaped and reshaped into patterns of agonizing implication. Shortly after my immersion into this world of Bosch-like nightmare flux, I consciously decided to relax my grip and just let go, to adopt a totally passive attitude about my surreal visions. I'd resist nothing and I'd be open to everything. I literally surrendered body and soul. But, as one horror piled upon the next, the density of despair became unbearable. Shattered, I felt beyond reintegration or reconstruction, and I prayed for a speedy doom.

Annihilation was forthcoming, but in a more profound and devastating form than mere cessation. Whereas at the moment of death my mind had so effortlessly and instantaneously found a peak of bliss, it now seemed headed for the opposite pole with a vengeance, taking the long, scenic route and excavating through all the layers and shades of dread that humans have faced through time. Ironically, when the bottom did fall out in a kind of black satori, it was not the presence of any kind of horror that was revealed but rather an absence. The miseries that had preceded had pressed in on me in an ever more confining manner.

Now, all confines exploded, and a gray immensity faced me. There was only the gray, sterile infinity aware of its own lack of warmth. There was a particular quality of warmth it lacked. I'm tempted to use the term *divine love* for the quality that was absent here.

When or how I emerged from this realm I don't remember. At some nonspecific point in time the flame reignited, and all experience was once again charged with the warmth that was entirely missing in the place

I'd visited. For several days I lacked the presence of mind to dwell on or articulate the experiences I'd had, even to myself, but I clearly knew and felt that I now housed an abyss, that I had become cavernous and hollow. Speculating on why these experiences—which could easily have remained an irreconcilable anomaly, an unbridgeable interval with the rest of my existence—didn't result in my disintegration takes me back to the Museum of Natural History in New York City.

As a very young child walking through the halls filled with artifacts from primitive societies, I started to suspect that these statues, masks, and totems were touching me, addressing me, if you will. There was a mysterious and dark aspect to the sensation, but a kind of titillating warmth emanated from them too. Like a child raised in a puritanical society who keeps all libidinal stirrings hidden, these feelings became and remained a secret part of my spiritual life. Being a child, I may have confused an aesthetic response with a religious feeling, but from that time to this, I have felt a compulsion to seek an ever more intimate convergence with the source of that noumenal presence, be it aesthetic, religious, or something other.

A devoutly Catholic youth, I, like the Haitian Hougans who add Christian effigies to their altars, found no contradiction in incorporating these seemingly pantheistic yearnings into my spiritual makeup. While the Catholicism was based on an esoteric faith, this noumenal quality I felt had the advantage of being a more tangible force, something that could actually, physically, emotionally, and psychologically "move" me.

Throughout my school life, I had contented myself by filling my room with carvings from Africa, Asia, and Latin America, but by the age of eighteen I wanted adventure, hands-on exotic adventure, physical, sexual, and spiritual. Disenchanted with the church, the Bronx, Irish-Catholic girls, and school, I was determined to travel to the most remote spot in the world. I didn't seek the sterile luxury of a tourist or student; I wanted to go like Sir Richard Burton or Sabu, in Lord Jim style, to get myself lost, go native, become enlightened, and achieve rebirth.

The jungles of Vietnam may now seem a grotesque choice of locale in which to realize a return-to-paradise myth, but, with its primeval forests, Stone Age mountain tribes, and all those Buddhas with their enigmatic smiles, it seemed like a place where some kind of revelation might be encountered.

So, in a sense, I saw then and see now all that happened to me as the result of a personal quest. An unclear but nevertheless strong feeling I had pursued since childhood led me to ask a simple, mystical question that—whether by God or devil, my own subconscious, or dumb chance—was answered in vivid apocalyptic terms. I had experienced both the gray nothingness somewhere at the center of my being, which had almost engulfed me, and the unexplainable warmth that brought me back from the brink.

Understandably, because I am a painter, a large part of a picture's value to me is the amount of this religio-aesthetic warmth that emanates from it and the degree to which it reflects the depth of human experience. Ultimately, the many hidden structures, the overlapping gestalts that hide behind and interpenetrate with the subject matter and the passion, feeling, and purity of its execution become a metaphor for humanity itself. It seems to me that when confronting a work of art, one should feel awakened in oneself a capacity for complexity, mystery, and an extraordinary intensity of feeling. Only through my experiences in Vietnam, my wounding, and my recovery did I come to understand this.

Even more than in previous American wars, petty politics worked to obscure and invalidate a mother lode of human insight that lay just beneath the surface of the Vietnam War and the hard-won experiences of its combatants. Intellectual fashion in the Age of Aquarius could accommodate—was, in fact, eager to embrace—the illuminations of every itinerant guru, maharashi, escaped Indian chief, psychedelic mind excursionist, and howling Jesus freak. Yet, through some odd prejudice, this same intellectual fashion found nothing worthy of scrutiny in the effects of sustained trauma on its veterans. The Vietnam veteran was merely assigned the role of depraved fiend in the twentieth-century's version of the Leyenda Negra, a being fashioned out of a complicated war. What might have been an enormous collective contribution was unexplored or buried. In fact, a huge granite block that builds to a black crescendo as you walk its length was thrown on top for good measure.

With thousands of years of warfare and holocaust as history, we should be as familiar with this dark human realm as we are with our own shadow, but each time our darker side intrudes into the arena of normal human affairs, it is treated as an aberration and given a new, misleading identity (shell shock, battle fatigue, posttraumatic stress disorder). Each reappearance is confronted by a psychological community that, though perhaps more sophisticated, is less in touch and familiar with the forces unleashed than our ancestors who painted themselves blue and pranced naked in the snow before Caesar's legions, challenging the absolutism, the dominion, of Rome. There is a criminal, spiritual cowardice in this evasion, because in examining the effects of war, we might well discover just what inveigles humanity to its blackest deeds.

Through a slight inversion of logic, I have come to see my war experiences and subsequent difficulties as a positive, enabling episode. As an artist, I have a responsibility to examine human existence on all its frontiers and to discover just how deep is deep. Furthermore, if all the unfathomable desolation I came to encounter was "all," was the total matrix of human experience, if it filled the whole circle, then humanity's plight would be an uninterrupted succession of Buchenwalds and Cambodias. It is not.

So I see my journey not as around the circumference of human experience, not necessarily even along the radius, but along a chord into myself, the length of which constitutes its own nourishing message as much as it does its darkness.

Postscript: Following my year at Walter Reed Army Hospital, my records were sent to the VA hospital on First Avenue and Twenty-Third Street in Manhattan. A clerical error placed me on a ward for plastic surgery patients, where I spent my last night of hospitalization along with a horribly burned and disfigured former marine. Like me, he had experienced a cardiac arrest. He remembered nothing of the moments following the arrest but said that for a week after resuscitation, small gray devils danced on his bed, variously entertaining and provoking him.

Voices

For many, the term *Vietnam* evokes memories of rice paddy and jungle, of warm rain, of being surrounded by an alien culture far from home, but these are not my images. I remember the parched plains of northern Texas and Oklahoma, the cowboy culture of Wichita Falls, Texas, an unlikely locale for an account of the Vietnam War, but a place that, nevertheless, connects many of its untold stories. These are the stories of Vietnamese pilots who lived a sequence that reversed the one American soldiers followed. Instead of spending a year in Vietnam and then returning home as their American counterparts did, the Vietnamese pilots left Vietnam for the United States, where they served their country for a year or so. Then they returned to Vietnam and to combat.

As a T-37 instructor pilot (IP), I taught fledgling Vietnamese student pilots at Sheppard Air Force Base starting in June 1974. My time teaching them was short, because less than eleven months later Saigon fell, and the Vietnamese flight training program ended. Still, as I reflect on that brief time, I'm astonished at how great an impact it has had on me. Here the abstractions of the Vietnam War dissolved, replaced by the faces and the hearts of young men who played a central role in a rapidly unfolding tragedy and played it with exceptional grace. Some days when the sun glints from my sunglasses the way it once glinted from my helmet visor, I remember instructing Vietnamese student pilots . . .

I hear my voice in the helmet's headset as it's transmitted on the T-37's interphone. "Pull back on the stick. Raise the nose. Back trim. Add power—now!"

I look to my left, at the student, sitting in the pilot's seat cocooned in a green flight suit and gloves. The green visor on his helmet and the green rubber oxygen mask with its hose dangling to the regulator give the appearance of an enlarged head with a single huge eye and long curled proboscis.

"My aircraft," I say, as I add power and steady the plane. "Look at how much power it takes," I point to the tachometers. "What happens if you don't add enough power?" I raise my voice. "What happens if you're low to the ground and don't add enough power?" He gives me the right answer: "Crash."

I shake the stick. "Your aircraft. Look at how high the nose is; keep it there. Cross-check the altimeter and airspeed. That's it. Relax. Get the feel of the controls. Just maintain your altitude and airspeed and heading."

While he practices, I look at the paved roads below us, etched into the plains of northern Texas and Oklahoma. The pavement radiates north, south, east, and west, stopping at the sea our students will cross when they return home.

In my mind I follow the ribbon of pavement that brought me to Sheppard AFB. The journey from an upper-Midwest adolescence to air force instructor pilot teaching Vietnamese air cadets how to fly involved more than geography, and it changed the landscape of my life. But the landscape of our students' lives changed much more.

The time I spent at Sheppard prior to the fall of Saigon was long enough to see a single class of Vietnamese pilots through the course of instruction, which included visual and instrument flying, formation, and navigation. Upon completion of T-37 training, these students received their pilot's wings and proceeded to combat training, typically in A-37 aircraft, the attack version of the T-37. I shepherded two students through the program, Long and Kai. Long had left medical school to become a pilot. He'd been born in Hanoi. After the Viet Minh killed his father, his mother fled to Saigon with him. Kai looked like he was about fourteen years old. One day my wife asked him if he was looking forward to going home to Vietnam. He said no. He said everyone he knew was dead.

But Long and Kai did go home, only a month or two before Saigon fell. By then, students no longer received combat training in the A-37 Dragonfly at England AFB, Louisiana, before returning to Vietnam. The money and time for training at England AFB had run out. Long and Kai went directly to Vietnam and to combat training—in combat. I never heard from Kai again. A few years later, I received a single letter from Long, who was lying low in Saigon. Later I heard from a refugee that Long had been captured trying to escape Vietnam and was never seen again.

But I did see many of their fellow student pilots again in 2003, when the 88th Flying Training Squadron, the unit we'd all flown with at Sheppard AFB, held its first and only reunion in San Antonio. I slept little during the weekend of the reunion. We spent most of our time gathered around a keg of beer, and I listened to the stories some two hundred former students brought with them. They told me in their still-broken English about how they trained, about how they flew combat, about how they escaped from Vietnam, about how they made new lives for themselves in America.

These were stories that told me something I needed to know about the war that defined my generation, about a war that casts a lengthening shadow on us as we age. Since the reunion in Texas, I've interviewed many of these former students, these former Vietnamese pilots. I've endeavored to give a voice to their stories that is faithful to their intent. Some stories relate a painful loss of country and identity; some describe agonizing hardship; yet others go beyond tales of endurance to glimpse a hopeful future for themselves and the next generation. What follows are but a few of the stories I've collected. All of them help us to see the Vietnam War from a perspective that's too often ignored, that of our allies, whose losses were far greater than the considerable losses we've experienced ourselves.

"One day you are in an aircraft doing loops and spins and flying formation; the next, you're on the ground washing dishes."

NGA P. DIEP, Class 75-07

My first flying lesson in the T-41, I learned how hard it was to taxi the plane. I'd never driven a car before, and here I was trying to keep an aircraft's nosewheel on the yellow centerline of the taxiway. But I learned and made it to Sheppard and flying T-37s.

Navigation training in the T-37 was a problem for me. When I flew my first visual navigation flight with Lieutenant Tanner, I had prepared the map I was to use to find my way through the nav route, but shortly after we took off, I realized that I'd left my map at the desk where we'd get our aircraft assignment and sign out of the squadron. Soon after the flight, everyone teased me about forgetting the map—the most important item needed for a navigation flight.

My problems continued on my navigation solo flight on Nav Route 5, which was over Oklahoma. I couldn't find one of the checkpoints. I should have just flown out my time for that segment of the route and turned to the heading for the next point, but my pride wouldn't let me miss a checkpoint. I flew back and forth trying to find it on the ground. Finally, I just headed off in the direction that felt right to me. When I called up Sheppard Approach on the radio, the traffic controller told me I was on the wrong side of the field and headed in the wrong direction. The controller told me to turn 180 degrees and asked if I was low on fuel, but I was ashamed to declare minimum fuel. I knew I'd have only enough fuel to make one landing attempt. After I pitched out to downwind, I tried to save fuel by not using the speed brake. It took a long time to slow to the gear-lowering airspeed of 150 knots. Finally, I moved my thumb to the speed-brake switch just as I heard two words on the radio from the runway supervisor who was watching me land: "Speed brake." I lowered the speed brake and kept going while the fuel-low light glowed red. I was determined to land even if the runway supervisor told me to go around. I landed successfully with maybe fifty pounds of fuel. As soon as I taxied clear of the runway, I shut down one of the engines so I'd have enough gas to taxi to parking.

At our graduation celebrations, everyone still remembered my forgetting the map on my first navigation flight. There was considerable laughter at my expense, but the joy of graduation and receiving our wings was diminished by events in Vietnam. We were scheduled to fly home on April 24, 1975. Exactly one month earlier, the ancient imperial city Hue had been lost. On April 21, President Thieu resigned. On April 23, the day before we would have gone home, Xuan Loc, just thirty-seven miles northeast of Saigon, fell to the enemy, and their path to Saigon was clear. That same day, President Gerald Ford announced in a speech at Tulane University that the war in Vietnam was "finished as far as America is concerned."

Our flight home was canceled. I stayed in Wichita Falls. All of us were in shock. We were allowed to stay for three months in billeting at Sheppard AFB, so that we could find a place to live and jobs. None of us had expected our training in the United States to end with our staying in America. Some of us hoped that we might be able to join the U.S. Air Force; others thought that maybe we'd have a chance to go to school and find civilian careers. Still others had no idea of what would happen next.

It was hard to find a job. I was only twenty-one years old when I came to the United States. I was now on my own, sure that I'd never see my mother or father or siblings again.

When I left Vietnam for pilot training, I thought I would be coming back home with wings. I would bring home proof of my accomplishments, something that I, my family, and my community could be proud of. Instead, something I never would have imagined happened: Saigon was lost. At first I didn't want to believe it was anything but a bad dream. I felt like I had to pinch myself until I woke up, but of course that never happened. Months before the fall of Saigon, I had been preparing for my homecoming: a new Zippo lighter for my father, silk fabric for my mother, chocolate candies. I even bought Levi jeans for my brothers so they could show off to the neighbors. But all of those items were useless and meaningless now. I would never be able to see my family again. I became a man without a country, without a home. I was an abandoned orphan. When Saigon was lost, my whole existence was lost. My piloting life no longer existed, my childhood dream was destroyed, and half of me died during that time. I spent many nights lying on a tear-soaked pillow trying to imagine the silhouette of each of my family members. A few months after Saigon fell, I was working as a dishwasher at a local restaurant. I would work late nights in a hot and sweaty kitchen. One rainy night, my coworker opened the door, said let's go home, and ran to the car. His statement caught me off guard. Where was my home? I stood there as the rain splattered on my face and mixed with my sweat, maybe even my tears. One day you are in an aircraft doing loops and spins and flying formation; the next, you're on the ground washing dishes.

A Vietnamese lieutenant I knew who had trained in the United States before I came had made friends with a family in San Antonio. When I was in language school in San Antonio, the lieutenant sent a letter to me and the family to introduce us, and I would spend free time with them. While I was working as a dishwasher, they told me of work in a quarry near San Antonio. I moved to San Antonio and worked with machines that sorted rock and sent it to a big kiln to make quicklime. After four or five years a Vietnamese friend of mine opened a gas station, and I went to work for him for a couple years, until my friend decided to sell the gas station and buy a shrimp boat. He asked me to go with him, but I didn't want to leave San Antonio. I found work with a steel company as a welder.

In the meantime, I met Nam, who would become my wife. She had escaped from Vietnam on a boat in 1979 and came to San Antonio. She found work at a local computer company. We saved our money so that I could go back to school to learn computer programming. I found a job as a computer programmer, but the company my wife worked for closed down. She heard about a Chinese restaurant whose elderly owner wanted to sell the business. My wife bought it and asked me to quit my job and become the cook. I've been cooking at the restaurant since 1990. Sometimes Lennol Absher, who was a T-37 instructor pilot at Sheppard, comes to the restaurant to eat. He tells me I should fly with him someday. I'd like to, but who would cook at the restaurant?

One of my brothers escaped from Vietnam in 1979 and my mother in 1984. In 1993 I took my first of five trips back to Vietnam. I visited my father and other brother. It had been twenty years since I'd left Vietnam, but it was as if the country had gone back two decades while the rest of the world had advanced. Since my more recent trips, though, the country has made a lot of progress. My father even received permission to visit the United States for six months in 2001. But after three months, he wanted to go home. It's hard for him to be old and leave his home. I can understand his love of Vietnam. If things can continue to improve in Vietnam, if there could be freedom and opportunity there, I'd go home to Vietnam too.

"We were rushing toward the ground, on the verge of losing control in a high-speed dive. I saw the lieutenant let go of the stick and reach for the ejection seat handles."

TRUONG TAI, Class 73-06

In April 1975, I was an A-37 pilot with the 532nd Black Bear Squadron. As Communist forces advanced, we had evacuated from Phu Cat Air Base to Phan Rang and then south to Can Tho, which was about eighty miles south of Saigon. In these, the closing days of the war, my wife, Lai, and my six-month-old son, Duan, lived in Saigon. The squadron operations officer, Major Vo Tong Linh, knew my family and thought I should go to Saigon to get Lai and Duan, but by this time, the highway running between Can Tho and Saigon was closed. I needed to find another way to Saigon. A pilot I knew in the 550th Black Spider Squadron, Second Lieutenant Hiep Nguyen, was scheduled to fly a mission that could get me there.

The mission was to take off at sunset from Can Tho in a two-ship formation, fly to an area about fifteen kilometers northeast of Saigon, and drop ordinance near Thu Duc, which was under attack. Hiep Nguyen flew in the left seat of the lead aircraft with First Lieutenant Tuan Nguyen in the right seat. There was room for me to fly along in the right seat of the wingman's airplane, flown by a second lieutenant I didn't know and whose name I've forgotten. Afterward, we'd land at Tan Son Nhut in Saigon for fuel. I'd stay in Saigon, meet up with my family, and we'd find our way back to Can Tho.

As the sun set, we took off from Can Tho, each plane carrying four bombs, two under each wing. When we approached Thu Duc, we began to receive heavy anti-aircraft fire. Normally, we would each make four passes, dropping one bomb on each pass, but Hiep Nguyen decided that to minimize our exposure to the ground fire, we would each fly but a single pass and drop all four bombs on that single pass.

We split up the formation, and Lead went in first. He released all four bombs at once and came off the target safely. Now it was our turn. We dived into the ground fire and released all four bombs, but the two bombs under the left wing didn't let go. The extra weight and drag on the left side turned us upside down. It was dark, hazy from the humidity and smoke. Ground and sky were indistinguishable, and the lieutenant didn't realize that we were inverted. He pulled on the stick, which increased our dive angle. We were rushing toward the ground, on the verge of losing control in a high-speed dive.

I saw the lieutenant let go of the stick and reach for the ejection-seat handles. Smoke from exploding shells surrounded us. I knew in an instant I didn't want to eject over the enemy's position.

I reached over and punched the lieutenant as hard as I could.

He paused, and I grabbed the stick, turned us upright, and began to pull. I felt the plane stalling as I pulled hard, and I had to ease off. We went through a few cycles of pulling hard, feeling the plane shutter, easing off, pulling again. As we came out of the dive and started to climb again, I could see the trees through the smoke.

We called Lead on the radio and told him about the two hung bombs. He slowed down so we could catch up. He also declared an emergency for us with Tan Son Nhut. The lieutenant took control of the plane again as we began to rejoin formation on the lead aircraft. But we were rejoining too fast. I took the stick again, pulled back on the throttle, and lowered the speed brake.

Tan Son Nhut cleared us for an emergency straight-in approach and landing. I gave control of the plane back to the lieutenant. We were now getting low on fuel. We'd have only one chance to get the plane on the ground, a landing that should be delicate so that the two hung bombs weren't shaken loose from the left wing. We came in high and fast. We passed the midpoint of the runway, and still we hadn't touched down. Land mines had been placed off the end of the runway to protect the field from intruders. We couldn't go off the end of the runway, and we didn't have fuel to go around and try another approach. Once again, I took the stick and poked the plane onto the runway. The bombs stayed on the wing, but the end of the runway was approaching quickly. I jumped on the brakes. All three tires blew out, and we slid to a stop just before the pavement ended.

Later, in the parachute shop where we stored our flying gear, I saw the lieutenant's face in the harsh fluorescent lighting. It was ghostly white.

At least I was in Saigon and near my wife and son. I found someone to give me a ride on a moped to where Lai lived with her family. She didn't know how close I came to not arriving. My wife's sister, Anh, and her husband, Ky Tuan—a good friend of mine who was a Vietnamese Air Force captain—were there. It was the evening of April 27, 1975.

The next morning, the twenty-eighth, we knew we needed to leave the city. Ky Tuan and I went to Tan Son Nhut Air Base, but the gates were closed. The MPs wouldn't let us pass on to the base. We came back to the house wondering what to do. Later in the day we noticed all the helicopters flying about the American Embassy.

The following day, the twenty-ninth, Ky Tuan and I went to the American Embassy, but once again we weren't able to get in. I worried about spending another night at my wife's family's house. It was about three miles from the center of Saigon, and guerillas could reach it at night. I worried that since I was a pilot and Ky Tuan was a captain, we'd be attractive targets that would draw their attention to the house. My wife's aunt, who lived in the center of the city, let us stay with her.

Early in the morning, about five o'clock on the thirtieth, we returned to my wife's family's house to get our wives and children. Ky Tuan went on to his father's house, about five miles away, to get him. We waited for him to return, but he didn't come back, and we knew we needed to get to the embassy before it was too late. We couldn't wait any longer. My wife and son and my wife's younger brother, Thao Tran, and I climbed on to a small Honda motor scooter and rode off to the American Embassy.

At the embassy, we found a crush of people trying to get on helicopters that had landed on the roof of the building. I made it inside the building, but the last helicopter left and we were still in the crowd of people. A Vietnamese police officer, a major, lay dead on the second floor, his .38 caliber pistol on his chest. He didn't want to surrender to the enemy and had chosen suicide when he learned that America had completely pulled out of Vietnam. Then came the tear gas.

Eyes stinging, I told my wife that we'd have to find another way out, maybe a ship. We went to the river, to the Bach Dang shipping dock. We still hoped that Ky Tuan and my wife's sister might meet up with us. At the docks, Thao Tran left us to take the Honda back to the house. We told him that if we didn't return that night, it would mean we had left Saigon. On that confused day, when Saigon was lost, I knew only that we must flee the city. Even as we boarded a ship next to the dock and then jumped from that ship to a second ship beyond it, I believed that I would find my way back to Can Tho. Even as we huddled on the deck of that crowded ship, I didn't think we were starting our journey to the United States. Had I known then what I know now, we'd have taken young Thao with us.

There were thousands of people, panicking as North Vietnamese rockets landed on the port. Rockets were exploding around us, on the land and in the river. There was a problem releasing the cable that attached the prow of the ship to the dock. A sailor came with a jackhammer and severed it. The ship, which normally carried maybe five hundred people, had maybe two thousand on it. Still, as it drifted away from the first ship, people tried to jump the gap between the two ships. Many didn't make it and fell into the river, which churned between the ships, stirred by their movement and the props. There was blood in the water. Two young women, just girls, sisters, were fortunate, because when they fell into the river, others threw them a rope and they were strong enough to hold on to it as they were raised to the deck and pulled on board. Later, we learned that the owner of the ship was left behind during this time of panic.

With most of the other people on the ship, we were on the exposed deck. A few wealthy people had cabins inside, but we were outside in the sun and rain as the ship pulled away from Saigon and began its journey down the river.

I worried for my infant son; I worried he might pass out from the heat and all we'd been through. I took him and my wife to one of the ship's cabins. A forty-something woman—an old lady to me then—who was part of the family who'd rented it wasn't pleased when we burst in and laid my son in the center of the cabin's floor, but I didn't care. Later, the two sisters who had been pulled from the river were brought into the cabin and laid on the floor to recover from their ordeal. We became good friends with the sisters. The younger one, then only thirteen, grew up to become a dentist.

Conditions on the ship were difficult. There wasn't enough food or water. Some squabbled over what normally would be trifles—a sip of water, a place to sit on the crowded deck. Nights were dangerous. One night the woman whose cabin we'd used was attacked by a small gang of young people. I was only a few feet away. I'd found a spot where I could sit down with my back against a wall. In that position, I'd lower my head and try to sleep. I heard the woman yell when she was hit. I jumped up and decked the guy who'd hit her. I told his friends I had some for them, too, if they wanted it. I was scared they might take me up on it, but they didn't. After that the lady liked me better.

The ship took seven days to reach Singapore. From there we went to Subic Bay in the Philippines, where we transferred to another ship that took us to Guam. We spent twenty-five days at sea.

Back in Vietnam, Ky Tuan was unable to escape. Like thousands of other South Vietnamese soldiers, he was reported to the new government and placed in a re-education camp. He tried to escape from the camp in

1977, but they shot him down. Thao Tran survived the motor-scooter ride from the docks to his family's house and grew up in Vietnam. On a trip I took to Vietnam in 2001, he told me about the ride home, when he was only a young boy, about how it took over three hours to travel the five-kilometer distance, about Saigon's streets, crowded with people and tanks as clouds and smoke darkened the city.

My wife's sister, Anh, still lives in Vietnam. She never remarried, even though she is very beautiful. She raised their three children, who were excluded from attending the public university because their father had been an officer with the South. However, they were able to go to a private school where they learned English and did well. As the years passed, their knowledge of English became important in the business world, and they all found good jobs in Vietnam.

"I knew that taking Quynh in an A-37 wasn't a good idea. Across the ramp, I saw a helicopter—a UH-1 Huey—starting its engine. We dashed to the helicopter and climbed in. About twenty people—all but five of them women and children—sat inside the helicopter on top of their luggage."

THANH DUONG, Class 74-07

During the 1968 Tet Offensive, Communists invaded our small village about fifty miles southwest of Saigon. They shot up the police station and burned houses a mile or two from ours. The townspeople worried that they might abduct some of the town's young men and press them into service as guerilla fighters. I was only seventeen, and the possibility of such an abduction was enough to convince me that, like my older brother, I should join the air force. I thought my chances would be better in the air force.

The air force sent me to helicopter mechanic training at Fort Eustis, Virginia. A few years later, in 1972, I was accepted for pilot training and another period of training in the United States.

Since I'd trained in the United States before, I had a pretty good idea what to expect at Sheppard AFB. My instructor was Captain Lou Campbell. Like most of my fellow students, I dreaded doing spins in the T-37.

On one training flight, I entered the spin, but before I could recover from it, the plane transitioned into an inverted spin. Captain Campbell took control of the plane and recovered it. He said, "Let's do this again." So I climbed the plane back up to altitude and entered another spin. The same thing happened again. I said, "I think I've had enough spins." But now Captain Campbell was curious. He wanted to know why the plane kept going inverted. So he said, "Let me take the plane and try this." The same thing happened again. And finally we gave up on spins and went home. Over the years, Lou Campbell and I have stayed in touch. We still talk about the day of the inverted spins.

At our T-37 graduation, he took a check from his checkbook, tore off the address, and gave it to me. He said to stay in touch. I put the small piece of paper in my wallet. It was there a year later, when I was in the refugee center at Camp Pendleton. I told him I was there with Quynh, who later became my wife, and we needed sponsorship.

Quynh lived in Saigon, where I had been stationed until the last week of the war, when my squadron relocated to Can Tho. The following Friday, the twenty-fifth of April, I took the bus to Saigon to see her. Once in Saigon, I went to my sister's house, and she told me that Quynh had left earlier in the day to visit me in Can Tho. By then, evening was falling and travel was dangerous, but I knew I had to return to Can Tho and to Quynh. I got back on the bus and arrived in Can Tho about nine o'clock that evening.

On Sunday, I took Quynh to the bus station for her return to Saigon, but the buses weren't running to Saigon because the highway had been cut off. We tried again on Monday and again on Tuesday, but still the highway was closed. On Wednesday morning, April 30, our commander met with our squadron and told us that the new president might take a neutral stance with the Communists. Almost as soon as we left the meeting, we learned that the president had surrendered. I was with a friend in the flight planning room. He said that guards had closed the base and wouldn't let us out. The only way out was to fly.

We hopped in a Jeep and drove back to the squadron. I got my chute and helmet. Then I went back to my quarters, where Quynh was waiting. We threw some clothing into my helmet bag and took off for the flight line. I knew that taking Quynh in an A-37 wasn't a good idea. Across the ramp, I saw a helicopter—a UH-1 Huey—starting its engine. We dashed to the helicopter and climbed in. About twenty people—all but five of them women and children—sat inside the helicopter on top of their luggage. The Huey was meant to carry only seven passengers. I sat behind the pilot, put on my helmet, and plugged in to the plane's interphone. The pilot told me that he flew for a general from Saigon and that he'd taken off the previous night from Saigon and was unfamiliar with Can Tho. He asked me how to get out of Can Tho's airspace and head for Thailand. Since I'd been a helicopter mechanic, I knew that the Huey wouldn't have the range to make it to Thailand. He said, "How about the ocean?" I told him about an island on the west coast that had been prepared as a last-ditch fallback location for the A-37s. We could go there and get more fuel.

We arrived at the island about one o'clock and were relieved to see the South Vietnam flag flying. But nobody was there: no maintenance personnel, no power. The base had been abandoned with the flag flying. We did find fuel, but we to hand-pump it into the helicopter. Even with a full load of fuel, we wouldn't have enough range to make it to Thailand. So we put more fuel into a fifty-five-gallon barrel and loaded it with all the people and all the bags in the small cabin of the UH-1. We were so heavy we had to do a running takeoff.

We leveled off about twenty-five hundred feet and headed for Thailand; we had to fly over Cambodia, which had already been under Communist control for two weeks. As we flew over the Cambodian jungle, our fuel was rapidly consumed. We needed to find a place to land so that we could refuel from the fifty-five-gallon drum we had. The fuel light came on. Then we found a place where a stream came out of the jungle and met the ocean. Here, a sandy delta had grown, giving us room to land the chopper. When we landed, I told the pilot to take out the guns and guard the plane while we refueled from the fifty-five-gallon drum. We had to use helmets to dip the fuel out of the drum and slosh it into the fuel tank. It was hot work despite the Cambodian clouds, and I was thirsty. I tried the stream, but its water was salty. A mist from the clouds coated the windscreen. I put my lips to it for the moisture.

After refueling, the engine wouldn't start. The pilot wanted me to push the blade, a dangerous proposition. I said to try one more time. I was relieved when it started. After we took off, we tried to contact Utapao control tower, but maybe we were too far away. The pilot switched to the guard emergency frequency and tried to call everybody. We couldn't tell if we were over Cambodia or Thailand.

Then, to the great relief of our pilot, an American 0-2 flew up to us. He rocked his wings and made a right turn. Our pilot's joy disappeared as he said, "He's leaving us." I said, "No, he wants us to follow." So we followed him, and then another American plane appeared, another Huey helicopter. He asked how much fuel we had and I told him that our low-fuel light had been on for about five minutes. He said, "See the rice paddy? Land now!"

The American helicopter had two barrels of fuel on board. He told us he'd been flying along the border for two days waiting for us. I don't know how he knew we were coming.

We split the remaining gas and the passengers. I went with the American pilots. We landed at a field where many Vietnamese waited. A cargo plane came and took all of us to Utapao. Then we went to Guam and finally to Camp Pendleton.

I still had the piece of paper with Lou Campbell's address in my wallet. He sponsored Quynh and me, and we went to Wichita Falls. His neighbor got me a job. A little more than a year after graduating as pilot at Sheppard AFB, I was working there again: in the mess hall as a busboy. We stayed with the Campbells for two weeks and then moved to our own apartment. A month later, Quynh, who had never been to America and didn't speak English, got a job too.

We were able to live comfortably, but I knew we'd do better if we had some skills. We moved to Waco, Texas, where I went to a technical school to learn how to be an instrumentation technician, the career I've had since 1982.

I think it was in 1985 that Quynh and I got our marriage license.

I had to apologize to Lou Campbell for not telling him from the refugee center in 1975 that we weren't married. Now when we laugh about the old days and inverted spins, we also laugh about how he says that had he known Quynh and I weren't married, he'd not have let us stay in the same room.

"I taxied around the hanger to the taxiway and picked up a major from my squadron and a crew chief. To make room for all three of us in the two-place cockpit, we left our parachutes behind."

SIMON LAM, Class 74-03

Next to the runway, my T-41 instructor pilot and a friend watched as I added full power and began the takeoff roll on my first solo. At high power settings, propeller-driven planes like the T-41 produce a lot of torque at high engine speeds, torque that can cause the plane to veer to the left if the pilot doesn't counteract with enough right rudder. Perhaps it was the excitement of my first solo, or maybe just my inexperience, but as the T-41 gained speed, it drifted to the left. Later, my friend told me that as the T-41 went into the dirt on the left side of the runway, the coffee mug my instructor held slipped from his hand. He stood there, fingers still curved around the now-dropped mug, as I continued the takeoff from beside the runway. Tower also noticed my nonstandard way of getting airborne and told me over the radio that I had run off the runway. It wouldn't be the first time that I took off or landed off the runway.

When I returned to Vietnam from pilot training at Sheppard AFB and A-37 training at England AFB, I was assigned to the 532nd Fighter Squadron at Phu Cat. The base commander, who was married to my aunt, already knew me, and when I reported in to him, he asked me what I wanted to do. I said I wanted to fly. As soon as I reported to the flying squadron, I began the combat checkout. Two weeks later I showed up at the squadron and there was my name on the scheduling board: I was flying solo as the wingman on a combat mission.

My last combat mission at Phu Cat came just before we evacuated for Nha Trang on March 30, 1975. We attacked a position just a short distance from the runway, maybe only five minutes away. After we dropped our bombs, we popped up onto an extended final approach in formation and prepared for a formation landing. We didn't do many formation landings, and it would be a treat for us to fly one. I maintained position on Lead's right wing. The runway was only a couple of miles ahead. I focused on staying in position, just a few feet separating my left wingtip from Lead's right wingtip.

I felt something graze my right leg, and then wind began blasting into the cockpit. The canopy was shattered, and I broke away from the lead aircraft and announced on the radio that I'd been hit. Lead continued with his landing, and I looked about the crowded traffic pattern—helicopters, a C-130, busy activity preparing for the evacuation of the base. I went around and pulled up onto downwind. I tried to lower the speed brake and the gear, but nothing happened. The gear remained up. The hydraulics had been hit, rendering the gear, flaps, and speed brake inoperative.

I asked tower to foam the runway, but they told me that it would take about forty-five minutes to do so, and I didn't have forty-five minutes of fuel left. On the ground, Lead was listening to the radio transmissions, and he broke in to suggest that I use the gear blow-down, an emergency gear-lowering procedure. I pulled the emergency gear-lowering handle, and a blast lowered the gear. The three gear-position lights glowed green, indicating that all gears were down and locked.

Still, I had no speed brake and no flaps. I crossed the runway threshold, but the plane continued to float. It wouldn't touch down. The end of the runway was protected by a minefield. I pushed forward on the stick, forcing the plane to the runway, and stepped on the brakes. But there were no brakes. The plane kept on its way toward the end of the runway and the minefield. The loss of hydraulics also meant that I didn't have nosewheel steering. The plane began to drift to the right of the runway and then dropped off the pavement. The landing gear hooked into the soil, and the plane's path twisted to the right. It slid to a stop in the dirt, not far from the runway's edge. I opened the canopy and jumped out of the airplane. A master sergeant I knew came out and picked me up. He took me straight to a Chinook helicopter that was evacuating personnel to Nha Trang. The disabled A-37 remained where it had come to rest beside the runway at Phu Cat.

Soon after the squadron's evacuation to Nha Trang, we moved again, this time to Can Tho. My last flight in an A-37 would be from Can Tho, on April 30, 1975, as Saigon was falling. I found an A-37 near the hangar that was fully loaded; it carried six bombs under its wings and wingtip fuel tanks, a good sign that it also had a full load of gas. I'd need a lot of gas to make it Utapao, Thailand. I taxied around the hangar to the taxiway and picked up a major from my squadron and a crew chief. To make room for all three of us in the two-place cockpit, we left our parachutes behind. The airfield was so busy that I took off from the taxiway. As soon as I was airborne—before I'd even raised the gear—I dropped all six bombs. Maybe it was shrapnel from these bombs exploding beneath us that damaged the aircraft's tires and the rudder. We'd not know about the damage until we landed at Utapao.

As we flew across Vietnam, we heard others on the radio. One radio exchange that still haunts me came from a helicopter that was over the sea. It was running out of gas, and the voice on the radio was a woman's, and in the background were sounds of children crying. They couldn't find a ship to land on. I also saw another A-37 flying, not with three people as we were, but with five. And I heard of a two-place O-1 loaded with seven people.

As we approached Utapao, we were low on fuel, but I couldn't find the runway. On the radio I heard an emergency B-52 inbound to Utapao with an engine fire. I looked up and saw the B-52 trailing smoke, so I followed him. Once I had Utapao in sight, the B-52 allowed me to go ahead of him because by then we were dangerously low on fuel.

When we touched down, I discovered that one of the tires was flat. The flat tire pulled us off the runway, and we came to rest beside the runway. We climbed out of the plane.

American personnel met us at the side of the runway. They took the pistol I always flew with, and they painted over the South Vietnamese insignia on the A-37.

"In Vietnam we didn't have amusement parks with roller coasters, and I didn't know what it would be like. After my first-ever roller-coaster ride, I said I wasn't going to do that again."

SANG X. VUONG, Class 75-07

I'd just finished high school in Vietnam and could have continued my education, but I wanted to become a pilot. I joined the Vietnamese Air Force in 1972 at the age of seventeen. After boot camp and survival training, I had to learn English. In high school I'd taken some English, but when I sat in the military English class listening to the audiotapes and to my instructor speaking English, I realized how little I knew the language. I wondered what I'd gotten myself into. I'd have to learn how to fly an airplane speaking this difficult language.

By the time I began training in T-41 aircraft, I'd received a lot of English training, but I still worried about my ability to understand the instruction. And the challenges of learning to fly became even clearer to me one day as I sat with my class at Hondo, the airport where the T-41s flew. It was early in our T-41 training; we'd not flown yet but were attending ground-training classes that would prepare us for our first flights. Outside, the T-41s buzzed in the traffic pattern, one of them being flown by a student in our senior class on his first solo. He touched down on the runway nosewheel first. The plane rocked back onto its main landing gear and then forward onto the nosewheel again. Each cycle of seesawing became more severe until the final rocking onto the nosewheel that caused the propeller to hit the runway. The force of the spinning propeller flipped the plane over and it slid to a stop, upside down on the runway. Fortunately, the student was okay.

The accident, however, didn't discourage any of us. Many times, though, I'd listen to the instructor but wouldn't understand what he said. I had to study hard and ask other students and just watch my instructor flying the plane and try to imitate his actions. We called it "monkey-see, monkey-do." I was the first person in my class to solo the T-41.

I arrived at Sheppard AFB for T-37 training in July 1974. My instructor pilot was Captain Greene, who had flown A-37s in combat in Vietnam. One holiday weekend, Captain Greene and his wife and another instructor and his wife took me and five other students to Six Flags over Dallas. Standing in front of a roller coaster, Captain Greene said, "You think you're so hot flying the T-37, see what you can do on this." In Vietnam we didn't have amusement parks with roller coasters, and I didn't know what it would be like. After my first-ever roller-coaster ride, I said I wasn't going to do that again.

Shortly after I soloed the T-37, we had to take a routine TB tine test. My skin around the test site reacted with swelling. The flight surgeon sent me to the hospital at Scott AFB near St. Louis for further evaluation. The doctors decided that I wasn't infectious, but they worried that the stresses of flight training might activate the tuberculosis. I never flew again.

I stayed as a patient at the Scott AFB hospital. The people there were very kind. They'd let me help with tasks—moving gurneys around, running errands for staff members. My English improved because no one at the hospital knew Vietnamese. They'd let me check out of the hospital, and I even took two trips back to Sheppard AFB. I went by bus. It was a long ride from St. Louis to Wichita Falls. My first trip back was at Christmas 1974; the second trip was for the graduation of my old pilot training class on April 24, 1975. It was an emotional ceremony. There would be no trip back home to Vietnam for this class.

After the graduation, I returned to the hospital at Scott AFB. The sergeant at the hospital told me to go to the Immigration and Naturalization office in St. Louis as one who had received asylum in the United States. They stamped my visa so I could get a job.

The hospital let me stay, telling me to stay as long as I needed to arrange a new life for myself. I stayed for about a month.

I learned that my parents and all my siblings except my older brother, who was also in the Vietnamese Air Force, had been able to leave Vietnam. My father had been a driver for the U.S. ambassadors—Lodge, Bunker, and Taylor. Because of his long association with the American government, the family received help leaving Vietnam. After I learned that my family was at Fort Chaffee, Arkansas, I sought sponsorship for them through various relief agencies. It was difficult to find someone to sponsor such a large group, but I knew it was vital to keep our family together. Finally, the Lutheran Immigration and Refugee Service found sponsorship for all of us. We moved to large, old six-bedroom house in St. Louis, where we stayed through two winters. I actually liked St. Louis, but my parents, used to tropical Vietnam, suffered through the cold. Friends from Dallas suggested we move there, and we did.

My older brother, who hadn't been able to leave with my parents, managed to hide from Vietnamese authorities for two years. He knew that they would imprison him in a re-education camp if they could find him. He tried five times to escape from Vietnam. Each time, something happened to foil the escape, but somehow he always managed to avoid capture. Finally, on his sixth attempt, he succeeded in escaping to Hong Kong and found his way to the United States and joined us in Texas.

"All of us knew what was happening in Cambodia as the Khmer Rouge began to slaughter anyone deemed an enemy of their state. We expected the same treatment from North Vietnamese Communists."

MIKE DOAN, Class 75-03

I graduated from pilot training at Sheppard in October 1974. Captain Al Viers was the flight commander. He was nearing the end of his tour at Sheppard and had been told that he would be assigned to a nonflying job as missile launch officer in Minot, North Dakota. He wasn't happy about spending his time underground in a missile silo instead of flying through the wild blue. We were astonished that America could afford to give pilots jobs deep under the ground instead of in the air.

Curt Emory, a young captain, was my instructor pilot. He took me up on my first T-37 flight. We were up about twenty-five thousand feet, and he was banking and yanking around, trying, I think, to make me sick. I kept my throat closed, and finally he asked me if I wanted to take the stick. Sure, I did. When I took it in hand, the stick was very heavy. Now I know that he had trimmed the plane nose down to teach me about the importance of trimming. On a well-trimmed plane, the pilot can let go of the stick and the plane will continue fly straight and level. I grabbed the heavy stick with both hands and yanked back with full force. The accelerometer registered 5.6 g's and Captain Emory blacked out. He came around and said, "Don't do that again." I said, "Don't do what?" When we came back, the plane had to be grounded for a structural check.

After a couple of weeks, Captain Emory was reassigned to Check Section, and I was assigned to a new IP, Captain David Shetter. Captain Shetter was a new IP, but he was very relaxed and even-tempered, and he spread good will. While he and his students knew that our first job was to fly, we could also talk to him about the day-to-day problems students in a strange land are bound to have. I didn't know then how I'd rely upon his good will even after pilot training. I also flew with many other IPs. I think the reason I flew with so many different instructors was because my English was better than that of many other students.

I'd been studying English since sixth grade. I was born in what became North Vietnam. My father was an army captain, and our family moved south before the partitioning of Vietnam. He had been French-educated, and after his discharge from the army, we settled in Da Nang, where I grew up and studied English in school. So, when I went to English language training at Lackland AFB, I found the studying easy. Since I already knew English, I took advantage of the time to learn about American culture.

None of us really knew much about the details of American life. Our first stop in the United States was Hawaii, where we learned about vending machines. One of the students put some coins into the machine, but without knowing the cost of an item. He began to think that the machine was just taking money without returning anything. A second student took a turn at the machine. He put in just a quarter, and the machine coughed up both product and change. The vending machines seemed more like slot machines to us. You never knew what you would win.

The contrast between what America had and what Vietnam lacked was especially apparent when I returned to Vietnam after pilot training. In February 1975, I had received my commission as a second lieutenant, but I never made it to a flying squadron. By then, there weren't the resources to invest in training new combat pilots. I spent my commissioned time assigned to headquarters in Saigon.

Only one time would I sit at the controls of a Vietnamese Air Force airplane, not an A-37, but a C-130. And it would be on a day I'll always remember.

The base came under attack on the twenty-ninth of April. Beginning at two in the morning, the base was pounded for four hours. I saw an AC-119 shot down. An SA-7 hit an engine, the wing came off, and the plane spun downward. A huge fireball punctuated its plunge. Three A-37s captured by the Communists at Phan Rang flew over the base and bombed it, damaging many of the aircraft. An F-5 scrambled in pursuit of the A-37s, but by the time it took off, they were gone.

All of us knew what was happening in Cambodia as the Khmer Rouge began to slaughter anyone deemed an enemy of their state. We expected the same treatment from North Vietnamese Communists. As Saigon's ability to repulse attack declined, we knew we'd have to face a painful decision: either suffer retribution from a brutal enemy or flee.

A crew chief asked if I could fly a C-130. I told him I couldn't, but I'd help. He'd managed to get family and friends together on a C-130. He found a Vietnamese major who was a C-130 check pilot, who also gathered his family together. We loaded onto the 130, the major in the left seat, I in the right seat. We left the troop doors open to invite anyone else to climb on board. By the time we took off we had about one hundred people—military personnel, family members, civilians—sitting on the floor of the cargo cabin.

We headed for Utapao Air Base in Thailand. The flight was short and we landed without incident. A blue pickup truck with a "Follow Me" sign met us as we taxied off the runway, and we followed it to parking. A crew chief marshaled us into the parking place and signaled to shut down the engines. We got off the airplane. While we stood on the tarmac next to it, American Air Force personnel arrived in a truck with a cherry picker. Spray cans in hand, they were hoisted up to the plane's Vietnamese insignia and began to paint them over. Tears in our eyes, we raised our voices to sing the South Vietnamese national anthem:

> O people! The country nears its freedom day.
> Together we go forward to the open way.
> Remembering our centuries of history,
> Brothers from North to South reunite,
> With hearts young and pure as crystal.
> Multiply our efforts and spare not our ardent blood.
> No danger, no obstacle can stop us.
> Our courage waivers not before a thousand dangers.
> On the new way, our look embraces the horizon
> And who can repress the soul of our youth?
> O people! Going until the end is our resolution.
> O people! To give all is our oath.
> Together we go forward for the glory of the Fatherland.
> We fight for the immortality of the Lac Long race.

An American Air Force captain came over and pointed to a roach coach, a van selling food and sundries. He said, "I'm very sorry."

I contacted Captain Shetter after I arrived at the Camp Pendleton Refugee Center. He sponsored me, and I went back to Wichita Falls. In my first week, I found my first job, working in a foundry. It was hard work, but soon I found another job. I went back to school, and today I work as a sales manager for IBM.

I traveled back to Vietnam in 1993 to visit my mother. It didn't feel right to me when we flew into the airfield I'd last seen when I fled the country in the C-130. The flag of my former enemy flew over the airport. Military aircraft bearing my former enemy's markings sat on its military ramp. I felt like I had to be careful with every word I said.

"I carried a .38 pistol in my waistband. My father had a Colt .45. He said, 'If worse comes to worst, we'll use the guns on ourselves.'"

CHAU PHONG NGUYEN, Class 74-06

In 1954, my father graduated from the Vietnamese National Military Academy with a commission as a second lieutenant. He was assigned as a finance officer in Saigon, where I grew up. Growing up, I saw many military people, especially pilots in their flight suits. I joined the Vietnamese Air Force and lived in the barracks while we prepared to go to flight training in the United States. Our English book had a story in it about the "quietest town in the U.S."—Fairfield, California.

My first impression of the USA came on my trip to Travis AFB in October 1972. We arrived at our quarters, and I thought it was like a presidential suite. America was so much more than I had expected. The little I knew about America came from what I'd learned after I joined the Vietnamese Air Force and had been selected for flight training in the United States. In Vietnam we lived in barracks far less grand than the quarters at Travis. We learned that Fairfield, "quietest town in the U.S.," was close to Travis, so I and my classmates decided to go see it for ourselves. On the way there in the cab, we came upon a nightclub with nude dancers. We had to stop and go inside. It was like heaven for us young guys. I'd never seen anything like this in my life. We never made it to Fairfield.

Soon, we left Travis for language school at Lackland AFB in San Antonio. The policy at the language school was to give Vietnamese students roommates from other countries so that we'd be forced to speak English as a common language. I was given a roommate from Iran. It was a bit vexing because he bragged about how he would be a fighter pilot flying a prestigious F-4 Phantom. I was just happy to become any kind of pilot for my country, and his cockiness got under my skin. His religious practices also bothered me because they interfered with my sleep. I'd stay up until about two AM studying and then go to sleep, hoping to sleep until six, an hour before class started for us. But every morning at five, my Iranian roommate rose, placed a piece of cloth on the floor, and began praying in a loud voice. For me that last hour of sleep, the hour I missed every night, would have been the best hour, but I suppose it did help me learn English a little better.

After language school came the T-41 flying phase of our training. My class moved to the Lackland Annex, called Medina, which also housed the air force officer training school. Here I made friends with the American students who were soon to become air force officers. As a Vietnamese air cadet, I wasn't allowed to join the Officer Trainee Club at Medina. This club was modeled after U.S. Air Force officers' clubs and was a popular place for trainees to let off steam. Even though I couldn't join the club, my American friends took me to it as their guest. We'd drink some beer and play the jukebox. We all had the same favorite song, and we'd raise our voices and sing along with John Denver: "Country roads, take me home / To the place I belong . . ."

Before taking the road home, I'd have to finish T-37 training at Sheppard. There, First Lieutenant Brian Spitzer had just come home to America after a tour in Vietnam flying C-7s. He called me Lima Delta, a nickname that sticks to this day when I talk to him.

I was finally able to take the road home to Vietnam after training at England AFB, Louisiana, in the A-37. On June 24, 1974, I finished A-37 training and was on my way back to Vietnam for further training. Eventually, I received an assignment to the 546th Fighter Squadron at Can Tho Air Base, Vietnam. I was able to get only a few training flights in the A-37, but I did get to sit in the right seat as an observer on some combat missions. I was really scared on the first combat flight. The captain, who was flying, told me not to worry, but it was hard not to worry when people were shooting at you and you were just along for the ride. But after a few times, I got used to it.

About a week before the country collapsed, my father—a 1954 graduate of the Vietnamese National Military Academy and now a lieutenant colonel—asked me to come home to Saigon, where he was assigned as a finance officer. Things had become bad enough that he wanted me to help evacuate the family members.

When the thirtieth of April dawned, we still hadn't gotten the family out. We received a tip that we could get out on a ship docked in Saigon. The extended family—about fifty of us—got on the ship, only to discover that the ship was disabled and couldn't leave the port. Vietnamese sailors went to work fixing it, but it wasn't seaworthy until two hours after the president had surrendered the country. Once it was repaired, there was another problem: two other ships had to be moved before we could get out of the port. We had to push those ships out of the way. There was little room, and those ships actually ended up being pushed into the houses that lined the opposite bank of the river.

There were about five thousand of us on the ship—standing-room only in the cargo hold. Outside, the hull echoed as bullets fired from the shore hit. Everybody was praying. I carried a .38 pistol in my waistband. My father had a Colt .45. He said, "If worse comes to worst, we'll use the guns on ourselves." As the ship traveled downriver, we survived on dry packets of Top Ramen. Once we were at sea, the ship's engine stopped running. Another ship came to the rescue, taking the women and children. My father and I and the other men had to wait another day for a ship to pick us up and take us to Subic Bay. We finally rejoined the rest of the family on Guam. Along the way, I always volunteered to help as an interpreter. I translated the safety instructions on the 747 that flew us from Guam to California. The flight attendant thanked me by giving me a brand-new Levi jacket. I was the only one at the refugee center at Camp Pendleton with a brand-new Levi jacket.

My immediate family numbered thirteen, and it was very difficult to find a sponsor who could take all of us. Finally, we were told that a Catholic church in Denver was willing to sponsor all of us. They rented a big six-bedroom house for us, where we stayed for a year. The church paid the first month's rent for us. We were able to find jobs and were able to pay the subsequent months' rent ourselves. I knew I needed to get more training so I could find a good job.

I talked on the phone with Brian Spitzer. He suggested that I get an airframe and powerplant certificate (commonly called an A&P certificate) to become an aircraft mechanic. I enrolled in a course of training for the A&P and worked full-time at whatever jobs I could find: house cleaning, dishwasher, busboy, room service, waiter, bartender. After completing my training, I found an aircraft mechanic's job with Frontier

Airlines. I was happy working there until August 1986, when Frontier filed bankruptcy. During the nine years I worked as a mechanic for Frontier, I kept pursuing flight qualifications, gaining commercial, instrument, and multiengine ratings.

One day after losing the job with Frontier, I was hanging out at the Aurora Air Park, a small airport just east of Denver. A guy asked me what I was doing, and I told him I was looking for work. He was from Evergreen Airlines, and he hired me as a professional flight engineer on Boeing 727s. Most airlines call this position the second officer. A flight engineer or second officer is the crew member who watches over the aircraft systems and manages the cockpit tasks that don't involve using the flight controls—things like transferring fuel from tank to tank, controlling the cabin temperature, monitoring engine performance, and running checklists. Second officer is the first crew position for an aspiring airline pilot who wants to move up to one of the front seats on the flight deck, the ones holding the captain and first officer. Professional flight engineers generally don't have a career path to first officer and captain, even though the duties of flight engineers and second officers are identical. I flew for two years with Evergreen, which subcontracted for United Parcel Service. Then UPS decided to start up their own flight operations, and I interviewed with them. They hired me as a DC-8 professional flight engineer in 1988. After four years, they upgraded me to 727 first officer, the pilot who sits in the right seat on airliners. Eighteen years after graduating from pilot training at Sheppard AFB, I was back at the flight controls of an airplane.

In 1994, I was promoted to captain. Since then, I've been a captain on the Boeing 747, Airbus 300, and McDonnell Douglas MD-11. My route is Asia: Shanghai, Manila, Singapore, Seoul, Hong Kong, and Taipei.

When I was a 747 captain, a new second officer came to work for UPS and was on my crew. We introduced ourselves; he asked if I was Vietnamese. He said he used to be an instructor at Sheppard AFB. It was Jim Wolfe, who had been a T-37 standardization-evaluation pilot. I told my first officer, I may be the captain on this plane and Jim may be just the second officer, but he was an evaluator when I learned to be a pilot. He decided if we were good enough to pass. If I do anything wrong, blame him—him and Brian Spitzer.

"I stayed in my country after the Communists overran South Vietnam. They captured me and kept me in a series of concentration camps for five years and six months."

DAO T. DINH, Class 74-02

In 1967, I began my military training at the Vietnamese National Military Academy. Like the American service academies, it had a four-year curriculum leading to a bachelor's degree and a commission. Unlike its American counterparts, its graduates went to all the branches of the military: army, air force, and navy. I graduated with a commission in the air force and became a fighter pilot, receiving my wings at Sheppard AFB as a member of Pilot Training Class 74-02.

I flew A-37 combat missions in the Delta region from April 1974 until the South fell in April 1975. Seven months before the South fell, in September 1974, I had married my wife, but most of the next six years, we would be separated while I spent my time in concentration camps. My captors would not tell my wife where I was. When they transferred me to other concentration camps, they would do so under the cover of darkness, I think, so that no one could know where we were.

The first camps were little more than an area of the jungle surrounded by fencing. The only structure was a guard tower. The branch of a tree was my bed. Each group of twenty prisoners was watched by two guards. The guards watched us as we cut down trees and stripped their branches and assembled their trunks into log buildings that would house sixty to one hundred prisoners. The camps would come to contain six to ten such buildings. Sanitation was a trench dug by prisoners. There was little food, even though we faced hard physical labor every day. They didn't even give us rice, just two bowls of corn a day. We were always hungry.

We didn't have meat. Once, a group of thirty of us was given a palm-sized piece of fish. We tried to figure out how we could fairly divide it. Finally, we made gruel of it; we boiled it in water and let everyone have a spoonful. Sometimes, when we worked with the soil, we'd find a root we would eat, or even a worm.

The last camp I stayed at was at Pleiku. One night, thirty prisoners escaped, but the camp was on a mountain and the surrounding terrain made it difficult to move quickly. We heard the guns of the guards firing in the jungle. The next morning we were assembled for a lecture on what would happen to us if we tried to escape. The visual aids for the lecture were the mutilated bodies of our former fellow prisoners.

We were never told how long we would have to remain imprisoned. Sometimes one or two of us would be released with no notice or fanfare. Perhaps they released prisoners whom they thought had become compliant enough to attend the daily meetings with probation officials, which were required of all who had served time in the concentration camps. My release came after five and a half years. I returned to my wife's home.

Every night after my release, I had to report to an official. They wanted to know how I had spent my time each day. Even worse, I found I was an outcast. People looked at me with disgust. Sometimes I'd be kicked. I had no money, no job. My wife and I knew we needed to escape from Vietnam.

I still had some friends from the old days. One, from my time at the military academy, was Van, who had taken a commission in the navy. A number of people who wanted to escape pooled what money we had to buy a twelve-meter fishing boat and fuel for it. Van arranged for the boat to cruise the water off the southern town of Rach Gia one night in March 1981, two months after my release from the concentration camp. Each of us had to find a small boat or canoe we could paddle under the cover of darkness to the larger fishing boat. As the boat cruised about two hundred meters offshore, many small vessels carrying two or three people slipped away from the shore to meet the larger boat at sea. Some became lost in the darkness and were unable to reach the larger boat. Still, thirty-two people made it. We spent three days and nights crowded on the twelve-meter boat before beaching it on the Thai coast.

After picking up the last group of people, the boat headed for international water. Government agents spotted us and gave chase. Perhaps they would not have respected international water had it not been for the passing of a large European ship.

Our first day at sea dawned, and many of us were still sleeping when sea pirates attacked. My wife and I had nothing, but others lost everything— the jewelry they hoped would fund a new start for their lives, everything.

When I say I had nothing, I'm not exaggerating. I didn't even have shoes. I don't remember when I lost my shoes, but when we landed on the

Thai beach, I remember how the sand burned my feet. I fashioned shoes from cardboard boxes so I could walk on the hot sand.

The Thai government let us stay on a section of the beach, where we built temporary shelter for ourselves from whatever materials we could find—fabric, cardboard, even palm fronds. I was especially grateful when United Nations relief workers gave me a pair of thongs for my feet.

After a week, we were moved to the Songkla Refugee Camp, where we stayed for four months. Here, I met officials from the U.S. Immigration Service. Because I'd trained for two years in the United States to become a pilot and spoke English well, they quickly accepted my application for settlement in the United States. My wife also had relatives in the United States. Her family had escaped when Vietnam fell in 1975 and were in Dallas.

We lived with my wife's family in Dallas for two months, until my wife got a job at a bank. I spent my time studying in the library, sixteen hours a day, to review the subjects I'd taken years before as a cadet at the Vietnamese National Military Academy: electronics, mechanical engineering, and drafting. I prepared my résumé and found a drafting job at a small company. I enrolled in night school to regain the bachelor's degree I'd lost with my country. School was easy for me, and we've been able to live a fine life in America, where we have a good house, plenty to eat, and have been free to follow our dreams. Our two daughters are growing up, the younger one a senior in high school, the older one a senior premed student at the University of Texas.

ROBERT MACGOWAN

A Boatman's Story

I have finally committed to tell my story. I am naked and in pain when I remember the war; yet, like all men, I must make sense of my memories or risk going insane—as I was for a time.

Mine is, first and last, a story of a father and his sons. My father was an infantryman in the European theater of World War II. I cannot know for sure the effects of that war upon him, for I did not know him before he went to war. Yet I knew well the contradiction of his sensitive and bright nature, his explosive rage, and his inexplicable withdrawal from loving his children. I see now the same mix in my older brother—and in myself. Like our father, my brother and I have seen our war, and it has changed us too.

It seems fitting that the three of us were in Vietnam at the same time. Only my youngest brother was left at home with my mother and sister. My father was in Saigon, an intelligence officer. My brother and I were in I Corps, he a helicopter crew chief, flying out of Phu Bai, and I a marine grunt, an infantryman, as my father had been in his first war.

Only once did I communicate in-country with either my brother or my father. I had walked out of my jungle boots and none could be found to fit me. Rather than stay behind—how then could I prove myself worthy of his love?—I wrote my father for his assistance. Knowing that he had suffered frostbitten feet during the Battle of the Bulge, I felt he would be responsive. Three days later, a helicopter landed on a hill north of the Khe Sanh. An officer disembarked; he handed me a pair of boots, no note.

My time in Vietnam seems now a dream to me, perhaps because I have striven to forget or to deny. Primitive events call for such primitive defense mechanisms, as I was to learn in my first killing.

I had joined a line outfit west of Da Nang on the day after Christmas 1966. I was handed a flak jacket and helmet and rifle. An M-14 rifle is quite a gift to an eighteen-year-old boy, an entrée to the responsibilities, and the sorrows, of a man. That first week, my platoon was on patrol in a rice-paddied area when a Vietcong jumped from cover and bolted. I ran after him. I squeezed off a round and hit him in the back, knocking him down. The dry paddy dust rose with the impact of his body. He arose and ran. Again I shot him in the back; again he fell and rose. The third time I hit him, he stayed down. When we reached him, he was still alive. We circled above him and he watched us. I could see the exit wounds in his chest. We had a staff sergeant with us we called "great white father." He cocked a .45 and shot the VC in the forehead, blowing his brains out the back of his head.

I recall my feelings that day: first, the surprising excitement of the hunt—an ecstasy that felt oddly sexual—the pride and awe at what I had done: hit my target, brought my man down. But I remember, too, disgust and shame at the shitty way the VC had finally been killed. I remember the look on his face when he was shot in the head: *Why are you doing this to me?*

Twenty-five years later, I can see how this first killing formed the manner in which I have dealt with the ending of many intimate relationships. In effect, I shot people in the head. Maybe this way the other person wouldn't hurt so much or I wouldn't feel so shitty. Probably I just didn't want to see the dust rise when these people fell and rose, then fell and rose again.

But back then, at eighteen, with the concreteness of youth, I was going to try to undo what I'd done. A week later, I had my opportunity. We were sweeping an area when a sniper shot at our team. He was hidden in a tree line, maybe three or four hundred yards away, and we were skirting the edge of an opposing tree line. My team jumped in among our trees and returned fire. I stood in the open and screamed at the sniper: "Fuck you, you lousy shot!" His next rounds hit the dirt a few yards ahead of me. I pointed and yelled, "Too low," and then "Too high" when the rounds zinged over my head. The third round was shoulder-high; a bullet passed by my neck. I yelled, "Fuck you," shot the sniper the finger, then strolled back to the trees.

I joked with my team that I had given the sniper the elevation, but goddamn if I'd give him the windage too. Now I know that I'd given the sniper a chance to kill me, to somehow make my killing of the VC in the rice paddy more okay. For a young man in time of war, it will always be "the best of times and the worst of times." For me, the "best"—call it pride—was ephemeral. The "worst"—call it shame—has endured.

Outside Da Nang, it was like Custer's Indian wars with back-and-forth raids and ambushes and mutilations. In other words, it was very personal. We had names for our enemies and their lands: the sniper who head-shot sentries with his purloined Starlite Scope was a VC we called Elvis; the guy who laid the mines at night was Zorro; the area of thickest concentration of VC was Dodge City. We moved out late one night to clean out Dodge and to kill Elvis and Zorro. I recall the feeling of powerfulness, walking in the dark, armed and dangerous, with other men. At dawn, our platoon—the moving hammer—had driven a group of VC into a river. On the opposite bank, another platoon—the anvil—awaited them. When we stopped firing, ten VC were dead in the water. We'd done our job well and done it clean, and I felt proud. The lieutenant asked for volunteers to drag the VC ashore, so a few of us stripped, then waded into the brown water for the dead soldiers. We cradled them to shore. Side by side on the red river bank, they looked more like dolls then men. A few minutes later, I walked back to look more closely. Someone had reaped their ears.

I remember the first time I felt rage. We were riding out on tanks, and the one in front hit a mine. The driver had a leg blown off at the hip, and someone had laid him out on an ant mound. He was alive and the ants were all over him, black on blood. I can't remember what I did—did I pull him away from the ants? I remember clearly, though, the feeling of rage. Even now, I cannot fully explain this barbarous equation: I felt pain, rage, and then I wanted to kill someone.

This feeling wasn't limited to seeing fellow marines fall. I remember feeling that same rage when dog handlers were carrying away a VC with a big hole in his hip. Their shepherd, his muzzle crimson with blood, was snuffling in the wound while the handlers laughed at the man's terror. I yelled, "Get that fucking dog away or I'll blow it away."

I remember, too, my rage whenever someone stepped on a mine and got trashed. When I turned in a prisoner to the Army of the Republic of Vietnam for questioning and they wired him to a field generator to torture information out of him. When we were test-firing LAW rockets and one blew the arm off a guy near me (I was sure the weapon had been sabotaged in the States). When I carried an old woman away from her home so we could have a free-kill zone, the sound of her death rattle in my ear. When an army helicopter dropped us ("Jump!") into a hot landing zone from a cowardly thirty feet above the deck (I fired off a few rounds at the pilot before he sped out of range). When a worthless slacker in the outfit tried to draw me into the racial violence that came to us. I held a cocked .45 to the man's head and squeezed the slack off the trigger. Later, the asshole stepped on a mine, one with a sharpened twenty-penny nail that went through his foot. The mine was meant to blow when you lifted your foot. I screamed at him, "Go ahead, you bastard, lift your foot!" But I felt ashamed, and I extricated him from his predicament.

I felt rage when I stepped on a "bouncing betty" mine with a wet fuse that only sizzled at me. When I fell in a punji pit (wide and deep enough for a helicopter) and clung by my forearms to a crosstree that held, my feet thumping against the tops of sharpened stakes. When I found one of the many scores of trip wires. When I saw dead marines in the regimental morgue hanging to drain. When the orderlies dropped a wounded man out of the helicopter we'd brought him in on, and he died. When we couldn't relieve a recon squad being wiped out, and we could hear in the comm bunker the voice of the last guy being killed, after the North Vietnamese Army removed the sandbags of the bunker to get at him. (At dawn, we flew to that bunker, killed off NVA stragglers, bagged the squad of dead marines, then packed them in a helicopter, in which the dead and alive were thrown against one another when the copter tilted, overweighted with the dead.) When we were held back from relieving a Special Forces camp being overrun by NVA tanks. Whenever I saw or expected to see people burned, shelled, shot, abused, or when I feared someone was working to do the same to me, I felt murderous rage.

In the war, that rage kept me alive, but now I look back at this time with very different feelings, as in this poem I wrote:

On the Plain of Jars I see men retreating,
leaving only wisps of smoke
in evidence of passion passing.
Now stunted oaks stand the sentinel

while the grasses sigh their duty
and cover the remains of men,
no eyes to see nor lips to speak.
All awaits a spark to become the flame
and uncover these fearsome frames
on the Plain of Jars.
And now, I am one of these men
returning, through smoke,
to hold these bones in older hands,
in awe and shame.

A few years ago, my older brother and I were in the Smithsonian's National Air and Space Museum in Washington, D.C., when we spotted a UH-34 (what we called a "shuddering shithouse" because of its vibration in flight). When my brother got within about twenty feet, he muttered, "They cleaned it up," then turned away and walked out of the museum. I caught up with him a block away; he told me he'd read the serial number on the fuselage and that he'd been crew chief on that helicopter. He told me then that his outfit flew Khe Sanh marines around during my time there and that I must have been on his ship more than once, but he had never recognized me.

I forgave us both, for I suspect we all were anonymous and the same in our smells and scared looks. To celebrate our discovery, my brother and I did what most marines would do: we got drunk together. And that's when he told me, my decorated older brother, of three tours in Vietnam, of so many missions to attack the enemy and to retrieve dead and wounded marines, all actions of which others might have thought he should have been proud. That's when he confessed his shame.

He said he'd been ferrying dead marines from a hill battle one day and that somebody had thrown in a roped prisoner among the bagged marines. During the flight, the prisoner had bitten my brother's ankle, and my brother went into a rage. He laid a heavy chain on the prisoner's head, pinning his face to the abrasive floor (embedded with grit so you wouldn't slide on blood or gore). My brother stopped his account then and would say no more. I can only guess at the damage done to the prisoner and marvel at what was done to us in that time and place: our humanity was abraded, our human faces changed.

My brother, my father, myself—in some fundamental way we are now the same. My brother went to war three times to gain our father's love; I went once and put the hope away. It came to me in a dream: my father is standing beside me, and we are looking down on the Khe Sanh Valley. He does not look at me, nor I at him. We are both looking down at the battered red earth below us. He says, "Now that you have returned, I can love you." I respond, "It's not worth it."

Had my father gone to war to gain his own father's love? I wonder, too, can anyone come back from a ground war without the albatross of shame about his neck? I never learned of my father's shame from his war, for he would only suggest by what I have since taken to be a metaphor: "They broke up priceless sets," he would say, looking saddened in his memories. Yet I do know his greatest shame since his war, and it is certainly mine: the failure to save the life of the youngest son, the one who did not go to war—what became the breaking up of my father's "priceless set," his children.

I left Vietnam during the early stage of the siege of Khe Sanh, running up the strip to jump into the back of a rolling c-130 (the pilots wouldn't stop for fear of being hit by NVA rockets or artillery). Maybe I should have paid attention to an event that happened shortly before I returned to the States. The first sergeant had gathered the company together and was screaming at us about the loss of two marines—one shot in the face, one bayoneted in the chest—killed by one old-man NVA because they were "out of their gourds on dope."

I was thirty pounds lighter when I hit the States, and my legs were still weeping from jungle rot, but I'd gotten back alive, though I hadn't fully inventoried the baggage I'd brought. The heaviest item was rage, and I was alarmed when it arose. I was apt to blow at the slightest provocation. It didn't take long before I nearly killed a man with my fists because I felt he'd insulted me. I supposed that is when I decided to put it all away, to tell myself that Vietnam never happened, for I felt far too dangerous for my own and others' good. In truth, for twenty years I suppressed Vietnam, never spoke of it.

But there was another thing I brought home with me: an infantryman's sense of smell, the knowing before it happens that something bad is about to occur. I say *smell* because this is as close as I can get to what it feels like, this sensitivity of the brain's limbic system to environmental cues that most people don't register. I suppose it comes from the need to know whether there is a mine under this dike, an enemy in that tree line, an ambush about to bust loose, someone somewhere preparing to kill you.

I smelled danger all over my younger brother, the one son who didn't go to war. I knew he would die, I knew it would involve drugs, and I knew I couldn't stop it.

My brother was a strong and sensitive seventeen-year-old kid who was acting out the pain and uncertainty of our parents' divorce by getting stoned whenever he could. I begged my parents to get him into counseling, had him live with me, even put him in jail, but all failed. Finally, while stoned with his friends, he fell, jumped, or was pushed from a forty-foot wall. He took nearly a month to die. I would work days and stand watch over him at night. His heart stopped one night, and the doctors worked to bring him back. I remember crying out for them to take my heart and put it in his chest—he'd never hurt anyone and I *had*. That night was the first time I cried since I'd left for Vietnam.

After my brother died, I quit my job, broke off an engagement to be married, and moved onto an island in a river. The police had told me that my brother had been with four of his friends when he "fell." In my grief, I became convinced that his friends had caused his death. The old equation came back: grief to rage, rage to murder. I found out my brother's friends' names and where they lived. I borrowed a hunting rifle and planned to kill the four boys, each in turn. I'd like to say I didn't kill the boys because I decided to keep death from the other children, but I know better. If I had gotten my hands on a military rifle—the familiar feel—I'd have killed the boys and I'd now be in prison or dead myself.

The decision to help others as a way to atone for my dead brother came later, when I ran a wilderness program for teenagers in difficulty. Ten years of working with kids finally seemed enough penance. But only recently have I become aware that on a level deeper than my conscious penance, I was also leading squads of young men into dangerous terrain and bringing them back, but this time with nobody dying.

Love for a woman finally brought me off my island. We married, created a daughter, and life went well for a while. For seven years, my wife gave me a sense of security, safeness, and normality. Yet I began to move from her, to withdraw from intimacy. It took some time for me to accept that I did not feel I deserved to be loved by her or by anyone. Once again I moved to live on an actual island, quit my job. I withdrew from contact with all others, except my daughter and a few friends. I still didn't know what was bothering me, though I had a vague sense of doing time for sins I could not or would not remember.

My isolation bred a deep depression. I dreamed of dragons that devoured me from the feet up, of having inadequate arms to defend others, of bodies floating in rivers. Once, on a riverbank, I hallucinated my wife and child floating by me, dead. I felt as if I were sliding into hell. One night I waded across the river to reach my island. The water was chest-deep and I pushed aside ice floes to make the crossing, yet I barely felt the cold. Instead of lighting a fire, I sat in the dark cabin all night looking at my moonlit hands. They seemed all there was of me. I was fragmenting. I began to wish for death.

There was a river falls a few miles upstream of my island. I began to go there every day to stand above the gorge and think of jumping into the deeper waters below. As each day passed, I got closer to making my leap. Only my not wishing to bring my daughter pain kept me on the cliff. One spring evening, I was standing in my place near the falls when a woman committed suicide. She had lowered herself into the fast waters above the big drop of the falls. I heard the cries of witnesses. I knew it would take the rangers time to lower their raft into the river, so I grabbed one of their old canoes and paddled up and down the gorge below the falls, now looking into the waters for the woman's life rather than for my own death. A helicopter joined the search, at one point hovering directly above me, its rotor wash threatening to capsize my craft. I began yelling at the chopper, "Fuck off!" I thought it was a gunship above me.

The woman's body was not found for three months. When I returned the canoe the evening of her death, a man told me this: "I saw her lower herself into the water. She tried to grab back onto the rocks at the moment the current pulled her toward the falls." If there is a time in life when one can see the hand of God, that was mine, when I was given a lesson by the Lady of the Falls. I gave up my thoughts of death and pulled away from the edge of the cliff, at least for a time. I visited my estranged wife (on the morning after she had been with a new lover); I visited my brother's grave for the first time since I had buried him. I lay on his grave and spoke to him and cried for the second time since I left for war.

The Dutch build three dikes in a row to keep out the sea; I've come to see this architecture as a metaphor for the defenses we raise to keep out painful memories that lie just beneath consciousness. I like, too, the names the Dutch give their dikes: the Guardian, the Sleeper, and the Dreamer. My own defenses, however, were not adequate revetments, as they were fast crumbling and I was flooded with memories—flashbacks by day, nightmares by night. The failure of my marriage was a signal bell, the reverberations of which set off a whole carillon of losses I had striven to deny. The first flashback, triggered by the helicopter looking for the Lady of the Falls, opened the doors for others of mounting intensity and duration. These in turn brought on full-blown panic attacks, which felt like heart attacks. I was back in the war. I moved west in hopes of beginning again.

I moved to a big city, in the hope that being surrounded with the stimulus of others would distract me from the war that ailed me. For varying periods, I was able to work, but then I would perceive danger about me, sense that something bad was about to occur, and I'd leave. There were a few times I experienced the twilight world of fugue, not knowing where I was or how I had gotten there. Work became a checkered affair. I was hospitalized when one of the panic attacks looked like a real-deal heart attack. Following my release from the hospital, I went through a period of homelessness. I felt like a man in a boat strapped to the gunwales, condemned to face always the sea of the past, memories rising to the surface unexpectedly. I was unable to sense or expect any joy in the future. Once again I moved to live on a river, for only rivers made any sense to me anymore. I was determined to figure my life out on the river or drown myself in it. At the time, I felt I must be the only man to feel so alone, the only man to go to the river for revelation or death.

I worked as a boatman, a man who ferried others down rivers. Once, on a river trip through a desert with a party of neophyte river guides, we came across a cow stuck in the mud of the bank. There were more than thirty of us, all young and strong, and only the one cow. Yet as we landed our boats, you could hear the ambivalence in the party, some wanting to free the animal, others wanting to leave it to its fate. Six of us set to work in the hot sun; the rest went to lie in the shade, to smoke pot or to make love, or to just relax in the desert. The cow had spent itself attempting to escape the mud, and the mud was mixed with its urine and its feces and the blood that had dribbled from its nostrils. We dug around the cow's legs and under its neck and belly, but the makeshift tools that we had were inadequate. We cut trees as lifting poles, but all broke. We called for help from the group. A woman called back that we should cut the cow's throat so it wouldn't suffer. One of the men handed her his long knife in eloquent refusal. In the end, the six of us who had worked were too exhausted to stand. The party demanded to leave, so we did. Shortly after we had gone (we learned days later), another boating company came along and marveled at the scene of a nearly dug out cow. They committed as a group to free it; they simply joined hands and lifted it out. That night, around a campfire, a younger guide asked me what I thought about our incident with the trapped cow. Of the cow we failed to rescue, I said, "That was our country in Vietnam."

The next day we prepared to face the most difficult and dangerous rapid on the river. I gathered the party onshore, and I drew a long line in the sand. I told them that the line represented how each of them felt about taking on this rapid, one end of the line being "great reluctance" and the other being "great commitment." I had them physically place themselves along the line according to how they felt about engaging the rapid. After they had done so, only the most committed were allowed to run the rapid; the rest were made to portage their boats around it. I don't think any of this group made the connection between the line of commitment and the cow, nor were they aware of the anger over the betrayal that had briefly surfaced in me, twenty years after the war.

One day, I paddled my boat downriver and, alone, came upon a large and twisted cedar, the trunk of which the river girdled at high water. I pulled up beside the trunk, leaned across the gunwale, and held on to it. I felt the force of the current against the cedar, saw how it had been shaped by that force, and identified with its twisted trunk. I looked across the river and saw an amphitheater, a curved hillside treed with cedars like the one in the river, as if these cedars were spectators to a single drama. And then I pronounced a name I cannot ever recall having said before. I said, "Orestes," and I cried for the third time since I left for war.

I did not know who Orestes was, but the name sounded Greek, and I guessed he was a mythic character. I looked Orestes up to find the story of a son who had gone to war with his father. Orestes's father, Agamemnon, returned from war and was killed by his wife and her lover. In a rage, Orestes killed his mother and the lover. For his crime of matricide, the gods beset Orestes with harpies, which wheeled about him and tore at his flesh—a fine description, I thought, of the guilt I felt over killing others, killing the love my wife had for me, and failing to save my brother's life.

There are variant endings to the myth of Orestes. In the version I like best, Orestes is brought before the gods, the harpies still wheeling and screaming and picking at his flesh. The gods expect Orestes to grovel and cry out that circumstances had made him commit his crime. He, however, claims responsibility for his crime. Struck by Orestes's ownership, the gods leave the harpies to wheel about him but not touch him. When I read this account of Orestes, I saw it as a sign of the conversion of guilt into remorse—for Orestes, and for me.

Knowing what ailed me, I was able to look about me and notice I was not the only twisted tree. There were hillsides of them all about me. I began to hear about them, about, for instance, the vet who had lived just down the road from me. He'd told his wife that he couldn't bear the nightmares of his war anymore, then drove his Harley into an oncoming semi. His wife told me this story one night as she waited on my table. She said their son was having trouble sleeping now, too.

Then I began to meet them, men who had retreated into these western mountains. I met them in a trailer set beside the river, in empty schoolrooms and churches, in a room in a courthouse, and in their homes and mine. When they trusted me, they brought their wives and children to talk.

There was the man who sat in the rain at night, his claw-hand upon the barrel of a machine-pistol, defending himself from horrors that had already occurred. There was the man who, on the anniversary of his wounding and the decimation of his company, sat in his car, alone in the mountains, gazing at pictures on the dashboard of his children, holding a knife to his own throat, on the brink of a decision, when he was found by a policeman who stopped him. This policeman's cousin had also gone to the war and then killed himself, in the same mountains.

There was a man who had won two Silver Stars for bravery, yet thought he was a coward because he had felt fear when his team was surrounded by a large force of NVA; his arm wounded by grenade fragments, he'd called in an air strike on his own position. When this man was a boy, his older brother had returned from the war in Korea and killed himself; when he first began to talk about the trauma of his own war, the man's therapist, another veteran, hanged himself. I would tell you more about these men I met, but I don't wish to jeopardize their privacy. I will tell you that they were some of the most wounded—and courageous—men I have ever met.

The largest concentration of veterans in the area I lived, however, was not composed of men who had chosen the solitude of the nearby mountains; it was made up of the veterans who had been sent to the prisons in the high valleys. The prisoners in turn drew other vets, whose work, as guards, was to keep them there. I went to the prisons to find the vets and counsel them. This was not a selfless mission: I went to these prisons, at least in part, to heal my own woundedness and to atone for my own sins. Anna Freud had me pegged when she said that men are not altruistic because they are so good but because they have been so bad.

One of the senior prison staff told me that ten years earlier, more than one-quarter of the inmates were Vietnam veterans (the Vietnam Veterans of America reported that more than 403,000 Vietnam-era veterans were incarcerated inside the U.S. criminal justice system in 1990). "Forget mental-health care—that never happened," the staffer told me.

The VA would never come in here to provide that, so we just tried to get assistance for medical problems. We had one guy who had had extensive bridgework as the result of a combat wound to his mouth. His mouth was falling apart, and we couldn't get the VA to get this guy fixed up. We didn't have the money in our budget, so we had to have all his teeth removed. We had a lot of problems with getting new prostheses for guys who lost limbs over there—they had to live with what they had that didn't fit, or we'd get them a cheap peg leg.

I was troubled by the stories of these men I never met. I knew them only through the recollections of staff and inmates who had known them and through studying the prison files. Frequently, I'd find the odd note in a file: a letter from a mother to a judge, pleading with him to understand that her boy hadn't been bad before he went to war, that war had changed him.

One of the stories has stuck in my mind—a prison report about a man who'd been a tunnel rat in the war. His pre-sentence report noted a repetitive crime: to gain entrance, he'd crawl through the air-conditioning ductwork of a restaurant, trash the restaurant, then wait for the police to come. The police kept putting him in jail, finally in prison. I wondered what nightmares he was reliving, what he had found in those tunnels, what crimes he must have felt he'd committed to seek atonement through incarceration.

I once asked a woman in the public relations office for the VA why they didn't investigate the situation of incarcerated veterans. She replied, "Wouldn't it make people sad?"

But isn't sadness a prelude to wisdom? Hers was not the only denial I encountered. I called the county coroner one day, told him what I was doing, and said I was interested in mortality rates of veterans versus non-veterans. "No difference, none," he said. Then, "You goddamn Vietnam vets, always crying about something. I was in World War II and we didn't piss and moan like you babies."

"What was your job during the war?"

His voice changed from an angry one to one of deep sadness. "I was a doctor on a hospital train in Europe."

I didn't blame the coroner for his anger; he was only trying to protect himself from his own fifty-odd years of pain, and I knew that we younger vets were ringing bells he was working hard not to hear.

I received a challenging message on my phone one day: "Just who the hell are you?" There was a number to call back. I reached a man who said he was a psychiatrist and that he was writing a book proving that posttraumatic stress disorder was a social phenomenon, not a psychological problem. In other words, PTSD was a falsehood, "not empirically proven," a myth we chose to believe in because we felt guilt as a society over waging, and politically losing, a war. In the midst of the call, he revealed that he'd served also.

"So what did you do over there?" I asked.

Once again, I heard sadness come through, "I was in Special Forces."

Denial was found also inside the prisons. When I accompanied the psychologist at one prison to meet the warden for permission to run a vet group in his facility, the warden met us with disdain: "Yeah, I'll let you do it, but understand that these are shitheads. I was there, and I didn't commit any crimes."

The warden's response was a rarity, though, in these prisons. Time and again I witnessed the reaching out of the veterans who wore blue, the guards, to those who wore green, the inmates who were veterans. A prison psychologist spoke to one of the groups one day. He'd been a battalion commander in Vietnam; in Korea he'd been the most decorated enlisted man in the U.S. Army. There were several men in the inmate group who'd been in the psychologist's airborne cavalry battalion in Vietnam. He spoke directly to all the men: "You just have to walk away from situations where you want to kill somebody. What you learned over there you cannot do anymore—unless you want to die in prison."

I ate lunch one day with a prison minister, and he told me his story:

> I wanted to be a grunt over there instead of a padre who'd tell his guys this was a just cause and then bury them afterward. So I'd go out in the field with them, carrying a rifle. One patrol, we were crossing a stream and I reached behind me to help a kid out of the water. That's when a sniper shot me in the guts. I can only hold my bowels for fifteen or twenty minutes since then.

I learned that there are three codes of conduct that rule the behavior of men in prison. There is the prisoners' code, which centers around getting things over on the guards and never snitching; there is the institutional code, which protects the institution by punishing prisoners for rule infractions and constantly reminding them that they have lost the rights of free men; and then there is an unwritten code known as the "heart," based on the integrity and courage of the individual, whether guard or inmate.

It was the presence of heart that made the veteran inmates' stories so powerful, and it was the guilt of Orestes that made these men so reluctant to share their stories. A psychologist I admire once explained the therapist's task to me. "Bob," he said, "every man has a story. Your job is to bring forth the saint from the sinner and the sinner from the saint and have them truly know themselves."

I met some great sinners in the prisons, and I want to tell you some of their stories. One of the first prisoners to come to a vet group was a medic who'd played God. In the group he projected a cynical self-deprecation and a lofty aloneness. "Just throw my food over the wall," he'd say. The son of a wealthy rancher, he'd chosen the army as a career and gone to war with an airborne unit. When he came back from the war, he divorced his wife, the army, and the family that raised him. The crimes that led him to prison were senseless. He'd go into a store, pull a pistol, demand money. Then he'd go to a bar down the street, play poker with the stolen money, smoke a cigar, and wait for the police, the trial, and finally the incarceration—seventeen years, all told.

He was a man that other prisoners would leave alone, for they knew he'd rather die than submit to any man; maybe they picked up on his wish to die. But he'd been a medic, and the other vets trusted him for that. He'd bring new men into the group and encourage them to tell their stories, or he'd pull me aside and say things like "there's a guy in C wing that needs your help." He made sure these other inmates were taken care of first before he told his own story. He spoke of the pain he felt over not being able to save many men, their wounds too severe. He spoke of the smell of a plane full of burned men, of watching a friend be decapitated, of the loss of other medics he'd admired. Finally, he spoke of his sin. Two men in his unit had raped a young girl, who was perhaps thirteen years old. He said that everyone knew about the incident but that no action had been taken against the guilty.

When the unit went back into the field, one of the men who had raped the girl took shrapnel in the groin, tearing his femoral artery. The medic ran to him under fire, as medics do. But when he saw who it was, he did not treat him; he cursed him and told him to die, then watched him die.

Two of the men the medic brought to the inmate group had been in-country neighbors of mine. One was a fellow marine who'd spent time in Dodge City. He said that his unit had lost a lot of men in that area. He told me of a new guy in the squad he led, of how he told this new guy not to take a trail because it was possibly booby-trapped. The new guy ignored the warning, and the VC triggered a buried artillery mound. The squad leader climbed a tree to rope down what was left of the torso. In a rage, the platoon swept a nearby village as a free-kill zone. The squad leader found a family in a hooch. He asked his lieutenant what to do. "Kill them all" was the response, and so the squad leader did. Even then the rage didn't end. The lieutenant brought in an amtrac. The bed was rigged with a catapult of sorts, and it hurled roped blocks of c-4 into the village, detonating all the blocks at once. When the smoke cleared, there was nothing left but charred ground. The squad leader went to prison, first as a guard, then as an inmate, convicted of assault in a dispute over a car battery.

The other marine inmate was a neighbor of mine from Khe Sanh. We'd both watched a "duster"—a quad 40 mm—blow during a rocket attack, either from a direct hit or because its overheated barrels cooked off a round. We figured out that we were no more than two hundred meters apart that night. Now he's in prison for murder. He sat in the corner in our group for months, wordless because he didn't trust anyone. One day, another man spoke about his own paranoia, which had resulted in his killing a man while in a cocaine psychosis. "Have a little Vietnam," the man said he had yelled. Dressed in camos, armed with an AR-15, he'd shot his "enemy" twenty-three times. The fellow from Khe Sanh, to our surprise, then spoke for the first time:

> I was wounded in the leg there. I lived in the mountains with my family. I don't like people. My dad was a cop and he used me as his personal punching bag. I did the same with one of my boys. I feel bad about that but I can't change it. I've made a decision to never hurt another human being. I only wish that I'd made that decision a long time ago.

A few months later, an inmate at the weight pile struck this man in the head with a free weight. The marine didn't kill the inmate who'd struck him; he let him go. Then they sent the marine to another prison, where they were collecting all the lifers. The rows of cutting wire around the perimeter evoked Khe Sanh for him, and he decompensated into psychosis. We got him back. He'd lost a lot of weight, but we put him back together again.

Sometimes in the prison group it was just plain scary. Once, two vets from rival biker gangs showed up and it got very tense. After glaring at each other, one stood up: "I'll be goddamned if I'll sit in the same group with him—too many of my brothers have been left face down in the street because of his guys. I won't deprive any vet of the right to be here, so I'll come back when he's not here." Another time, when a vet shared that he was in prison for molesting a teenage girl, another vet put his finger in his face and screamed, "I'll kill you, pervert."

Remarkably, though, for a prison group, the vets tended to embrace rather than reject the traditional outcasts in a society of outcasts—the sex offenders. A man who murdered turned one day to a man who molested and told him, "I'm not one up on you—at least your victim is still alive." The vets even brought to the group a man who was not only a sex offender but hadn't even gone to Vietnam; he'd buried the war dead though, in little towns throughout the South. That was good enough for the vets to include him and protect him and help him with his bad dreams. They brought in another vet, a bad cop—a bank robber—and protected him from men who wanted to kill him. And they brought in vets from other wars too.

They brought in an old man. He was having trouble adjusting to prison and dealing with his guilt about running down a hunter while driving drunk on a mountain road. He told his story:

> I was in WWII as a belly-gunner on a bomber. My brother was in my squadron. I was in my turret when I saw his plane get shot down. I guess I started drinking a lot then, but I've worked all my life and never been in trouble until this happened. When Korea came around, I was fishing in the middle of a lake and I saw the sheriff drive up. He got out and was yelling something at me. So we yelled back and forth until I heard him say something about my uncle wanting me. "Uncle who?" I yelled. "Uncle Sam," he yelled. So I got drafted and sent to Korea in the infantry. Maybe I have been drinking to forget some things. God, I wish I hadn't run that poor man over. I feel ashamed, and I don't think I'm ever going to feel okay again."

The men in the group brought in a Korean War vet who reminded me of the Marine Corps ethic: Never leave your dead on the field.

> I was there at Chosin Reservoir. I was wounded, and when they were hauling me out, a diesel caterpillar passed by on the road, loaded with dead marines, frozen and stacked like cordwood. I went to the hospital in Japan. While I was there, I got a postcard of Santa and his reindeer flying over a map of Korea. It was signed by all the guys in my unit. By the time I got that postcard, all of them were dead but one [he begins to cry]. Jesus Christ! I haven't thought of that in forty years.

He next said that he deserved to be in prison for his crimes, "no bones about it."

The groups were mixed by race, too—blacks and whites and Hispanics —and for a voluntary group in prison, this is a rarity. Whereas the medic was the clear leader in one prison group, a black man who'd been a recon marine was the leader in the other. He'd killed a man in a dispute over a car radio. At his trial, the prosecutor made sure to bring up his military past: "This man's a trained killer," he said.

The recon marine became the leader of his group in prison because he exemplified "heart." One day three men, including the marine, came late to the group; usually they were early. Finally, one of the men said that the recon marine had just stopped a killing in the prison yard. A man had been striding into the yard with a sharpened spike in his sleeve, intending to kill another man. Without speaking, the marine had put his hand on the armed man's arm, and the man let the killing go. When the recon marine was ready, he told us of how ashamed he was—for killing a man for a car radio, for having failed to live up to his potential, for having hurt his family by withdrawing from them, for being one more black man in prison.

One day he came out with what had happened in Vietnam:

I led thirty-eight long-range recons. I always brought my team back. I was the only black man in the outfit. There were rednecks in the outfit, including some officers. They kept sending me out, and after a while I thought they wanted to get me killed. So I refused to go out—thirty-eight times seemed enough. A buddy of mine asked me to point for his team, but I refused. Yeah, he got killed because I didn't help him out.

He got real quiet, then got up and walked out of the room. I didn't see him for a few weeks, so I looked him up in his cell. I told him I needed his help with another vet. So he came back to group. A while later, he caught me alone and said more: "This week I remembered something I'd forgotten. One day I was in the ready room to brief the chopper pilots on an area we'd just reconned. They were all officers and they were all white men and they were all listening to me, a black man. Damn, that felt good."

One story led to another. The recon marine's story encouraged another black man to tell his story:

When the presidential elections came up, they took anybody who wanted to vote to the rear. I was the only one in my team old enough to vote. I didn't care about voting, but it was a good excuse to get to where the women and booze were. While I was in the rear having a good old time, my outfit went on patrol. Bobby got shot in the head, and Terrible T got wounded from grenade fragments. So Bobby was dead and Terrible T hit, maybe because I wasn't there to help out. When I mustered out in Chicago, I was an El driver. Terrible T was living on the street. A lot of nights when I reached the end of my route, Terrible T would be waiting for me. I'd give him food and sometimes money. He'd be standing there in rags. He really looked terrible now. I felt like I was keeping him alive. Then I got sent to prison. I'm sure he's dead, just like Bobby, because I wasn't there to back him up.

The prison psychiatrist would send men to me who had not been to war but who had PTSD from childhood beatings and sexual assaults, or assaults upon them as adults. The first man to come was too paranoid to sit in a room alone with me. He'd been stabbed twenty-seven times and saw the face of his assailant on those about him. He and I met beside a low wall, in the open, where he could see all who approached him. That wall became the place where men who would not come to the group could speak with me. Regardless of the weather, they sat at the wall and spoke of their pains and their fears, of fathers who'd attempted to kill them as children, of parents who'd used them as sexual toys, of the rage they'd displaced on others, of the shame they felt.

These men reminded me of an essay William Saroyan published in the newspapers, at his own expense, during the Vietnam War. His were the only welcome-home words I ever got, so I treasured them. In part, he wrote as follows: "Remember that every man is but a variation of yourself; no man's guilt is not yours, nor is any man's innocence a thing apart. Despise evil and ungodliness, but not men of ungodliness or evil; these, understand."

I want to tell you one final prison story. Routinely, I'd get the men to request copies of their military records for me. I followed this procedure to keep the wanna-bes out of the group, to exclude the sociopaths who'd never been to Vietnam but who would lie about serving there—frauds who wanted *in* the war, whereas the actual vets wanted the war out of them.

The black recon marine's record came back. It cited his combat time in Vietnam, as well as the two Bronze Stars he'd earned for bravery under fire. There was also a notation that he'd been wounded, but no record of his having received a Purple Heart. I told him I thought we could get the medal for him. "It'll never happen," he said, "and what difference does it make anyway?"

I contacted the county's veteran service officer, a grizzled ex-gunny who'd been a dog handler in Vietnam. His leg had been all but torn away when he jumped out of a helicopter onto a mine. He'd been a cop also, and he'd put some of the men in my vet group into prison. He said he wouldn't go into the prison. "I'll help these guys out, Bob, but I won't go in there, because some guy I put there might want a little revenge." While he chewed on a handful of aspirins for the pain in his leg, he wrote the letter. "Dear Commandant of the Marine Corps."

Time passed with no response, until one day the marine received his Purple Heart—which, by regulation, requires a formal presentation— in a box, in the mail. "I'm a vet, I'm a black man, and I'm a convict," he said. "What did you expect?" I called the local base and got a first ser- geant. After a few excuses, he came out with it: "I'm not bringing marine blues into any fucking prison!" As it turned out, the top got his way and I got mine: he sent his gunny and a navy chief down. A local paper ran a picture of the ceremony, hosted by the warden—the one who'd told me "they're all shitheads."

Some of the men are out now, some are still in prison, some are dead, and some have returned to prison again. I just received a letter from one who's still there—the black recon marine—about to be released after more than twenty years of incarceration. He tells me he thinks he's just one of many "shadow warriors," as he describes them, from Vietnam: "You know, the prisoners, homeless, mentals; there ought to be another wall for us."

Last year there was a ceremony at the memorial wall in D.C., a gather- ing of the marine defenders of Khe Sanh. I couldn't afford to go, but a buddy told me about it: "We all read off the name of somebody we knew who died there. Then it got real quiet. Then a sound of a small explosion; a bagpiper was on the wall and he'd slammed his heels together. Then he played 'Amazing Grace' and most of us began to cry."

Oh yes, the prisoners built their own memorial—it's a helmet on a small concrete pad in which they've embedded their medals from their wars. They pass by the memorial each day while they pull their time, remembering.

As for me, I find that telling my own war story has diminished the weight of the memories that I carry. The harpies do continue to accompany me, but I am more trustful that they may not touch me. The river bottom sometimes still beckons, but I believe I can resist the leaping impulse. And while I am not rid of my sense of aloneness in pulling the oars of my own boat through time, I am no longer tied to face only one way. I am now just another boatman, involved in, to paraphrase Anne Sexton, "the terrible rowing toward God."

As for my older brother, he is somewhere in the Gulf War zone, for he feels safer in the zone of war than he does in the zone of intimacy with others. His retreat from his marriage was accelerated, I think, by the death of his wife's younger brother. The boy had hero-worshiped my brother as the warrior he wished to become. The boy had joined the marines, then died in a training flight. I believe my brother blames himself for the boy's death. I think I'll try and find my brother to share my story with him; perhaps he can begin then to share his.

As for my father, he has recently finished with his rowing. I knew of his death in a dream. In the dream, my father and I were again in the war, on a hill. This time, though, I saw him attacked by his own harpies, in the form of lions. With an ax I chopped at them, but to no avail. They would not touch me, but they ate his heart while I cried.

I was never able to share my war story with my father, nor to coax his from him. But he did leave me with a map of sorts, a genealogy of the family, which he'd crafted over the years—in silence, as was his way. The progenitor of the clan, Robert, Duke of Normandy, tops the list; his son, William the Conqueror, is next. As I read the names, with dates of birth and death and vocations—in hexagons and circles linked with lines— I note that each generation had its war. From Hastings to Agincourt, I can know that the fathers and sons of my lineage were there. Some were royal, but most were farmers and blacksmiths who went to war. As my name denotes—MacGowan—I am also the son of a smith, who went to war. Above my own name, I read my father's description of himself: "Soldier." Alongside my own name, I read my father's comment on my brother and me: "Marine."

Reading my father's gift jogs the memory of my father taking my older brother and me, when we were boys, to the Smithsonian to view a general's sword, wielded at Chickamauga, Tennessee. "The river ran red with blood that day," my father said. My brother and I, uncertain of this obeisance to the sword of our relative, looked at the sword for the blood we knew must still be on it, but they'd cleaned it up, just as they'd cleaned the helicopter in which my brother had ferried me in our war, the same machine which today sits in another Smithsonian museum, across the mall.

My father rests now at Arlington, on the grounds of Lee's old mansion, across the river from the helicopter and the sword. We were never able to talk about our respective defining wars, his in the Ardennes Forest, mine in the Khe Sanh Valley. There are things I wished I'd told him, and things from him I wished to know:

> Were you so inured to the dead and cold
> that you sat atop black hummocks in the snow—
> men whose blood no longer flowed—
> and ate your rations?
> Was your battlefield commission gained
> in those Ardennes forest and plains
> because you were so brave, or
> because you were of the few alive?
> Did the terribleness of the cold
> and the hummocks in the snow
> reach around your heart
> to numb it like your toes?
> Was it your memories of your war or
> the unfealty of your wife that caused
> those starbursts in your brain?
> These I would have asked you.
> Though, of all I might have told you,
> listen, I learned this from the river—
> I am your son, Orestes. You are
> my Agamemnon.

There, I have finished my war story. I have told it so that I could also tell you the stories of some other men I have known, men who went to war and then went to prison, stories you might not want to hear at first.

I think their stories are part of a larger story that needs telling—the one about why so many men who went to the Vietnam War later went to prison.

What is life but a story? And what is history but our collective stories and the ways in which we have met one another?

Shadow Soldier

I met Donald Clay on a visit to prison. As a writer and teacher of writing, I accompanied a psychologist, both of us hoping to encourage the prisoners he met with to write their stories. What follows are excerpts from Donald Clay's work.

—Donald Anderson

In July 1970, Lance Corporal Torres was mortally wounded. I was not a member of that patrol. Torres had been my mentor, training me in the nuances of the lead position as point man. In my experience, point men are either foolhardy and reckless or extremely courageous. It can be said that the life of a team is in the hands of this individual. Torres epitomized the qualities and skills necessary for the position. Torres's instructions were feats themselves. He had only a rudimentary grasp of English, but seldom, if ever, did a fresh hunk of grinder meat receive the full breadth of exact instructions such as I received from Torres. In the bush, as well as in the compound, he could admonish and implore me to use my eyes, ears, and sense of smell to detect the presence of enemy booby traps and troops. More important, he was instrumental in my learning to acknowledge and act on my intuition as a means of recognizing potential dangers, thereby minimizing the threat to men and mission.

When I look at a cherished photograph, I am reminded of just how young and full of patriotism we were. Death, dying, or permanent disability were no concern; this sort of thing was what happened to other people. We did not know, or choose to accept, that we were *all* other people.

In time, I was given the honor of leading my own team of six. Grim Reaper was our moniker. Walking through the compound one night to round up my team to prepare for a patrol, I heard the revelry of marines taking a break from the stress of war. I approached the noisy hooch only to overhear a braggart: "Can't wait till I get back to the world. Why, back home, we'd get drunk and go nigger busting for real fun."

I entered the hooch. The revelry was replaced by a deafening silence. As I surveyed the hooch, I saw that two of my guys were part of the crowd. Here I am, a black team leader in a battalion with no black officers and but one black staff NCO. What was it that hurt so intensely? I knew. Although daily risking my life for American principles and South Vietnamese freedom, I was to be reminded that despite any risk or patriotic conviction on my part, I would always be a nigger, and Torres, an exceptional marine, now dead, would always be a spic. The incident would affect me in ways I wouldn't begin to fathom until years later.

In addition to all else I ever felt in Vietnam, I also felt like a self-conscious twelve-year-old with a loaded weapon. Nonetheless, as Grim Reaper's leader, I had a responsibility to protect and ensure the safety of the team: Dietrick, Miller, Knuth, Hooker, Doc, and Hughes. Grim Reaper was a collection of personalities that learned to function as a single-minded unit. I am most proud of one achievement in Vietnam above all others: Grim Reaper lost not one man.

I was reared in Mississippi until age fifteen. Our small town was a sequestered enclave, underdeveloped and racially gerrymandered. Jonestown was a totally segregated section of Hollandale, Mississippi. The boundaries were rigid—physically, socially, and psychologically. Besides the railroad tracks, our community was bordered by interminable fields of cotton and soybeans. I worked in the cotton fields at an early age. Besides the stifling heat and work, there were the ubiquitous snakes. Rattlesnakes, copperheads, and water moccasins sure helped me develop survival instincts early. Sometimes the fields would be so parched they hardened like cement. Each swing of the hoe sent reverberations through my body like vibrations through a tuning fork. Conversely, whenever it rained, the mud would literally suck the tattered boots or worn shoes from my feet. I earned three dollars for a ten- to twelve-hour day.

My formative years in Mississippi were spent going to school, playing, and learning about the dos and don'ts in a segregated society. School was fun and my curriculum work exemplary. My parents stressed the importance of obtaining a quality education; they were not disappointed. I was a courteous and attentive student and actively involved in student government.

When we were ten or twelve, my friends and I were playing a rowdy game of football on our major league field of dreams. Three white kids appeared and joined in the fun. Toward the end of the game, as we were reveling in the experience, our celebration was interrupted by the rumbling sounds of a dilapidated Ford pickup approaching. Screeching to a dusty halt with its brakes locked, the vehicle disgorged its cargo. Before the truck had come to a complete stop, the first man yelled out at the scrawniest of our new playmates.

> "Boy, what ya'll do'in playin wit dem dar niggas?"
> "We's jest playin football, mister," the child answered. The child was clearly shaken.
> "Well ya'll ain't a playin no mo. Com'mer and we's gon see you folks 'bout dis. Hey," he continued, now directing his vehement disapproval at us, "Ya'll nigga boys a bettin never play wit these har boys again—ya'll har me?"

We didn't say a word. I wonder why. Fear? Whatever, I have never forgotten the vile epithets and degradation of that moment. Why do I believe that isolated incident belongs here? Among the many influences in my life, that one remains a poignant reminder of a social lesson I had to be exposed to.

My parents divorced about the time of the football game. Mom moved to Michigan, and we—my two sisters and I—joined her nine months later. Upon arrival in Michigan, I experienced a severe case of culture shock. Change is always difficult, especially with the loss of childhood friends. Still, I wasn't prepared for the challenge of attending a high school with a black enrollment of less than 10 percent. Up to this time, I had spent my nine fruitful school years in the security of a totally black student body.

Dowagiac Union High School was an exceptional school, however, and I again excelled in my schoolwork, graduating with honors in 1968. Moreover, I was skillful enough in sports to garner the attention of many Mid-American Conference colleges and universities. (One of my classmates, Chris Taylor, went on to earn an Olympic bronze medal as a heavyweight wrestler.)

In dire need of an identity check (having come of age in two disparate environments left me with a host of unanswered personal character questions), I volunteered for a four-year enlistment with the United States Marine Corps. The date of my enlistment was September 19, 1969, a month shy of my ninteenth birthday. It is important to note that the decision to enlist was based solely on finding a means to define my worth and character. That is to say, there was no juvenile misconduct that precipitated the decision.

I survived marine boot camp! Oh my, the indignities one faced. Another story for another day. Suffice it to say, and this is worth repeating, *I survived boot camp.* This quest to become a man wasn't progressing as well as I'd anticipated. I still lacked self-confidence. After a few additional weeks of advanced combat training, I volunteered for Reconnaissance School, Camp Pendleton, California. This training was even more physically and mentally exhausting—so tough, in fact, that I gave serious consideration to withdrawing from the service. But despite any personal reservations I may have been harboring about my military abilities, I gave all I had.

Upon successful completion of recon school, I had earned entry into an elite fraternity. Later, while in-country, I would attend another recon school. But before that, I had begun to feel and think like a marine. It was a feeling of incomparable mental and physical readiness and toughness—in a word, *invincible.* It was then when I first heard this philosophy: "Challenge your fear. If you sense a threat, close and incapacitate the threat." Without a doubt this mode of thought is directly responsible for the survival and call to duty of me and my men. It has also been the bane of my civilian existence.

War by its very nature—designed destruction—is a traumatic experience, even for the professional participant. I arrived in Vietnam as a cocky, red-white-and-blue nineteen-year-old. A year later, I left as a disillusioned bundle of perceptions: a psychological and social liability. As I look back I can see that there were indeed a set of situations and circumstances that contributed to my inglorious metamorphosis into a shadow soldier.

As a point man in Vietnam, I had gained considerable respect and noto-
riety. Grim Reaper was standing down for a well-deserved rest, so Sergeant Fink, a veteran of two prior tours, approached me with a proposition. He asked if I would walk point for his upcoming patrol. I declined.
As insistent as he was over a three-day period, I was equally adamant
in refusing. On his way down to the LZ for insertion, Frank stopped by
my hooch: "Claymore, if anything happens to me I am coming back to
haunt you." We laughed; I reassured him that this patrol would be, in the
vernacular of the day, a cakewalk.

Soldiers often experience premonitions, most of which are only flights
of fancy. Less than three hours after being inserted near a VC enclave
hidden in the Que Son Mountains, Fink was felled by a single AK-47
round. He had just deployed his team and was moving to cover when the
sniper struck.

I felt responsible for his death. If only I had walked point, Fink would
be alive. In my mind I heard the whispers: "Clay is a coward; Clay should
have helped out." Like Poe's character in "The Tell-Tale Heart," I thought
surely everyone was aware of and convinced of my guilt. Unlike the fictional man driven mad by shame and guilt who at last screamed out, I
bore the visceral imprint of cowardice. Doubt, particularly of one's com-
petence, is devastating.

I snapped. Where before I had experimented with drugs, I now began
to depend on them for the modicum of solace I rarely obtained. Professional cautiousness was supplanted by recklessness in the bush. If I
could die in a fierce firefight, my courage, I felt, would be unquestioned.
I invited death. I wore a flesh-tone Band-Aid on my forehead in marked
contrast to the layered camouflage on my face and neck. During fire-
fights I protected my men by placing myself in exposed positions. I wrote
to my mother:

Dear Mama,

Because you haven't written, I'd like to say—I am still alive.

Don

P.S. Only for the moment.

During October 1970, we were operating in the Quang Nam province,
an enemy-controlled territory. I was walking point twenty to twenty-five

meters ahead of the team. Signs of recent VC/NVA presence in the area were undeniable. In addition to the broken twigs and discernable sandal tracks on the trail, I felt the enemy's proximity. I could smell a faint odor of boiled rice. I moved back toward the team and gave them instructions to be extra vigilant. Moreover, I told them that we'd be "in the shit" this particular morning. "Like real soon," I said.

Again I moved out ahead of my men. As I turned down the well-utilized trail, two VC irregulars appeared. They weren't but ten feet in front of me. The lead soldier was laughing, obviously having just shared something with his companion. Alerted by the perplexed expression on his companion's face, the lead man turned in time to see a fleeting image of me, then a muzzle flash that signaled the ejection of a 5.62 mm round. The soldier's head exploded, covering foliage and his friend with fragments of skull and pulverized brain.

Never had I seen an expression such as his prior to his abrupt demise, nor do I ever wish to see it again. It was a smile of gelid terror, disbelief and acknowledgment that life was over. The other soldier was mortally wounded with the next volley. In less than a second—from sighting to firing—I had killed two men.

After we'd secured the area, we again set out along the trail. I resumed my position at point. We wouldn't have to worry about complacency. Thirty minutes later, attempting to find the best fording route across a stream, I came under intense small-arms fire from enemy troops positioned among rocks above our position. Apparently the VC had not seen my men, who began emerging from their concealed spot on the bank of the stream. The VC had a strategic advantage, as they were behind boulders firing down. I was in the middle of a rock-strewn stream without cover. I could hear the rounds whiz past my ears and splash into the water around me. One of the first rounds knocked me face down into the stream. The round had entered my backpack and been altered when it hit the C rations. My consequent wound was minor. While I drew the VC fire, I shouted to my men to saturate the area with fire. I was able to move from the stream.

Resuming the line of march, we set out once again. We'd traveled about two hundred meters when we decided to take a short breather. I moved ahead again, taking a position some twenty meters up the trail. I was exhausted, but the adrenaline flowing through my body ensured a vigilant awareness. I noticed a barely perceptible movement in the dense foliage off to my left flank. Peripheral vision enabled me to see a figure moving stealthily toward my position. As he inched closer, I casually retrieved my weapon that was propped against the tree.

In a minidrama, the soldier rose to toss a hand grenade. I swung my weapon at the same instant and fired. Once, twice, three, four times. My victim was unable to run or walk, so he began to claw his way through the tangled underbrush.

The grenade the soldier had thrown exploded—a violent thud—further disturbing the eerie quiet of the jungle. Hearing the gunfire and muffled explosion, my team began firing in the direction of the injured soldier. I shouted above the cacophony of cursing and small-arms fire for my men to cease fire. The air was chocked with cordite. I entered the bullet-torn brush. When I reached down to turn the man's small frame, the arm detached itself from his Raggedy Andy body. I remember yelling, swearing, and weeping. I was nineteen-years-old, trying to be a marine, a man. The child (he was twelve or fifteen) at my feet was simply gone.

In less than two hours, I had figured in the deaths of five human beings. Can anyone fully comprehend the effects of the power, the God complex, on a young man with a license to kill?

Dennis Dietrick and I were moving through a VC base camp. Grim Reaper was part of a combined operation being used to harass and extricate the VC from the region. Lollygagging and inattentive, I, the skillful point man, felt the telltale tautness of a trip wire slacking around my ankles. As if he'd heard or sensed my stark realization telepathically, DD knew we would be body-bag material in a few seconds. We didn't have time to panic or run. We stood transfixed, like two ducks struck on the head with a rock, dumbfounded. One second, two, three seconds . . . it was a dud. "It" was a U.S. 80 mm mortar round lying prone eighteen inches to my right. With a disbelieving shake of our heads, we gingerly exited the spot. Neither of us uttered a single word about what had just happened—nor did we ever.

Fifteen minutes later I walked into a disheveled structure to investigate its contents. During my search, I discovered nothing out of the ordinary. There were baskets filled with grain, discarded clothes, and an empty storage chest of varying dimensions and questionable craftsmanship. I walked across the straw-strewn floor to check a large upright vase when the floor caved in. I landed on my face in a huge open cavern filled with grain and other stores. Difficult though it was to see in the dim light, I couldn't help but notice a shadowy recess. Protruding from the earthen dugout was a barrel pointing directly at me, attached to a tripod. My weapon was lying three feet in front of me. I now knew exactly what the lead VC soldier must have experienced in the instant before I shot him.

The machine gun was unmanned. Even today I am haunted by that frozen moment; I often awake terrorized, my heart pounding, my kidneys throbbing like bellows gone awry. The one consolation was the realization that the unoccupied cavern was a cache. AK-47s, SKSs, ammo galore, and numerous other weapons were recovered.

Though I never used drugs or alcohol in the bush, I did use the two when not on patrol to deal with my pervasive thoughts of death and constant danger. To further desensitize myself, I incorporated the resignation that I would die in Vietnam. My mind was invaded by morbid flights of fantasy. When I would search lifeless and often-mangled bodies of VC/NVA soldiers, I would wonder whether their families knew about or appreciated the sacrifices these dead soldiers had made, or the danger they faced daily, or the destruction they wrought.

Because I had resigned myself to die in Vietnam, I was unprepared to return to "the world"—there had been no contingency plan for alive-and-not-well. Still, I had more than two years remaining on my enlistment. After a strained leave with my family in Dowagiac, Michigan, I was assigned to Cherry Point, North Carolina, a Marine Corps air station.

At Cherry Point, the first rent in my personality appeared. The rage, repressed as it was, surfaced, and I began a cycle of unintentional aggression I was ill-prepared to handle. What happened? A fellow in a car nearly ran me down as I entered a crosswalk on base. The near collision didn't upset me; it was the driver's insolence and aloofness about almost hitting me. When I approached his vehicle, he sped away, showering me with dust and grit, laughing.

For the next five days I canvassed the base looking for the vehicle and driver. All my recon skills were employed in this hunt. On the fifth day, I spotted the car outside the base PX complex. I positioned myself next to a vehicle one row behind his. An hour passed before the man emerged from the Dairy Queen. He carried a milkshake, and a cigarette dangled from his mouth. While he fumbled for his keys, I got into a low stance and circled around to the passenger side of the car. I had hoped to catch him unaware and enter through the passenger door.

The door was secure; I'd compromised the mission. Recognition was established, words were exchanged, and a litany of racial slurs was directed at me. I recall vividly what transpired next. The man attempted to flick his cherry red cigarette into my face. To accomplish this he had to extend his hand outside the driver's side window. I timed perfectly, grabbing his hand. I pulled the man's arm through the narrow opening and broke it. The only reason I didn't rip the appendage from the body was the instant recollection of that horrific moment (the arms and food cache) a scant few months earlier in the jungles of Vietnam.

My actions at Cherry Point earned me a psychiatric evaluation, the first of four before I was given an honorable discharge under medical conditions. Specifically, I was diagnosed and discharged as a "schizoid personality." My rage continued. The outward projections weren't as vicious as the incident at Cherry Point, but my mental disarray undermined my ability to function in a positive and consistent way. Suffice it to say I became increasingly aggressive, combative, and withdrawn.

Marking the beginning of an imprisonment was my ignominious discharge from the marines. This discharge confirmed my deepest fear that I was, indeed, a failure. The excerpt from my medical evaluation captures my despair: "21-year-old Marine is bright and articulate. Outward appearance cannot mask his profound sadness. On the ward this Marine remains withdrawn and depressed."

My depression was authentic. I had been reduced in rank twice in less than two months, from sergeant to lance corporal. In addition, I'd been psychologically poked and prodded by doctors from Brunswick, Maine; Portsmouth, New Hampshire; Bedford, Massachusetts; and, now, the U.S. Naval Hospital, Philadelphia, Pennsylvania. I had been experiencing severe headaches; moreover, the frightening chimerical visions kept me anxious and unnerved. Sleep eluded me, and when I did fall asleep I always saw Sergeant Fink's face or the bloodless corpses of men brave enough to dare to be men. My erratic behavior was episodic, my ability to cope waning.

Ordinarily a desired marine attribute, my combative tenacity was now unacceptable. The crowning insult was the assertion that my detrimental behavior was a preexisting condition. This diagnosis was approved. On March 23, 1973, I left the corps.

Civilian life provided no miraculous cures; in fact, my symptoms worsened, and I vacillated between periods of extreme confidence and an almost total moroseness. Fueling my debilitating neurosis was the sixth sense to intuit danger. In the bush, this acuity had saved lives; now a life was being consumed. My intuition was a liability. Too much noise! Too many signals to process! Like the person who has only a hammer and treats everything encountered as if it were a nail, I treated every movement as a threat, real or imagined. Something was needed to jam the signals. In addition to the drugs and alcohol, I learned to use avoidance to my advantage.

Regardless of the negatives I have shared with you, the Marine Corps does build men, which is to say I was not without some acceptable, socially redeeming qualities. In fact, as a direct result of lessons learned in the corps about commitment and goal orientation, I came into contact with sensitive and intelligent women.

During the summer of 1973, I met such a person. We had known each other as early as 1969; however, at that time, the relationship was platonic. Even the best of my many relationships throughout this time was no better than mediocre. This one with Pamela was the best. In the beginning, ours was a blissfully idyllic relationship. We regularly socialized and made adult plans for the future, including the fenced yard and children. I cared deeply for Pamela then, just as I do today. I would be her security, was my thought. I would never abandon her. Although my intentions were genuine as well as chivalrous, the reality was, sadly, far removed.

I can't say with any certainty the moment our friendship began to deteriorate. I became more withdrawn, paranoid, and sullen. Compounding my problems was the specious belief that alcohol and drugs could ameliorate my depression, anxiety attacks, guilt, and sleep deprivation. At times I would weep like a widow; other times found me in fits of unwarranted rage. Nearing the end of our tumultuous relationship, Pamela had to be awakened from a horrible nightmare. When I roused her, she screamed louder. Following two weeks of constant badgering, she said she'd dreamed I was strangling her. Given my mercurial nature—which frightened me on occasion—her fears were not unfounded. Was I an abusive mate? Yes, since I often intimidated her both verbally and physically. We did not part friends. This would be the heaviest monkey I'd ferry for fifteen more years. My deepest regret, other than the anguish I subjected Pamela to, is not seeking professional help at her behest. Also never sharing my Vietnam guilt with her. My time with Pamela was the only long-term relationship—six years—I've entered into. All the rest, like the jobs I've held, were short, necessary, and doomed to failure. Not every aspect of every relationship was bad. In between displays of masochistic machismo, I was considerate, caring, jovial, magnanimous, and hardworking. However, there was no consistency, except the inevitable depression and humiliating, unprovoked fits of tearfulness and rage.

Jobs: I've held many. When I wasn't among the unemployed and homeless, I consciously limited my employment to low-skilled or unskilled jobs requiring minimal contact and interaction with others. Case in point: employment as refuse collector, laborer (farm, railroad, foundry, construction), tavern sweep, ad nauseam. At the first hint of possible management consideration, I would abort employment.

Criminal conduct had never been my way of life; my parents taught me respect for life, law, and property. It wasn't until 1984 that I came into contact with the justice system. My on-again, off-again affinity for drugs earned me a controlled substance charge. I received probation.

At the time I was arrested and officially charged with second-degree murder, I had been completely drug and alcohol free for more than six months, though my mental state was far from normal. I was still plagued by the classic symptoms of posttraumatic stress disorder. Two weeks before the confrontation that resulted in murder, I'd willingly contacted a community mental health office in Aurora, Colorado. I explained that I was afraid I couldn't contain my temper. Most days I couldn't leave my house. I was held captive by a fear of self and others. The doctor prescribed Thorazine. The order was filled and I took the 100 mg tablets four times daily, as prescribed. Now I was a lethargic, hypervigilant individual with recurring nightmares, guilt, a fear of crowds, anxiety. It was impossible to shake my feelings of doom and disaster.

Throughout this time I was trying desperately to ensure the success of a relationship I had been in for thirteen months. It had seemed a promising arrangement. My private inner war aside, in the presence of my companion and her five-year-old daughter, I enjoyed more pleasure and peace than I had had since being with Pamela. These two people were all I had. I wouldn't betray or allow any harm to befall them. Regrettably, someone would challenge my resolve. The domestic dream of middle-class predictability was dashed when an individual decided my and my girlfriend's interracial living arrangements were unacceptable.

I had met Kurt twice before the July 8, 1985, confrontation. The first time was at my baby-sitter's apartment. He happened to be there when I stopped by to make arrangements for my girlfriend's child. A couple of days later we ran into each other when I purchased a late-model van from another man, obviously a friend of his. Kurt, at the end of the transaction, quite affably offered to sell me a stereo. His friend verified Kurt's contention that the stereo was indeed Kurt's own. His car had been totaled, I was told.

"Okay," I said. "One hundred dollars for the stereo. Here's ninety. Can I give you the ten later?" I told Kurt I'd probably see him at the sitter's home. He agreed.

Two days later I heard that Kurt was upset. Among other things, he'd been sharing his philosophy on the wretchedness of interracial relationships. The next morning I saw that my van had been vandalized, tires flattened, and the new stereo gone. Even though only my property had been vandalized, all the years of my own repressed racial enmity surfaced. Too much repressed anger! Too many unresolved issues! My rage wasn't about Kurt specifically. I now think it was far more insidious and wide-ranging. It was about Vietnam and Mississippi, about Torres and Fink, about being a marine and decorated vet, about being tired of avoiding, being tired of being slighted, being tired of feeling a failure. It was about it all.

The sixth sense that had served me so well in Vietnam interpreted my van's violation as a dangerous intrusion, a clear and definite threat to my family's security. If, I reasoned, this person were brazen enough to commit his act of premeditated vandalism during the wee hours of the morning while I was present in the nearby house, what would this person entertain to act upon if my family were home alone, unsuspecting and unprotected. This question I sought to answer later that night when I located Kurt at his motel residence. Foolishly, I obtained a weapon.

The thirty-two-caliber automatic was in fact the first and only time I'd handled a firearm since my military discharge twelve years earlier. The consequences for so arming myself were predictably catastrophic.

I approached Kurt. When I asked him about my van and the theft, he pleaded ignorance. As I became more adamant, he admitted to the act, let loose with a barrage of racial slurs, then swung. I blocked the blow and pulled my weapon from the pocket of my windbreaker. During our struggle, a single round was inadvertently discharged. Three weeks later, Kurt succumbed to the head wound.

Within hours after my deadly scuffle with Kurt, I would be apprehended and charged with first-degree assault. The charge became first-degree murder with Kurt's death. On the day of my sentencing, the district attorney pronounced that I was a "time bomb."

"Your Honor," he announced, addressing the court, "we believe Mr. Clay's high incidences of combat during the Vietnam have made him a walking time bomb; therefore, we believe he should be remanded to the Department of Corrections for twenty-four years."

WAYNE KARLIN

Wandering Souls

Family and friends wondered why we were so angry. What are you crying about? they would ask. . . . Our fathers and grandfathers had gone off to war, done their duty, come home and got on with it. What made our generation so different?

As it turns out, nothing. No difference at all. When old soldiers from "good" wars are dragged from behind the curtain of myth and sentiment and brought into the light, they too seem to smolder with choler and alienation. . . .

So we were angry. Our anger was old, atavistic. We were angry as all civilized men who have ever been sent to make murder in the name of virtue were angry.

MICHAEL NORMAN, from *These Good Men: Friendships Forged from War*

On March 18, 1969, Homer Steedly, a young American infantry lieutenant, turned a bend in a trail in Kontum Province and came face to face with a North Vietnamese soldier, his weapon slung over his shoulder. The soldier, who Steedly first took for an enemy officer, was a twenty-four-year-old medic named Hoang Ngoc Dam, from the village of Thai Giang, near Hai Phong—a fact the lieutenant would not discover for more than thirty years. There was no time then for more than a quick glimpse of each other. As soon as Dam saw Homer, he snatched his weapon off his shoulder and brought it around. "I shouted *Chieu Hoi*, the phrase to surrender," Homer wrote in his journal, "but he continued to draw down on me. I fired just before he got his rifle on me. If I had not been so scared, I might have had the presence of mind to just wound him, but in my adrenalin-rush panic, I killed him with one shot through the heart."

For a time he stared in a daze at the body. The man he'd killed was young, his pith helmet clean, his uniform starched, and the SKS rifle clutched in his hands new, the greasy cosmoline used as an antirust still gooped on its bayonet hinge—someone new to the war, Homer concluded. He bent down and went through the dead man's pockets, drawing out a notebook with a colorful picture of a man and woman in what he took to be traditional or ancient Vietnamese dress on the front cover, and a daily and monthly calendar grid labeled with the English word *schedule* on the back; a smaller black notebook; and a number of loose papers—letters, ID cards, some sort of certificates. The spine and corners of the first notebook had been neatly reinforced with black tape.

Thirty-five years later, as I handed that notebook to Dam's brother, I was struck again with the care Dam had taken in binding it up. He was a soldier in an army in which nothing could be thrown away, nothing wasted, and I thought, not for the first time, of what the appearance of that book must have meant to Homer as he looked through it on that dark trail. Raised on a small, hardscrabble farm, Homer knew the preciousness of things that could not be replaced, knew how to shepherd them. The way he had shot Dam was unusual—a gunfighter duel in a war in which more often than not the enemy remained faceless to the Americans, only sudden flashes of fire from the jungle, targets to be annihilated. That invisibility was frustrating to the GIs, but at least it allowed the comfort of dehumanizing the enemy, making him ghost, demon, target. To see not only the face of the man he'd killed but also the carefully rebound covers, the force of will that the meticulous writing and drawings inside the book revealed, confronted Homer with a mirrored and valuable humanity. He tried not to think about it. There was scarcely the time anyway, and later that same day, he'd have one more encounter with a soldier who wanted to shoot him—this time, an American whom the war had broken, who had already had shot and killed another soldier. Homer was able to talk that man into laying down his weapon, and so that day he had taken a life and saved a life. He couldn't dwell on the former. It was, in any case, a killing justified by custom, law, and the need to survive.

Homer sent the documents to the rear area, where he knew they'd be assessed and then burnt. But later that evening he changed his mind, contacted a friend in S-2 Intelligence and asked him to bring everything back. He couldn't bear to have the documents, the last evidence of the life he'd taken, destroyed. "I kept his personal documents and will send them home," he wrote to his mother. "Someday, perhaps, I will be able to contact his relatives." By refusing to let go of the notebooks he'd taken from Dam's body, Homer somehow understood, though he could not put it into words or coherent thoughts until years later, that he was hanging on to a grief that was the price of remaining human.

The shy son of a South Carolina sharecropper and his German war bride, Homer considered himself an unlikely officer. He had grown up poor in the rural South. Unable to afford more than a year of college, he enlisted in the army in order to get training and save money for his education. But the army saw leadership potential in him, and in 1967, he was sent to Officer Candidate School, graduating as a second lieutenant. One of his classmates was William J. Calley, who, exactly one year and two days before Homer would shoot Dam, led and participated in the massacre of more than five hundred women, old men, and children, all civilians, in the village Americans called My Lai, far from the arena where Homer fought his war.

"It's a strange thing to say, because combat was so much heavier where we were in the highlands, fighting the regular NVA," Homer said, "but for me it was a blessing not to be in those areas where you couldn't tell the VC from civilians." He was spared from ever having to make the moral choices the soldiers who were at My Lai did or did not make. His enemy was the highly trained, well-armed regular forces of the People's Army of Vietnam. Homer's unit, the 1st Battalion of the 8th Infantry Regiment, 4th Infantry Division, was engaged not in the guerilla war of rice paddies and hamlets, where most casualties came from mine and booby traps and Americans couldn't tell enemy from civilian. Instead, they had humped ninety-pound loads in ninety-plus-degree heat and humidity, and they were locked for months in savage jungle fighting in rugged mountain country where the thick triple-canopied trees made it dark at midday.

It was as clear-cut as a war could be. He and his men killed, as he had killed Dam on that mountain trail, in order to stay alive. He came to see that goal as his main job. By 1969 it was obvious to all of them that the war was only a holding action. Homer did his best, even extending his own time in the field (army officers were required to serve only six months in combat), unwilling to let his company be led by an inexperienced commander. And then he had come home. There was nothing he needed to feel guilty about. He had committed no atrocities, was no baby killer. He had been promoted and decorated. He had participated in the defining history of his time. He had experienced the close camaraderie of combat soldiers, had fought bravely and led competently, and had come back relatively intact. There were men who would and did take such experiences as the high-water marks of their lives. There were others who were foolish enough to envy them.

"When I came back," Homer said, "I tried to talk to people. But I could see they changed toward me so I just shut up, threw myself into work." He threw himself into a bottle as well, and at the same time, he began engaging in solitary and dangerous sports—cave- and sky-diving, small-plane piloting, motorcycle racing—activities in which a careless or irresponsible move could get him killed, but could get *only* him killed. "The deaths and injuries [that occurred] under my leadership still haunt my memories," he would write. "I expect they will be among the memories that flash before my eyes when I lie on my deathbed. Somehow I feel guilty for having come back alive."

He had sent the documents he'd taken from the body of the man he'd killed to his mother. She had lived through a war and its aftermath herself, and she understood his need to preserve what he had taken and what had been taken from him. She carefully stored the documents in a box that she placed in the attic. They remained there almost three decades, locked away in a space of contained darkness, a physical anamnesis of the memories of the war itself that Homer locked away inside his own mind. He had seen and done things that he knew the people around him did not want to know about or would not believe. His ears rang continuously—the result of a 105 mm shell that had landed in his fighting position and splattered him with the blood of the two sergeants with him—a thin, constant scream in the middle of his mind that never, to this day, went away. There were certain images burned into his brain, certain smells seared into his nostrils, certain tastes still on his tongue, and he felt they composed a wall between himself and those who had not seen, felt, smelled, and heard what he had. He was afraid that difference made him monstrous. He was afraid that he would turn anyone with whom he truly shared those tastes, those sounds, those sights, into himself, and there were some people he loved and he wanted to protect, so he remained silent.

Besides, he knew that nobody would believe him.

He might tell people, for example, of the time when one of his men out in the jungle on a listening post had been seized by a tiger, felt without any warning the terrible clamp of the animal's jaws on his skull, its hot breath and slobber encasing his face. As he was being dragged off into the trees, the soldier had had the presence of mind to bring the barrel of his M-16 up to the animal's flank and fire. The tiger, wounded, dropped him and disappeared. The GI was left with its mark: two perfect indentations on either side of his forehead. Homer could tell the story, but people would stare at him, say nothing, or, worse, say, sure, they'd seen that in *Apocalypse Now*, and think he was making it up. They had the illusion, in their safe lives, that there were no beasts. They didn't understand that the tiger had come into him, Homer, into all of them, eventually, had left its mark on them and in them and in him. *Here there be tygers*, the old maps marked unknown territory. Once, on a jungle trail, he had been the tiger.

He could tell how from March 21, two days after he'd shot Dam, to March 30, he—a twenty-two-year-old country boy, sharecropper's kid— had commanded an understrength company that held a hill against an overwhelming enemy force, his men with little and then no water or food or ammunition, shelled constantly, sometimes by hundreds of rounds of 105 mm howitzer fire, as well as by uncounted mortar rounds landing inside their fifty-meter perimeter. He could tell how the North Vietnamese tried to swarm the hill, about their insane bravery as they were chopped to pieces in the American cross-fire, about the insane bravery of his own men fighting them off, and about his own insane bravery—he could never use that noun without that adjective. He could tell of the true insanity of a battalion commander who countermanded his urgent request for ammunition, food, and water and instead risked helicopters to bring them rations they couldn't even use without the water they didn't have and so desperately needed. In spite of that, his men fought on for days in that heat, their throats swollen and parched, one man going berserk and trying to drink from a canister of diesel fuel. He could tell how a door gunner had vomited when he saw a corpse's eyes come alive with maggots when the helicopters finally were able to take out the wounded and dead, and how on the final day of the siege, after he had made sure all his men were evacuated in the helicopters, there were so many enemy soldiers pouring into the perimeter that he thought he and the last three men with him would have to make a run for the jungle. He could add that an also insanely brave helicopter crew disobeyed orders and extracted them in a hail of gunfire, and he looked down from the door of the helicopter to see the North Vietnamese covering the hill "like angry ants" and saw his rifle's hand guard and magazine guide scarred by gunfire, saw bullet holes in his rucksack and through his radio, saw the crease in his helmet.

Sure, people would say; they'd seen that movie too. So he kept his mouth shut, sealed his lips, swallowed it. Once he had lain in the elephant grass and saw grass when his company had been ambushed, and the boy next to him—who had pushed Homer down when the firing started and saved his life—had the top of his own head blown off. Homer had stared into the empty pink skull cup as the sheltering grass was being mowed down as if by a giant scythe. He knew he would die then, and then he went away, the smell of the bullet-mulched grass suddenly wonderfully evocative of peaceful summer lawns, the sun warm and gentle on his face, the noise fading and then suddenly back again, deafening, and then again fading away. Inches away from his eyes he saw a line of ants carrying bits of insect corpses and pieces of a strange pink fungus to their nest, their normality, their indifferent life, comforting and amazing him. He slowly felt his body, the details of his own physicality; he could even taste, feel with his tongue, a large chunk of the C-ration ham and eggs he'd had for breakfast still lodged in his cheek. He idly chewed it and swallowed, detached from the sounds of mortars and grenades and AK-47 rounds cracking over his head. He focused again on the ants, so busy, and he glimpsed again the empty skull of the boy who had gone down near him, and it came to him in a wave of bilious nausea what the strange pink chunks carried in those mandibles were, and what that glob of breakfast meat and eggs he'd felt in his cheek and swallowed really was, and he screamed, ignoring the bullets, getting on his hands and knees and giving in to projectile vomiting. He didn't tell that story. Even years later, when he wrote it, he put it in italics and a red font and warned people not to look at it if they didn't want to be changed. It was the kind of story you sealed behind your lips. How could you kiss anyone again, ever, seal your mouth to the mouth of someone you loved; how would you not be afraid to let her taste what you had tasted? It all stayed inside of him, like the box in the attic, not to be opened until he opened.

Trauma, according to Dr. Judith Herman's seminal work *Trauma and Recovery*, occurs when a horrible event or events cause a break in one's own life narrative. On the other side of that break, you can no longer see yourself in the same way. Recovery from trauma starts to occur when you are able to tell your story, in sensory detail, to people willing to listen without judgment and willing to be changed by what they hear—in other words, when you can be taken back into a community that is willing to be wounded itself, willing to break through a comforting shell of protective myths and learn what you have learned. If you can't do that, if they can't do that, you remain forever alienated, forever outside your community. You are what the Vietnamese call a wandering soul.

That is what Hoang Ngoc Dam became to his family. In the Vietnamese belief, the spirits of those killed far from home, through violence or accident or war, wander the earth aimlessly, far from the family altar. There were 198 such souls from Dam's home village of Thai Giang, one of them his older brother, Hoang Ngoc Chi. They'd gone south, disappeared into the war as if they had stepped off the earth. Dam's family, in fact, had more knowledge than most about his fate through Dam's hometown friend Pham Quang Huy, who had fought in the same area of operations in the Central Highlands.

Although the two were not in the same regiment, they tried to see each other periodically to exchange news and pass on letters. Huy found out about Dam's death from a nurse named Sinh a month after it occurred. Dam had been in a unit that had been trying to overrun an American outpost (probably what the Americans called Fire Support Base Twenty—Homer's base). When they failed, he was attached to a small reconnaissance group whose mission was to scout out other attack routes. They were engaged in that activity when they had fallen into the ambush Homer's company had set up; it was in the pursuit after the ambush that

Homer had come across Dam. Later, Huy had asked others in the unit about what had happened to the body and was told that Dam had been buried by some local guerillas. After the war, his body and three others were excavated and reburied at the A Giun Pa military cemetery, in Gia Lai province. But the excavators had not properly identified any of them, and Dam's remains were now among the other unidentified bodies in that cemetery. Huy and Dam's brother-in-law, Hoang Ngoc Dieu, visited the area in 2002, hoping to find the body and bring it home to be placed among the family tombs. But all they could do was grieve for all the anonymous dead in that place. There were no remains, and no objects to be put on the family altar, to draw his soul back to the family hearth.

Dam had become one of the three hundred thousand wandering souls—the missing in action from the war—that still haunt Vietnam. Without their remains being brought home and the proper ceremonies being followed—without, that is, commemoration, a physical knitting back into the community—they cannot find peace. "Strangers have buried you in careless haste," writes the poet and war veteran Nguyen Du, addressing all of the missing: "no loved ones near, no friend, no proper rites . . . and under the wan moon, no kindly smoke of incense wreathes for you."

What were left were memories and family mythologies. Dam had been, they remembered, a bright, studious, and very neat boy who at seventeen had taken very seriously the role of eldest brother. They remembered the tenderness with which he had bathed the youngest, best-beloved sister of the family, Tuoi. For the first years of her life, she had suffered from a skin condition, probably eczema, that marred her and caused her to be teased cruelly by the other children; and the adults, though they pretended to be indifferent to the ugly lesions, would often hesitate to touch her, hold her, pick her up. It was only Dam, his clothing always meticulously pressed and neat, his hands and face always scrubbed, who would hug her without hesitation, pick her up, kiss her, wash her, dress her. But it was that same neatness that would later haunt Homer, who had looked at Dam's clean, well-kept uniform and assumed he must have been an officer or a new guy who'd become a family legend. "We were very poor," Dam's brother Cat said, "so I never understood how Dam got a white suit, but he wore it whenever he went out. And he studied very hard. We

did not have paper, so we would take used paper and soak it in lime water
and use it again as scrap paper. But Dam always kept his books in order,
and he was very careful; he was neat from his hair to his way of walking, to his clothes. We did not have many clothes, but his clothes always
looked pressed, even though we did not have an iron."

And then one day he had disappeared beyond the village gate, as all
the other young men had, and Tuoi was left alone. The love she felt for
him left an emptiness and an ache that would never go away, like the sadness of his wife, Phan Thi Minh. They'd been married ten days before
he'd gone south; she never saw him again. A month before he'd gone
south to the war, he had written to her to come visit him at his training
base; other women from the village were coming to be with their hus-
bands for a few days—it was a last chance, everyone understood, to leave
behind a child. But she was too shy, only seventeen, to go there, to have
everyone know she was going for that reason, and instead Dam stood
guard for the other couples as they made love. It is something she regrets
to this day: "I wish I could have had a daughter with him; I would have
never married again. My current husband was also a soldier, wounded in
the war, but he is an alcoholic and I'm miserable. I keep thinking, if only
I had a daughter with Dam, then my life would not be this miserable."

What would Dam have been if he'd returned? What had been lost?
Dam became what each of the three hundred thousand was—a lingering
question, a question that his mother, Hoang Thi Thuy, tried to answer
by going to a fortune-teller.

Besides his wife, Dam and his brother had left behind their parents—his
father, Hoang Dinh Luc, a farmer, like Homer's father. There were also
his two younger brothers, Luong and Cat, and three sisters, Thi Dam,
Tham, and Tuoi. They worried constantly, but their hometown was only
nominally a rear area, a safe haven. The town's closeness to the port of
Hai Phong made it a target of American bombs: at one point an errant
bomb fell on the schoolhouse, killing thirty-six children. Most of the
young men went off to the war; some hung back. A postscript in one of
the letters in the packet of documents Dam was carrying speaks archly
of another young man who used his influence to keep himself out of
the army. "When I think of him, I get embarrassed for myself and the

neighborhood," the writer says. Loyalty—accepting one's military duty unquestioningly, fighting when the country called—was as expected of young people in Thai Binh province as it was in Homer's South Carolina. The families of soldiers who were "war martyrs" were compensated with stipends, job advantages, and, mainly, honor.

What the fortune-teller told Dam's parents was disturbing. Their eldest boy, Chi, was indeed dead and lay somewhere under the ocean. It was an assessment that proved accurate when they finally got an official notification of death. Apparently, Chi had been taken prisoner of war and had died in an island prison, his body flung into the sea. That accuracy stabbed like a knife when they heard the second fortune: Dam, the fortune-teller said, was in America. It was a fate they couldn't imagine. Had he somehow survived and gone over to the enemy? Or was his soul there, waiting to be commemorated and reborn? The consultation was supposedly only between Dam's mother and the fortune-teller, but soon some malicious people in the town were whispering rumors about the former possibility, spurring an outraged Huy and Dieu to go south and try and find his body.

It was an issue Dam's parents did not live to see resolved. Both had passed away before we were able to return Dam's documents and allow the family and the rest of the village to finally understand exactly what the fortune-teller had seen.

For a number of years, I've been involved in projects with Vietnamese writers and filmmakers, traveling at least once a year to that country where I had spent my own youth as a marine. Early in 2005, I met another writer, Tom Lacombe, also a veteran, who asked me to use my contacts in Vietnam to help a man who was trying to return some documents he had taken from the body of an NVA soldier he'd killed.

Over the last decade, Homer's life had changed to the point where he had become ready to confront his past. In the late seventies, working toward a master's degree in sociology, he had become fascinated by the then-new field of computers and had made himself an expert in the early days of information technology, finally securing a position as assistant director of the computer lab at the University of South Carolina's College of Liberal Arts. It was an occupation challenging enough to fill his time and his thoughts, and it kept him from dwelling too much on the past. It was also one that allowed him to be alone, a workaholic, until one day he met Tibby Dozier, a fellow employee who consulted him about some problems with her computer. He fixed it, and they fell in love and were married in 1995. Tibby, the soft-spoken daughter of a WWII general and Medal of Honor–winner, understood the nightmares and secrets of soldiers. With her encouragement, Homer began to open up and find a measure of peace in his life. He stopped drinking and reached a point, with Tibby's urging, where he needed and wanted to examine the war that in so many ways had formed him as a human being. He needed, in Dr. Herman's model, to tell his story in a way that would make his community listen and be changed by it.

It is a need that predates the psychological terms developed to describe it. Phil Caputo, in his Vietnam memoir *A Rumor of War*, writes of the tradition of the battle singer, whose role was "to wring order and meaning out of the chaotic clash of arms, to keep the tribe human by providing it with models of virtuous behavior—heroes who reflected the tribe's loftiest aspirations—and with examples of impious behavior that reflected its worst failings." Homer became what his given name called him to be—a battle singer—but he did so on his own terms by creating a Web site that provided photographs and detailed accounts of his time in the war. Now, ready to retire, assessing his past, he had come across Dam's documents, forgotten in his mother's attic.

Although the face-to-face encounter that had taken Dam's life was rare in that war, Homer's impulse to hang on to the documents was not. Nearly all North Vietnamese soldiers and Southern National Liberation Front fighters, those the Americans called Vietcong, kept journals or diaries in which they wrote and copied poetry, their thoughts, the events of their days, and it was common practice for American GIs to take and keep these or to give them to intelligence. So many personal documents were captured that eventually thousands were put on microfiche and are now stored in the National Archives. No one knows how many thousands more were taken by individual GIs, to be brought home, stored away, locked up. The lag between locking the documents away and bringing them into the light again—the need, decades later, to not only confront and tell the unfinished past but also to redeem it through concrete acts—was also a common reaction. Over the last ten years, many veterans have made the effort Homer vowed to make back in 1969: to find the families of the men and women whose documents and diaries they kept and return them. To this date, more than nine thousand have been returned to veterans' organizations in Vietnam through the Vietnam Veterans of America Initiative program.

Homer had spent hours scanning those documents into his Web site, and when I wrote to some friends in Vietnam—Phan Thanh Hao, a journalist and director of a social agency, and the writer Ho Anh Thai—I sent along the scans as e-mail attachments. They both told me that the best solution was to bring the documents in May, when I was planning to come to Vietnam anyway, and hand them over to the Vietnamese Veterans Association. A week later, I received an email from Hao. She had written an article published, with photos of the documents, in the newspaper *Giao Duc and Thoi Dai* (*Education and Times*), and Ho Anh Thai had also gotten an article published in *Lao Dong* (*Labor*), a major paper. The Hoang family had read the articles on the anniversary day of their mother's death and had immediately called Hao. They were very excited. They wanted to get the documents back, and they wanted Homer to come himself—"to place them on the family altar." They had no bitterness or anger toward him, they said. It was war, and they understood war. All they felt now was gratitude.

On April 22, 2005, Homer e-mailed the following letter, through Hao, to the brother of the man he'd killed:

Dear Mr. Hoang Dang Cat,

I would love to have given the documents back personally, but I can't possibly afford a trip to Vietnam. I am retired, on a fixed income and with recent health problems, just don't have the money. Even if I did, I am afraid I am far to shy to meet with strangers, whose language I do not even speak. I was raised on a small farm and have always been very shy. I still do not know how I managed to be a Platoon Leader and Company Commander in the Army.

I am very touched that you have an altar that keeps Dam's memory alive. It makes me feel good to know that his brave soul is still honored in such a wonderful manner. It hurts to think of the hundreds of thousands on both sides of that tragic war, who still mourn the loss of their loved ones.

Sometimes the guilt of surviving can be overwhelming. What will I say, when I enter into eternity? Is there a little known footnote to the commandment "Thou Shalt Not Kill," that forgives killing in combat? Look what I did in the ignorance and folly of my youth. I thought I was a true patriot. So why doesn't that give me comfort at age 59?

Dam and I met by chance on a trail. He and I saw each other and both of us attempted to shoot the other. I lived. He died instantly. For over a quarter century I have carried the image of his young body lying there lifeless. It was my first kill. I wish I could say it was my last. Why did a medic die and I live? I don't know.

Maybe someday humanity will gain the wisdom to settle conflicts without sending its youth to kill strangers. Know that my website www.swampfox.info is an attempt to educate those who have not lived the horrors of war. People should know what our leaders are doing when they resort to armed conflict to solve political problems.

In my dying moment, Dam and many of his comrades will surely call to me. I am not afraid . . . only saddened. Perhaps we will meet again as friends.

Respectfully yours,

Homer

"I just can't do it," Homer told me. He asked if I would bring them instead. A day later, the documents arrived at my house by express mail. He had let them go.

I hesitated a long time before I opened the padded envelope. In the Vietnamese belief, a male contains seven souls, a female nine, and I knew that for the Hoang family what I had now was literally a piece of Dam's soul. For a moment, I felt a kind of resentment, fueled by an atavistic fear. What was I releasing into my home? I had not killed this man. As soon as the thought came to me, I tried to struggle against it. One of my Vietnamese friends had written me when I told her Homer might come over that she would not want to meet the man, was not sure she could look into his face. Homer could have been me, I replied to her. He could have been any of us.

I opened the envelope and drew out the notebooks and papers, the smell of very old, very dry paper wafting to my nostrils. Everything had been kept in pristine condition. I looked through the documents as carefully as if I were an archaeologist examining an ancient and precious text. On one of the title pages, Dam had drawn an elaborate red and green orchid and his name, Hoang Ngoc Dam, under the date 1-1-1966, in the kind of ornate lettering teenagers will use to inscribe their school notebooks; a previous page was decorated with a hand-drawn pair of surgical scissors. The book was divided into sections concerning treatments for different types of wounds, though, surprisingly, the first section was on midwifery. Page after page was illustrated with beautifully done medical drawings: head and neck arteries, bones of the leg, the hip, and so on, as if he had copied an entire medical textbook. The work is beautiful in itself, and it is astonishing to think of Dam doing it in jungles, tunnels, and caves, under bombardment and artillery fire. On the last page was the only drawing that did not seem neat: scrawled grids, five squares per line. I wondered if they were tactical positions, battle plans, but when I showed them to a Vietnamese friend, he grinned and told me they were Vietnamese tic-tac-toe; he had played the same game when he was a kid.

Seeing and touching Dam's neat, precise handwriting—letters tiny, using as little space as possible, the exquisitely done anatomical drawings—I thought of Homer's anguished cry in his letter to Cat: "Why did a medic die and I live?" What could Dam have become, what would he have accomplished, who else had been taken from us? Dam's book raised the questions war has always raised, that war should always raise, the questions that should always be asked before a war and never are. But what stabbed me then was the hope those meticulous drawings and notes revealed; the book was an amulet, bound and filled by a young man trying his hardest to give himself the illusion of a future.

The notebook was not the only document. Inside it were four separate "Certificates of Commendation" that Dam had received. The earliest one, dated October 20, 1965, cited his model performance in serving the wounded soldiers of an unnamed artillery unit. He was elected (named) "outstanding individual" for the year 1965. The second, dated December 22, 1966, commended him for having "contributed to the building of a good unit during the first six months of 1966." The third citation was issued September 1, 1967, for "accomplishments in the first six months of 1967," and the fourth commended Dam for his accomplishment "during the general offensive and uprising of 1968," that is, the Tet Offensive. It was dated February 10, 1969, a little more than a month before Dam would be killed.

All the other documents belonged to another man, apparently an army truck driver named Nguyen Van Hai. The first was, in fact, his license, affixed with his photo. Hai was a very handsome young man, and one of the other papers seemed to be a love letter and a poem to him from a girl he left behind:

When you left I was speechless; I couldn't find the words to say. In every step you take away from here, I carry with me the feeling that I have. . . . Our feelings for each other are as wide as the ocean. What is in your heart is also in my heart. Your image has faded away beyond the bamboo hedge, but you brought me to life. I was so moved when you told me to wait and do my duty, so touched that I didn't know how to reply to your words. . . . Now you have left to fight the Americans and I must stay here to build the country. But I will see you again one day.

As long as there is still Heaven
As long as there is still earth
As long as there are still clouds
You and I will meet again.

When you left I didn't know who to talk to, to be with. You left behind your spirit, which inspires me to keep strong. Now that you are on your way, I wish you good health and success in the fight against the Americans to save the country, so that we can be reunited one day. I promise to fulfill my duties as a younger sister should while you are away, and when you sit to your meals, remember that there is still a younger sister who waits for you.

Had Nguyen Van Hai been one of Dam's patients who had died? We hadn't found out anything else about him, though now I would bring his documents also to Dam's family. There were other letters to him in the packet and a black notebook filled with high school math problems and copies of poems by Ho Chi Minh, in tiny handwriting. A friend had written as follows: "I miss you like a son misses his father. I bought some cloth, and will buy some for your family if they need it. On August

26–28 the hamlet was bombed and children and old people had to be evacuated. Remember to write to me." On the bottom of that letter is a note from Nguyen Van Hai's mother: "Your departure had made me miss you so much; I will never forget you, son. I feel sick with missing you so much."

We left for Dam's home village of Thai Giang, in Thai Binh province, at six in the morning on Saturday, May 28, two days after I flew in to Hanoi. Phan Thanh Hao, who had written the article that the Hoang family read, had made and received literally hundreds of telephone calls arranging the visit. The village is located deep in the countryside south of Hai Phong, and we rode out in a small van, past the new textile and clothing factories lining the Hanoi-Hai Phong highway, their products destined for Wal-Marts and Targets all over the territory of the old enemy. They were the incarnate forms reconciliation took on when it occurred between nations, and they were raising the standard of living here, we were told, but there was something bitter and mocking about them to me, about the unanswered question they evoked: What had all that killing been about? The reconciliation we were engaged in now was smaller, more personal; it was the only kind that could bring a true peace. We rode deep into the Vietnamese countryside, away from the new factories and into an older time.

With me were Hao, another writer named Y Ban, who is the editor in chief of Hao's paper, and George Evans and Daisy Zamora, two poets who had come on the trip to help interview Vietnamese writers for another project we were doing. George is also a Vietnam veteran and had also been a medic. He had arrived in-country in March 1969, the month Dam was killed and a year after George's best friend, also a medic, had been killed. It was George's first time back in Vietnam since the war. His wife, Daisy, is also a veteran of the other side of a different war: in her youth she had been a Sandinista guerilla. Her presence seemed appropriate in another way.

It took us more than three hours to get to Thai Giang, even though it is only, as the crow flies, about forty or fifty kilometers from Hanoi. There were no direct roads, and on the way we made another stop that also seemed to take us back into the war. Y Ban's father had died the month before, and we stopped at her family's house to pay respects and light incense at the family altar. When I asked Y Ban how he had died, she hesitated, and then she said he had suffered from the effects of Agent Orange all of his life since the war; now it had finally taken him.

Some of the members of Dam's family had arranged to meet us at a bridge near the main road, so they could lead us to the village. We stopped the van at the top of the bridge and waited. After a few moments, another car drove slowly past us and then pulled in front of us and stopped. Dam's brother and sisters were wearing the white headbands that signify mourning. They were all weeping. They clutched my hand, the depth of their grief surprising me—it was as if Dam had died yesterday instead of so many years ago. They asked us to follow them in but for me to keep the documents for now. As we drove through the lush green countryside, surrounded by rice fields, they would from time to time throw pieces of green and orange paper from their windows—Buddhist symbolic currency. They were leading Dam's soul back to his village.

I had come to Vietnam with a small National Public Radio crew to do an interview project, but I had asked that they not come out with us: I expected that there would be a small, private ceremony just for the family, and I didn't want to intrude. But as we came into the village, I was stunned to see that the street was lined with people, hundreds of them, most wearing white headbands and many were weeping and keening. I got out of the car and walked alone for a time, into the gauntlet, the rest of the party hesitant to get out of the car. I was there for Homer, as his surrogate, as his brother, and I was walking into the village of the man he had killed holding the documents in front of me like an offering, feeling the naked vulnerability of a man walking point, as if I were offering my body to something, as if I were a surrogate for more than Homer.

The others in our party had come out of the van now and caught up to me. George looked dazed. Dam's other relatives gathered around us—an entire extended family of aunts, uncles, nephews, nieces, cousins. His sisters, Thi Dam, Tuoi and Tham, his brothers, Cat and Luong, were all weeping, touching the book, as was a woman I found out later was his wife, Phan Thi Minh. "I know war," Phan Thi Minh would say later, "It was horrible—all the young people had to go. My biggest memory of that time was when we had ceremonies to see young people off to the front. Families and everybody would come see them off, and we all cried, even the officials. We did not have much hope that they would come back, and so it was as if we were parting, forever parting. The war ended more than thirty years ago, but I don't know when its consequences will end. The war still lingers, like blood trickling in our hearts."

Surrounded by a small sea of grieving people, we walked in procession to the community center; its veranda was ten-deep with people. They crowded around us, needing to touch us, the women petting Daisy. Inside, on a stage, an altar had been set up; it contained incense and flowers and a large photo of Dam and was flanked by two Vietnamese veterans, standing at rigid attention, in dress-white uniforms. The small, hot hall was packed with men, women, and children.

A series of village and district notables mounted the podium and made speeches. Finally, Dam's brother Cat rose. His voice breaking, he thanked Homer for allowing the family this release. He bowed toward me as he spoke, and when he was finished I climbed onto the stage and presented the documents, wrapped in the national flag, to him. He placed them on the altar. Many in the crowd were wailing, crying out. Dam, folded back into his village now, was himself a surrogate, a point man, for the two hundred that had been taken from this small place.

When the ceremonies were finished, we rose and walked through a soft rain to the Hoang family's compound. Thi Dam, the second-youngest sister, had been weeping throughout the morning continuously, her face so suffused with pain that I couldn't look at her. Finally, Daisy, unable to bear it, put her arm around her shoulder, and the two collapsed against each other. She had been drawn back, Daisy told me, into the griefs of her own war.

At the house, dozens of people had crowded inside, and more were on a kind of patio area under some fruit trees outside, where tables and chairs had been set up for a huge feast. The family altar was against the wall; it contained photos of Dam, his other brother, killed in the prisoner-of-war camp, and their parents. People kept filing in to see and touch the documents, and children stared at us, softly pulling the hair on my arms and George's, the way I remembered Vietnamese kids in the war doing, amazed at our monkey hairiness. I sat next to Cat, Dam's brother, and next to Pham Quang Huy, the veteran, Dam's friend, who would later tell me details of Dam's death and burial. I had brought the papers of Nguyen Van Hai, the truck driver, along with Dam's, and I asked Huy what could be done with these. He looked at me as if in surprise, blinking. But hadn't anyone told me? Hai was alive; he would come to the village soon and collect his things.

We ate with the family for about an hour and spoke about simple things—our families, our homes, and the losses of war, the price of hatred. I was told many times that they wished Homer had been able to come. They would always welcome him, they said. The village had even offered money to purchase a plane ticket for him. He was now a part of them.

After I returned from the village, it was a few days before I could get myself to sit down and write to Homer. A day later I received two e-mails in return. One was from him: "I have a huge lump in my throat. I am sure I would have been a basket case, if I had been there. I am still trying to comprehend the totality of your e-mail. . . . I know it must have been difficult. Knowing that the family has the documents gives me great peace of mind. . . . will get back in touch later, after I stop sobbing." The other came from his wife, Tibby: "When I asked Homer how he felt after reading your e-mail tonight, he said, 'Complete.'"

Two months later, sitting in the Steedlys' living room in western North Carolina, an area in some ways not unlike Vietnam's Central Highlands, I told Homer again how eager the Hoang family was to have him visit them. The Steedlys' dog, Dottie, pushed her forehead against my side, and I scratched her ears. Moments before, Tibby had told me the story of how the small black dog had come into the family. Homer had noticed her cowering under a low bridge, starving, and, from her reaction to his advances, obviously abused. He had sat with her for five hours, talking softly, and had finally stuck his hand out; and when she sank her teeth into his thumb, he had not reacted, just let her grip him until she understood he would not harm her, and then she had come out and become their dog. It was something, Tibby said, that she wanted to tell me.

I'll go there, Homer said to me. He was ready now.

Quarry

Years ago, this rock quarry was a factory, producing rock and gravel for all towns around. I'm walking on a new road at Gibbs Army Airfield near Tirana, Albania, and I wonder if the towns which surround us take pride that this quarry is producing gravel again.

The rust-black metal structures of the quarry loom like a foreclosed amusement park. This is Albania, and like the quarry, every aspect of the country's infrastructure has disintegrated. I detect decay in the buildings, old factories, and in the faces of people.

Gibbs Army Airfield is here to support the war efforts in Yugoslavia. They named the airfield for a helicopter pilot who died, along with his copilot, during a training mission. So far, they are the only casualties of the operation.

An old Chinese-built dump truck puffs past me, lifting dust and dirt, and I'm forced to look away. Strategically positioned U.S. Army tanks hunker behind new earth berms.

We're roughly a month into the bombing campaign to regain control of Kosovo; we're beyond the strategic bombing of darting fighters and cruise missiles. B-52s have been added to the arsenal. We heard that, two days ago, a series of cluster bombs caught two groups of Yugoslav soldiers in the open.

Serbian military casualties are to be expected. But there have been others killed. Weeks ago, we bombed a bridge near Sarajevo and killed people making their way home from market. Then there was the incident when our bombs struck a convoy of ethnic Albanians—the Albanians we are committed to protect. The headline read, "Unavoidable casualties of an air campaign."

My job is to monitor the quarry operation, to ensure this part of our mission, this production of rock and sand for the warfighters' base camp, is "up to snuff," is "making the grade," is an operation the general will be proud to call his own.

Inside the gate of the quarry, children run beside a moving troop truck, jumping to the floorboards, begging for chocolate and Meals Ready to Eat (MREs). Across the way, two children chase a dog away from a pile of empty green MRE packages. The dog carries one of the torn green plastic containers, runs behind a pile of crushed pea gravel, and under a strand of concertina wire. The dog clears the tight roll of barbs, and the children stop at the fence and watch the dog run across the field. When the dog sees the children trapped behind the fence, it sits and begins working on the filthy package.

Then there is a child atop a large pile of sand. He triumphantly sprays his friends with a water bottle. He swings the bottle round and round—the water like a moving whip—as if the water were supplied by a garden hose.

The children screech. When the bottle empties, one of the boys races over to soldiers resting beside a large truck and begs for another water bottle. The child motions with his hands, pleading. The soldiers stop work and ask him how old he is, ask him his name. Another soldier gets a friend to take a picture of himself and the kid. The Albanian child hams it up and forgets about the water bottle. His friends join him. Every soldier wants a photo taken with the smiling Albanian children.

The quarry used to sit outside Gibbs Army Airfield's perimeter, which proved inconvenient. So the army real estate office bought the quarry and then bought the road leading to the quarry.

One older woman, whose home included a hand-painted door, rose bushes, and a patio covered with grape vines, wasn't impressed with money. Eventually, the combination of money and pressure convinced her otherwise. Her front yard now houses port-a-lets and green tents. Her flowers and vines are neglected.

The quarry first produced gravel for the primitive roads in camp, though it has now degenerated into sandbag production. The soldiers and local Albanians have piled up thousands of bags for the camp. They have thousands to go. The higher-ups initially ordered twenty thousand bags, then forty thousand, military intelligence highlighting threats of indirect fire, snipers, terrorist bombs. I think of African safari movies, where hunting parties collect piles and piles of wood to keep fires burning day and night.

There have been rumors of Serb Special Forces and expected mortar attacks from the hills. We've seen the pictures in *Stars and Stripes* of what the Serbs have done to Kosovars.

The quarry is bordered by road, river, and pastureland; the quarry yard is roughly the size of a large supermarket parking lot. Bottles, plastic bags, used utensils, strands of wire, potato chip bags, and other trash lie everywhere. Stationed near the front gate, the port-a-lets stink. Paper towels, newspapers, used Handi Wipes, and toilet paper are trapped in the barbed wire.

At the moment, some twenty sandbag teams are at work. Unlike the neatly aligned tents or the orderly rows of parked military vehicles, the sandbag teams are spread around the yard: there are eight army enlisted groups and twice as many Albanian teams.

The Albanians wear dress shoes (loafers for the men, heels for the women) or plastic sandals. Some of the younger workers don't wear shoes at all. Sweatpants and dress slacks are popular, as are dress shirts, T-shirts, and tank tops.

Albanians seem to prefer shirts featuring a sultry Marilyn Monroe or a Rocky Balboa in victorious pose. Many of them wear clothes advertising Harley Davidson or Marlboro. I told a woman wearing a Yosemite National Park T-shirt that I lived in California, near the park. She looked at me with a blank stare. She said she bought the shirt because of the cotton; she made me feel a sleeve.

The GIs wear their camouflage pants, combat boots, and army-green T-shirts. Their pants are faded on the thighs from struggling with fifty-pound sandbags. There are GI women in some of the crews. These women look much like the men, with short hair and arms built to handle the long shifts.

I walk between the piles and working people carrying a digital camera in one hand, a notebook in the other. I'm here to observe the sandbag operation process.

The GIs give me the worst looks. They love to hate me: a cleanly attired air force officer snapping photos. I grunt hellos, try to keep ridiculous questions to a minimum.

But I break down and ask one group how many bags they think they've filled. Finally someone says, "Four trucks full." Then another, "Too many." To make the point more clear, another GI adds, "Too fucking many," which I take as a cue to leave. A soldier asks if I'm a reporter for *Stars and Stripes*. Before I can tell him no, he tells me there are machines that do this work, sandbagging machines. He wants to know why the army doesn't use them. He says that'd make a good story. He says I should write that one.

The GIs employ an assembly line. Four shovel, four hold the bags upright, two tie, two stack. When a squared pile of bags is complete, a truck is requested, and the crew passes the bags, person to person, to the bed of the truck.

The Albanians mount a frenzied attack on the sandpile. They use the group, all ten or twelve of them, as many as possible around the large mound, and work furiously, some with shovels, others kneeling and scooping with their bare hands. One of the teenagers has taped his hands like a boxer. These people without shovels, with or without taped hands, are closer to their work, are more efficient on their knees and hands, scooping sand. The Albanians with shovels have as much sand at their feet as they do in a bag.

The filled bags lie haphazardly around the Albanian crew. Then, in one seemingly coordinated movement, half of the crew goes to the shade while the other half ties the bags shut. When the truck comes, each person takes one or two bags and heaves them up onto the truck, stacking the pile of bags in the fashion of a slash pile of scrap wood.

In one way, the two crews, the Albanians and the Americans, are the same: they both suffer from the hard work. Shirts and pants, of whatever sort, are sweat stained, and when they rest, both crews squeeze in to tiny slivers of shade. Half-demolished concrete walls offer relief, while a few GIs lie close to parked trucks. But many just put shirts over their heads and pour water down their backs.

Some Albanians sleep in wheelbarrows. An American lies outstretched, his head on a brick-hard sandbag. And there is an Albanian asleep on a sandpile, curled like a homeless person on a park bench.

One of the GI teams passes around a water bottle. It's shared by each soldier, and then the last soldier gives the little remaining water to one of the begging children. The child runs away, splashing at his friends.

A child approaches a GI team on break. The team is drinking water.

The boy is small, with a large head. The boy approaches the group and asks for water, even using the English word. The Americans yell at the child in Albanian. The child runs back to his group of friends. I go to the group and ask a soldier what they said to the child. The soldier says, "Don't know exactly. Something like, 'Get the hell away.' Whatever it means, it works."

The friends are angry with the small boy, upset that he returned with nothing. The boy twists at his Spiderman shirt. I look at the boy with his friends and I understand that it's not the children who have changed: it's the adults.

The children's never-ending energy has ignited something awful in the worn adults. The Americans now yell at the children in foul Albanian slang. When that doesn't work, they throw empty water bottles. The children shield themselves, then steal away with the bottles. And when the children approach their Albanian fathers or brothers, the men lunge at the children, grab them by their hair or arms and scold them, slapping their faces with their hands. The children approach the adults less and less, choosing instead to sit by themselves or walk around in small gangs.

Three weeks ago, I visited a refugee camp. There were families just arriving at the camp, and the children tagging along behind their families, or their newly adopted families, acted similarly.

I climb up onto an old concrete wall. Below me, people move slowly—the adults, the children, even the dogs. The workers have another four hours until quitting time.

The children stay clear of the workers. I watch one of the small gangs. A barefoot child sneaks up to a stash of MREs. He hides behind a truck's wheel, then jumps around and snags two packages. He runs, and a GI runs after him. The child throws the MREs to his friends and the friends scatter. The soldier doesn't know whom to chase, so he curses in English and stops. He goes back to the other soldiers, and I can see his expressions and gestures complaining of the thieving local kids, of how you can't trust them, of how primitive these people are. The Albanian workers hear the American's excited language and understand the problem. They stand still and look blankly at the soldiers.

The children who stole the MREs are running through the quarry yard. They weave through the mazelike, trailer-high piles of sand.

They eventually group again on the backside of a large gravel mound. A few of them are ripping at the MREs. Brown cardboard and green plastic containers are thrown on the ground. The boy who stole the MREs runs up and starts wrestling with two other boys for parts of an MRE. The children fight and run and stop and fight more. It reminds me of a nature film about hyenas—the segment in which the lion is supposed to be the star, but then the crazed hyenas flash into the frame, nipping at chunks and stealing the spotlight. I watch the children, and I can hear the hyenas yipping and chewing at the spare zebra leg, blood on their snouts.

Things to Pack When You're Bound for Baghdad

> In an airplane there was absolutely no place in the world to go except to another part of the airplane.
>
> JOSEPH HELLER, *Catch-22*

> Literature is history with the truth left in.
>
> RALPH PETERS, *Fighting for the Future*

Missouri, 19 March 2003

The clock is punched for war in Mesopotamia—six hours until midnight, the day before the sudden flourish of air combat. I am suited, armed, and briefed for a twenty-thousand-mile flight. The middle 208 seconds of the journey will be over Baghdad. Tomorrow's strikes will compose the first salvos of "shock and awe."

Our war birds are carbon-fiber and titanium Stealth Bombers. They idle, topped with fuel, preflight crews tending aircraft systems on the rain-damp tarmac of Whiteman Air Force Base. In the course of the next two days, I will stiffen my backbone against exhaustion and battle with air force–issued amphetamines, a half-case of canned espresso drinks, and forty thousand pounds of steel and high explosives. And books.

The Northrop Grumman B-2A Spirit is a flying wing, a sixty-year-old concept writ lethal in composites and computers. In profile, it is racy—a falcon stooping on distant prey. From the front—a menacing, winged whale; from overhead—a wedge-shaped Euclidean study in parallel form. The plane carries aloft a crew of two pilots with the necessary life-support systems—oxygen, heating, air-conditioning, and cockpit pressurization. The pilots sit next to each other in twin ejection seats. The running joke is that the seats don't work because you'd rather be dead than face an accident board having crashed a $2.14 billion national asset.

Satiny charcoal in composition with a smooth, blended body, the B-2 is simultaneously rounded and angular. The skin is "exotic" [designed to elude radar] and top secret. The wingspan is 172 feet, two-and-a-half times its 69-foot nose-to-tail length. It is rare—only twenty-one were built—but not endangered. It threads the 3-D envelopes of missile defense networks. Stealth has the same effect on defenses as speed has, rendering reactions ineffective because they are too little, too late, if at all. This plane will bring us home.

The payload consists of sixteen weapons mounted on two eight-position rotating launchers in each of the three aircraft of our flight. My primary weapons are thirteen one-ton penetrator bombs for hardened targets and runways. The three remaining launcher stations carry the 4,617-pound GBU-37 Bunker Buster. These two-and-a-half-ton monstrosities are targeted against deeply buried, steel-reinforced, concrete command centers in a planned effort to "decapitate" Iraq's leadership. In the lingo of combat aviators, these bombs will "prosecute" targets. Rarely—unless talking about Saddam or his sons—is killing mentioned. We are distanced. We make "inputs" into a network of flying computers. I manage the ghost in the machine.

Our enemies label us the Great Satan, moral descendants of the paladins of Charlemagne, Protector of the One Church. I don't know if those we aim to liberate call us anything at all. We are armed to strike from the air, over the land, between the two rivers.

I have brought a bag of books and journals to pass the hours of tedium. I am bound for desert places.

Over Indiana at thirty-five thousand feet

Our wingmen in position two and four miles behind us, stacked up in altitude, we have settled into our roles and tasks. We have momentum. I boost out of the left seat and leave the colonel in the right to control the stick and throttles. A thick Bible is cradled in his lap.

The cockpit is brimming with electronics, maps, target photos, food, bottled water, and standardized military duffels containing "comfort items"—sleeping bags, air mattresses, pillows, black foam eye-masks to darken the day, noise-cancellation headsets and extra earplugs to stifle the rhythmic thrum of the engines. I sort the mounds of bags to locate my combat survival vest. There it is, folded and resting for war, against a circuit-breaker panel. It is choked with maps for evasion on the ground, water packets, radios, night-vision goggles, a fixed-blade knife, compass, fire starter, handheld global-positioning system (GPS), and a 9 mm handgun with three full magazines. I pull the vest on—right arm, then left—zip it, and try to locate specific items with my eyes closed. It weighs twenty-eight pounds.

I have supplemented the standard equipment with my own essentials, stashed throughout the seven pockets of my flight suit:

Three tubes of ChapStick, medicated
Toothbrush, floss, and travel toothpaste
One-ounce tin of Bag Balm—cow-udder salve for dry hands
Nail clippers
Aspirin, acetaminophen, ibuprofen, vitamin C, multivitamin,
    Imodium, iodine, Band-Aids, saline nasal spray, eyedrops
Baby wipes in a plastic sandwich bag
Sunglasses
Swiss Army knife
Duct tape

In a stained and ratty duffel bag, I have a small library of books and personal journals:

Heartsblood: Hunting, Spirituality, and Wildness in America—David
    Petersen
The Shape of the Journey: New and Collected Poems and *Just Before Dark:*
    Collected Nonfiction—Jim Harrison
Winter Morning Walks—Ted Kooser
Nine Horses: Poems—Billy Collins
A Timbered Choir: The Sabbath Poems 1979–1997—Wendell Berry
West with the Night—Beryl Markham
Fire Road and *Aftermath: An Anthology of Post-Vietnam Fiction*—Donald
    Anderson
The Things They Carried—Tim O'Brien
Winter: Notes from Montana—Rick Bass

Burning the Days: Recollection and *Dusk and Other Stories*—James Salter
Blood Meridian: Or the Evening Redness in the West—Cormac McCarthy
The Vintage Book of Contemporary American Short Stories—Edited by
    Tobias Wolff
A Voice Crying in the Wilderness—Edward Abbey
The Art of Living and Other Stories—John Gardner
Hunting the Osage Bow—Dean Torges
The Norton Book of Classical Literature—Edited by Bernard Knox
Don Quixote—Cervantes, Walter Starkie translation
Gilgamesh—Herbert Mason translation
Thoughts of a Philosophical Fighter Pilot—Jim Stockdale
Wind, Sand, and Stars—Antoine de Saint-Exupéry
The Longest Silence: A Life in Fishing and *Keep the Change*—Thomas
    McGuane
The Nick Adams Stories—Ernest Hemingway
Gray's Sporting Journal—August 2001 and November/December 2002
The *Iliad* and the *Odyssey*—Homer, Robert Fagles translations
Beowulf—Seamus Heaney translation
Four leather-bound journals in various states of wear

At the bottom of the bag, among the books:

Stainless-steel Colt 1911A1, .45 ACP with custom night-sights and four
    loaded magazines, in a nylon chest holster
Four pairs of wool socks, black silk long-johns, three brown undershirts,
    two pairs of flannel boxer shorts
Blue, fitted-wool, logo baseball cap "YALE—*Lux et Veritas*"
Black-and-white photo of my wife, son, and daughter

These things, these books, are a measure of security, a redoubt in war.
They bring me comfort in their many ways. The books have all been
read. That is the point. In the middle of the Atlantic, I won't be interested in the cheap plot-twists of the latest bestseller. I'm in need of art—
recklessness, patience, wisdom, passion, and largess. I rifle through the
titles, grab five, and return to the seat. We are over Ohio—me, my books,
and the colonel.

Much later, the Med, splitting the Strait of Gibraltar

To the north, Spain. From the library bag, Cervantes: "But all this must be suffered by those who profess the stern order of chivalry." And: "My judgment is now clear and unfettered, and that dark cloud of ignorance has disappeared, which the continual reading of those detestable books of knight-errantry had cast over my understanding."

Don Quixote was, and remains, redemption for a maimed veteran of the Battle of Lepanto and seven-year prisoner of the Saracens. Four hundred years later, we are bestowed the unwisdom of the knight and the fidelity and candor of his man Sancho. I pray he squires me now.

To the south, the Atlas Mountains heave up through the sands of North Africa. Over the water—low, scattered, vivid white cumulus clouds. Time, distance, and history are crammed into the fourteen kilometers severing continents. The sea below is a Homeric wine-dark against the early afternoon March sun. Our Mediterranean flight plan ushers us through international airspace to minimize the political complexities of trucking weapons to war.

Valencia.

Barcelona.

Marseilles. The lilting music of a female French air-traffic controller's voice. She knows we are USAF bombers. Our documentation conceals nothing. I expect contempt in her voice but hear none. Her warmth suggests a kind of condolence. A sadness floods me when she hands us off to the next controller.

Italian-controlled airspace over the Tyrrhenian Sea

Mindful of the *Iliad*'s great tactician and diplomat, Odysseus. Hunkered at the Siege of Troy for ten years, he brokered the egos of Agamemnon and Achilles. With the deployment of his Trojan horse, he became the technological progenitor of the plane my enemies won't see. Unbeknownst to Odysseus, during his twenty-year absence his wife, Penelope, would weave a death shroud during daylight. In the eventide, she would unweave this tapestry and forfeit her art, more in fear than in hope. She gave twenty years of her life to a war at the eastern edge of the known world.

My wife is named Diane, the Roman conflation of Artemis, goddess of the hunt and daughter of Zeus, and Leto, sister of Apollo. In seven hours, back in Missouri, she will press Record on a machine tuned to CNN's live coverage from Baghdad. One of my targets is Saddam's main presidential palace. It looms in the backdrop across the Tigris River from the hotel where journalists shoot their footage. At 11:04:25 Central Standard Time, a long series of cracking explosions will send dust and fire into the sky in a televised close-up. Diane will cry when she sees anti-aircraft artillery and missiles racing skyward. She will hide her tears from our young children. She will claim that I didn't warn her.

Eleven hours in, steering southbound thirty miles east of Sardinia toward the Strait of Messina between the toe of the Italian boot and Sicily

Odysseus's six-headed Scylla and devil-vortex Charybdis hunger five miles below the pregnant bellies of bombers. A couple of times an hour, someone in the formation offers a joke on our discrete radio frequency. We laugh and make smart-ass comments even when the joke isn't funny. We are all reluctant to resume the silence.

I snap open my fourth lukewarm Starbuck's DoubleShot. I can smell the coffee through my dry skin. In the preceding thirty-six hours, I have "flown" the bomb runs four times on a computer simulator back in Missouri and hundreds of times since in my head. Two weeks ago, we practiced the Baghdad portion of our bomb runs over Omaha at two o'clock in the morning. Method, repetition, and judgment. One human part of a vast system set in motion.

The colonel twists in a crouch over green computer displays, a technophile living a technophile's dream. The computers are his decorous armor for any debate over the consequences of our words and deeds. Me and the colonel. We're different. We each need the other.

Ionian Sea, west of Greece

Again, Homer, the "blind poet." When this thirty-nine-hour mission is over, I will have seen three "rosy-fingered dawns," and like Apollo the Archer, I will have "come down like night" over the skies of an ancient city.

As Homer's prelude to western history suggests, virtually everything revolved around honor and courage in battle for the warring Greeks in their *poleis*. Death and the horrors of war were acknowledged as tragic, but their constancy and proliferation paled in comparison to the everlasting honor gained through a display of fierce strategic genius, the first virtue. The *demos* elected and impeached the *strategos*—generals—who would lead them into battle. The electorate rewarded skill, intellect, courage, compassion, and wisdom. They had their politics. They had their heroes. Both were accountable to the people.

I lift Stockdale's book from where it rests on the glare shield. Handwritten on the inside cover is a note I penned six years ago when I was living in rural northern Japan, flying "Wild Weasel" missions in the F-16. It is from Clausewitz's *On War*: "The soldier's trade, if it is to mean anything at all, has to be anchored to an unshakeable code of honor. Otherwise, those of us who follow the drums become nothing more than a bunch of hired assassins walking around in gaudy clothes . . . a disgrace to God and mankind." Admiral Stockdale survived seven-and-a-half years as the senior ranking officer in Vietnamese prisoner-of-war camps. Malnutrition. Torture. Fear. Guilt. *Four years of solitary confinement.* He had no books, nothing physical to anchor himself. In his mind, he bore the great Stoic philosophers Marcus Aurelius and Epictetus. "Character is fate." After the war, he received the Medal of Honor; but more than that, he was possessed of honor.

The colonel breaks the silence over the intercom. "I'll be heads-down in the navigation systems for a while." I nod.

Ezra Pound once suggested Homer was an army doctor because of his keen descriptions of the honor displayed and the horror rendered in combat deaths. I seek honor in my posthistorical air war, but it is difficult to match deeds with the ancients. I am cloaked in the conceit of technology.

I look down at a map and figure angles and distances in my head based on our current heading. The Greek Peloponnese is off our nose, out of sight, over the horizon. Ancient Sparta. I look up and left, past the wingtip. Honor is, at best, diluted in the binary code of the most advanced airplane in the world. I place maps and mission papers in a lidded case behind the throttles to my left and pull out the *Norton Book of Classical Literature*. I linger on a highlighted section of Hesiod. By his description, the Olympian gods were petulant, arrogant, inhuman. When brilliant—yet inevitably flawed—mortal heroes approached the gods in deeds, their deaths were tragically orchestrated. But they lived on in myth. They reflected great truths, truths that were refined with the first spoken art—an art that began around campfires, in caves, in long halls, on wooden ships: the poems and stories we have always needed to bring meaning to the random acts of man and nature that thwart our best plans.

Tonight, I will shoot Apollo's silver bow, which never misses. I will be miles above the Olympian mountaintops. The skin of the airplane that shields me from my enemies' eyes also shields me from renown. Popular stories of pilots are more often about machines pushing the limits of human capacity and endurance (I almost let the F-16 kill me numerous times) than about the nature of the individuals who fly them. Technology trumps our shared human nature. I tell myself that my actions will help save the lives of soldiers who are racing north out of Kuwait. This is honorable. It is not honor.

Socrates, Sophocles, Aeschylus, Thucydides, Pericles, Xenophon, Demosthenes—all clarified their moral, physical, and intellectual courage on the fields of battle. The immediacy and closeness of war led them to believe that they would rather die fighting than live as another man's slave. As the ability to project power over great distances has advanced with technology, the question I must now ask is this: Will I *kill* to free another man's slave into a world that may be more chaotic, anarchic, and dangerous?

Aeschylus's epitaph mentioned nothing of his considerable poetic legacy, only his having served as an Athenian officer at the Battle of Marathon against the "long-haired" Persians. "In war," he wrote, "the first casualty is truth."

The radio hums and barks. I don't recognize a word the Greek air-traffic controller is saying. Apparently my wingman can translate his English, so I swallow the pride of a flight lead and let him have the radios until we get handed off, southbound, to the controller out of Cairo. The Cairene and I are talking over each other. Clipping transmissions. He orders our flight to climb above thirty thousand feet. After we do, he no longer answers our queries. The radio silence is peculiar, and I wonder if he is searching for a supervisor to turn us around and give us back to the Greeks. The coast looms. Southeast on the veiled horizon I can see a brown cloud of civilization mixing over the Nile delta from the pollution of Alexandria and Cairo, Egypt's two largest cities. The cloud trails off to the east as it rises and meets the lower reaches of the jet stream. The sky above fades to the deep blue of altitude.

Nineteen days past was my thirty-third birthday. I am two months older than Alexander the Great when he died in Babylon, the age of Christ at crucifixion.

A handwritten fragment of Heraclitus from a small black notebook carried in the thigh pocket of my flight suit reads thus: "Fire of all things / is the judge and ravisher."

Egyptian airspace, twelve miles inbound

The coast that bears down is thirty miles west of El Alamein and another thirty miles from Ptolemy's Alexandria, where, according to Plutarch, arrogance and betrayal among Roman factions led to the destruction of the greatest library of the ancients. A fire at the Temple of the Muses, the most extensive collection of the genius of the Hellenes—gone. Who can forgive Julius Caesar his "collateral damage" when Alexandria burned?

Nothing but sand in all directions now. The pressurized, treated air in the cockpit tastes coppery. The B-2, like every aircraft I've ever flown, blows hot air in your face while your feet are bitten by frost. I have learned. I am wearing merino wool socks so thick that I have been shoeless since shortly after takeoff. Quite probably, this is against some regulation.

Ninety minutes later

Still only sand. Saint-Exupéry and the Sahara Desert country of *Wind, Sand, and Stars*. Somewhere east of our current position he crashed an old prop-driven airplane in 1935 while trying to set the speed record from Paris to Saigon. He made wonderful art from his ordeal in the desert that nearly consumed him. "It has become impossible to say whether love or hate plays the greater part in this setting forth of the warriors." My mission is not to establish speed or endurance records. I carry bombs.

I safe the ejection seat and unbuckle the shoulder harness and lap belt. I tap the colonel's shoulder and gesture to the food in coolers behind us. He passes a thumbs-up, and I press out to stand in the eighteen square feet of real estate between the chemical toilet and the port bulkhead of the cockpit. The cooler lid creaks as I lift it and pass a roast beef and cheese sandwich forward. Needling pain in my lower back and legs. I dance a jig—elbows bent tight, fists clenched chest-high, feet bouncing heel-toe, Scottish war pipes ripping my imagination. I twist from the waist and jab-jab, right-cross, dip-duck, feint, left-hook, combo upper-cuts to the liver and chin. Arms raised in victory, I declare myself the undisputed welterweight champion above thirty thousand feet. I shake out, roll my head left, then right, and crumple to the nonskid rubberized floor. I build a nest with a camping air mattress and a drab, canvas sleeping bag. I unwind into the bag and compel myself to relax. The lower third of my body rests on the closed interior door of the entry hatch. Even though it only opens inward, I imagine plunging through every time I step on it; disgorged from the aircraft. Wind-tossed terminal velocity. Shoeless death.

I roll up to a sit, reach around to the map case, and grab the last book I was reading, Cormac McCarthy's *Blood Meridian*. I fan the mangled and tabbed pages. Highlighted passages and penned marginalia flick past my eyes like a grade-school notebook cartoon. Without reading the words, I recall tempers and thoughts that came to me as I knew the book for the first time: undistilled violence promoted to high art; Ares—god of war—come to the 1840s southwest border country as the mercenary Judge Holden. He never sleeps and never dies. He speaks all languages. Artist, scientist, shaman, preacher, liar, killer of children—eventually, he will have us all.

A yellowed, grocery-list bookmark falls from page 248, where orange highlighting burns the judge's explication of war into the page:

It makes no difference what men think of war, said the judge. War endures. As well ask men what they think of stone. War was always here. Before man was, war waited for him. The ultimate trade awaiting its ultimate practitioner. That is the way it was and will be. . . .

War is the ultimate game because war is at last a forcing of the unity of existence. War is god.

I lay the open book across my chest. I'm over Egypt, land of pharaohs. In two hours we'll arm and test the weapons. In the colonel's jargon, a "function check." I yawn continually because (I forecast) I am spiraling into oxygen debt. It unnerves the colonel in the right seat because he imagines I am unserious about my duty. I rise and gaze out the port-side windscreen, leaning forward from behind the seat.

Eastbound

Fifty miles ahead is the narrow-gauged Nile River Valley, a shock of vegetation. The ground shadows highlight the Valley of the Kings just across the river from Luxor and Thebes—the Great Temple of Amun and Ramses III, the Temple of Isis, the Necropolis. The pyramids at Giza are over the horizon to the northwest.

I grab a leather-bound journal from a duffel bag stained with hydraulic fluid and engine oil. Crossing the great river of Africa reminded me of a quote I copied into the journal a couple of years ago from an essay by the Korean War fighter pilot and author James Salter. There it is, written in smeared blue ink backed by faded yellow highlights: "Literature is the river of civilization, its Tigris and Nile. Those who follow it, and I am inclined to say only those, pass by the glories." I will overfly both of these rivers—twice—within a matter of hours. Farther down the page, Jim Harrison: "Great poems make good prayers."

Over the engine noise, I hear the colonel order the trailing wingmen to stack up from our altitude in five-hundred-feet increments to compress our reserved air-traffic block. The wingmen check their air-to-air radar as a precaution against the coming night. We are lit from below by a sand-blown, blood-orange sun that is waning below the horizon. The sun god Ra has already set for those in the valley beneath the plane. The late purples and reds of the desert contrast with the underwhelming gray and black of the cockpit glare shield and switch consoles. The only colors stab out from eight cockpit computer displays. Through these we manage our mortal cargo.

The desert air cools rapidly, generating light turbulence. The plane pogos every few seconds. I return to the seat and buckle down until the sky darkens and the chop calms. The night is a quiet blessing. The world closes in as the sky opens with stars. The radios grow silent with the dark. Beryl Markham wrote that there is no twilight in Africa, only night's sudden reclamation of the land. This reclamation is the haven of stealth. We own the black sky and the radar spectrum over distant countries.

The arid emptiness cleaved by the sudden, green river valley over the left wing looks like a *National Geographic* photo. Glancing back to the darkening horizon, I imagine a Saharan nomad tending his camels and searching the sky for the low, quiet booming of three B-2s en route to a war that has not yet begun. In words and deeds, what of our humanity do we apportion? My flight coveralls are designed to protect me in a fire. For these long hours in the air, my religion is fuel. My spirituality is speed. Every tanker who gives us gas is my muse, pushing me onward. I breathe supplemental oxygen at combat altitudes (sometimes switching to 100 percent oxygen in a rush to gather my thoughts). My great-grand-parents, early in the last century on the unbroken plains of Nebraska, were the last of my American family to struggle hand-to-mouth for survival. I cruise at high-subsonic speeds, 10 percent of the distance to the lower reaches of orbital space. What of the gazing nomad? Does he carry books with him in his travels, or does the weight come at too high a cost? Would he fight an enemy with a sword, the curved scimitar of a mounted warrior? Yes? He would have to watch his adversary breathe his last, watch his eyes glaze, *feel his death rattle on the tip of his blade*, knowing that he must protect his family, his tribe, his very life. Rubbernecking up, would he recognize me as a man in this black machine six miles above the desert? Would he think me a bat-winged demon?

Pacing again, I center-up between the seats and look forward over the aircraft nose. The colonel is still banging on the data-entry computer and bumping the throttles periodically. I should try for another twenty-minute nap while he has the controls.

Back into the nest. I won't doze until well after the Baghdad fire-walking stunt; a pretender to sleep and dreams.

Eyes closed, I cross into the territory of mind.

Clarity, courage, ambiguity, context—these perceptions gain meaning and momentum through the processes of literature, the one thing, I believe, that burns through the veneer of civilization to gift us glimpses into the eternal truths of human nature. *The things we know but cannot name.* The books I pack in my flight gear: poetry, short stories, the world's classics, collected essays, glossy hunting journals with ads for forty-thousand-dollar shotguns, and poetry—poetry first and last. At the controls, you can't disengage for more than about thirty seconds at a time. Darting attention and wandering thoughts: a prescription for lucid, brief, simple, and majestic words with the strength of memory. These words and their accompanying images provide thoughtful inter-ruptions to the method and repetition of long-range flying. Life is given nuance between the lines, between the soulless aircraft checklists de-signed to protect you from yourself.

Perched crossways on the half-zipped opening of my book bag is the frayed copy of *Heartsblood*, by David Petersen. On the cover is *The Hunt-er*, by N. C. Wyeth. With eyes still closed, I focus the image in my mind. The painting renders an idyllic Ojibwa hunter standing ankle-deep in water. He quarters right, toward the viewer, naked but for skins wrapped around his waist and a red cloth tied close about his hair. Over his left shoulder is slung a Canada goose, wings askew, black-beaked head hang-ing limp by the hunter's knee. The hunter looks away, over this burdened shoulder, toward barren trees and a V-formation of geese flying south for the winter. He is wildness, simplicity, freedom, and hope. In his right hand, a wood selfbow with a buckskin-wrapped handle.

I am that hunter. I build and hunt with primitive bows. I scrape wood with stone blades. It is experience stripped bare, and it brings me, wrapped in stealth technology, closer to that hunter, closer to existence and the actual costs associated with living. It is the opposite of meaning-lessness or absurdity. On the ground, I am a living mixed metaphor of radar-absorbing material and the ancient woods of bows—hickory, ash, osage-orange, yew. I fancy a bow in my mind.

A straight-grained limb with no twist, cut to an arm-span's length; the face, or "back," of the bow under tension, wider near the grip and tapering toward the nocks that hold and center the string; width con-trols draw weight. In profile, thickness is uniform, excepting the buck-skin-wrapped palm-swell at the handle. Thickness controls the bend throughout the length of the limbs. Unstrung, after the bow is finished and shot-in, there is a slight string-follow where the wood "remembers" the compression stress put upon it. When the bow is strung, there is a gentle, even curve throughout, the string seven inches from the belly of the handle. At full draw, the bow is a crescent, a new moon. If the wood is well seasoned and I honor the craft, my bows pull forty to fifty pounds at a twenty-eight-inch draw. They will cast heavy, wood arrows flat and fast.

Universally similar to the hunting bow just described, the selfbow of hunter-gatherers is simple and streamlined, the perfect weapon a stealthy woodsman might use to kill large prey animals reliably inside of twenty paces. With a dried stave, a passable hunting bow can be made in hours. These weapons of survival became more complicated when they evolved into the implements of warring pastoral and agricultural societies rather than tools of food procurement for nomadic peoples. The ancient Scythians did not perfect their high-performance sinew and horn horse-bows to hunt the steppes. The building process would have been inefficient for a man struggling to feed his family. These weapons were purpose-built for defense and brutal subjugation at range. Without hitting a major bone, these bows could be shot through two lightly armored footmen lined up in ranks. From the back of a rushing horse, they were more accurate than a GPS weapon with zero collateral damage. Warrior nomads like the Scythians became specialized and wedded to the geography that bore them. Primitive rituals evolved. Organized warfare became a principal ritual over and above the struggle to survive and protect resources.

Centuries later, the Athenian general Thucydides commented on war as a function of fear, honor, and interest. The agricultural and pastoral Greeks sought decisive battle in the open field as a cultural expression of strategy. They were known for their disciplined and courageous infantry. The Greeks favored spears and short swords in close-contact fighting. In contrast, the weapons of loosely organized cavalries were primarily bows. Archers control distance in a tactical engagement. The Scythians, and later the Huns and Mongols, were the people of stealth, deception, and hit-and-run, guerilla-style warfare. Marauders on horseback, they treasured the bow in war and were deadly at range. They were undisciplined, individualistic, and tribal, but rarely were they lured to fight Western forces in a decisive, pitched battle.

The cultural effects of bows start early. At the age of seven, Tatar boys were no longer provided food by their family. They ate only what they could steal or kill with a bow. If they lived to adulthood, they were vicious archers from horseback.

The Persians were bowyers. They were more culturally decadent than the warrior nomads, but they knew the spiritual value of archery. During adolescence, the sons of Persian nobles were sent to live with shepherds and farmers. They left the courts to learn horsemanship, to learn to tell the truth, and to learn to shoot straight.

The bow is complete, and I carry it now in my ritual. It is osage, the most difficult, most rewarding bow wood. Locating a tree straight enough and long enough is to find one in ten thousand. Snaky and twisted, the bow is orange-brown with dark, closed grain. It pulls forty-eight pounds and has a rawhide string. The smooth-burnished wood is conditioned against weather with melted beeswax. This bow is a bridge to another world or at least to what is real in this world. It shoots true.

Once a week, during the lunch hour, I drive west out of the gate at Whiteman Air Force Base to the south parking lot in Knob Noster State Park. If any cars are parked in the lot, I leave. If no cars, I park my beater pickup in the shade of an old-growth Shagbark Hickory. In spite of any weather, I strip from my uniform and hop-step into a pair of black nylon running shorts that my wife thinks are unfashionably high-cut. I remove the smooth-worn truck key from the key ring and place it, solo, under a rotting railroad tie in the dirt parking lot. No shoes. No watch. No thing. I cross the unnamed creek that borders the lot and join a trail that will draw me deep into the hardwood forest. If I plan on gathering river cane for homemade arrows, I pause on the creek bank to scrounge a good piece of flint. I rough out a stone knife to cut bent cane close to the ground. I will carry it with me to where I know the cane grows straight and then toss it when I have six good stems. The spiritual rewards of inefficiency.

If it is hot and humid, I linger in the relief of a light breeze on the ridge tops. If the mosquitoes are swarming, a light coat of creek mud, a quickened pace, and an end-of-run dip in the flowing creek keeps me bite-free. If it is snowing or raining, the pace is faster, breath blowing through my nostrils like a horse. Steam rises off my shoulders. My stride changes without shoes blocking me from the earth; I glide low and smooth on the balls of my feet down a game trail. I see wild turkey, whitetail deer, red fox, possum, cottontail rabbits, and coyote. If the ground is quiet from a recent rain or the wind is blowing—if I measure my approach among the shadows—I get close to deer. Mere feet. I listen to the rippling alarms of songbirds and squirrels as I skim along the trail. My mind is quiet, movement purposeful and clean, wood bow light in hand. The deer calmly survey, tails flicking. I am a hairless wolf, an unburdened predator. My kill comes clean and quick from one fire-hardened, stone-tipped arrow cast from full brace. I overcome distance with an arrow to compensate for the weakness of my instincts. It is *my* arrow that vaults from *my* bow and kills the deer, whose eyes I look into as it breathes a final breath. I possess the deer and become the deer when I feed my body. My hands are dry. Feet cold. Armpits stinking. Owning the death I brought. Purging the toxins of a plastic-wrapped, military–industrial complex life.

I am stealth. I am time and distance.

Scandalous shorts, mud camouflage, calloused feet, a bent stick, and lithic tools. My ritual.

The harmonic buzz of the turbofans prods me out of mind to the dimmed Egyptian desert. Recurring questions about the task at hand: What have I forgotten? Do they know I'm coming? Are the surface-to-air missile operators trained and rested? Are their minders leaving them to a futile chore, or are they pointing pistols at the back of menaced heads, ordering them to launch the surface-to-air missile or face an apostate's death? "Shoot down the Yankee Air Pirate and your family will be esteemed for seven generations."

Your feet are cold, your skin is dry, you eat and eat, but you hunger still. You smell like coffee, sweat, beef jerky, and fouled shearling seat-cushions.

Back on task.

The Kingdom of al-Saud

The darkened Red Sea approaches. With it comes temporal dilation, demarcation. A few hundred miles northeast lies a city that will soon spit fire and become fire. Swirling fighters will haunt the periphery of southern Baghdad while I ghost-in through the back door and bring hell from northwest to southeast. The city will hunt me down, but in the radar dark it will not find me. The city will not know I'm there until I'm gone, and gone's too late.

I twist into my chest holster and rack the slide on the old 1911. I thumb the safety up and slip the comforting heft into the tight holster that is now under my flight suit. The firearm will be covered and secure should I have to eject at upwards of 80 percent of the speed of sound. At .80 mach, the B-2 technical manual states, "moderate to severe injuries are likely." If I am shot to earth, my library will burn in a Heraclitean fire. If I am shot to earth, Iraqis will hunt me. If I am shot to earth, the smart thing is to bury the handguns, because grounded pilots are most brutalized and likely to be killed with their own weapons by their initial captors. To the government and the military, I am a political weapon. To the people living under a state-controlled press, I am Satan's proxy. These are men and women who have cowered with their families in ditches and alleys from Saddam's thugs and American bombs.

I am back in the seat, and the jet-stream winds are rapidly swinging between west and south and back again. The nose of the B-2 hunts left and right to maintain the planned track. I get a status report from my wingmen, Raccoon 32 and 33. The jets are in great shape, with almost no oil consumption, weapons and aircraft systems tight. No target or route changes. All as briefed.

I can avoid the drudgery of the computers no longer. I reconfirm the latitudes, longitudes, and altitudes of targets to the third decimal point of minutes of degrees. Crossing into Saudi Arabia, I will power all sixteen weapons with three switch actuations. The dedicated weapons computers will begin a deadly calculus of delivery. Within seconds of release, the latitudes and longitudes will be sent to the guidance units on the bombs. The most complicated drops involve the three "Bunker-Busters." In their parabolic flight, the eighteen-foot missiles will have accelerated to fifteen hundred feet per second when they strike within feet (often, inches) of the intended objective. Upon sensing the deceleration associated with impact, the internal electric fuse will begin the countdown to detonation-charge ignition. No one will hear the bomb's supersonic approach to the target. Milliseconds later, the earth under Saddam's presidential palace will shake, and fire will shoot from the domed roof. A special issue of Time will portray this on the magazine cover one week from now.

Written in yellow chalk on the dark green steel bomb casings are words. Traditionally, weapons loaders and aircraft crew chiefs write sophomoric death taunts, love poems, and eulogies for friends lost to terrorists or to combat in the Middle East:

"If the house is a rockin, don't come a knockin."
"Forgive us our trespasses and forgive them their sins."
"For all you do, this bomb's for you."
"When it absolutely, positively has to be destroyed overnight—USAF"
"For A1C Brian McVeigh—Khobar Towers 25 June 1996"
"All you need is love. Love is all you need."
"Saddam—Mess with the bull, get the horns! Johnny T.—Dumas, TX"
"If you'd stop gassing Kurds and Shiites—stop torturing your own
    people—we wouldn't have to shove this candle up your ass and light
    it. Love, Tiffany S."
"May freedom follow chaos.—Chief"

The colonel, earlier in the flight over Nova Scotia, told me that he inspected every weapon the day before we took off, now two days past: every steel lanyard, bomb-fin configuration, power connection, and fuse setting. He told me he wrote a proverb on a bomb body and took digital pictures "for the squadron history books."

The Saudi coast passes right, then left, out of sight under the aircraft as we angle over the coastline.

Standing now, the colonel fiddles with an obviously nonfunctional piece of satellite communications equipment. He has spent at least five combined hours of this flight resetting and rewiring various components. There is no dead horse that he believes a proper beating won't revive.

From the right seat, I snap up the colonel's worn, leather-bound King James Bible, with a silk bookmark in the Psalms of David, chapter 25, verses 19–21: "Consider mine enemies; for they are many; and they hate me with cruel hatred. O keep my soul, and deliver me: let me not be ashamed; for I put my trust in thee. Let integrity and uprightness preserve me; for I wait on thee." I could have criminal charges brought against me by Al-Madina, "The Authority for the Promotion of Virtue and Prevention of Vices," if I were standing on Saudi sand and caught in possession of this Bible, interrogated and beaten as an infidel—a forced confession, but for the grace of altitude.

We have the fuel to complete the mission and hit the poststrike tanker. Our timing is spot-on, which means our bombs will hit on time, to the exact second. The British controller passes word to us that all support aircraft have checked in. There will be no timing slips. The war is to start on time.

Northbound now for our piece of it, we push far to the west, flanking our support aircraft. Serving deceptive ends, as we crossed the border into Iraq, our call sign changed from Raccoon 31 to Squeak 31. It doesn't much matter because we are radio-silent, a roving black hole of electronic emissions. We are over the moonscape Iraqi desert, southwest of Baghdad, over the nothing. It's quiet from without and from within. The winds have settled strong from the west. The weapons computers are grinding. We wait.

The books are stowed. My mind is still darting.

I read to rage against the constriction of my profession—the barbarity of all overspecialized professions. I look east to the kingdom of Uruk—the city of Gilgamesh—through the green haze of night-vision goggles. I know the first story written down, the oldest story in the world, one thousand years before the Old Testament, one thousand years before the *Iliad* and the *Odyssey*—*Gilgamesh*: "As when one senses / Violence gathering its force, / Soon there is no sound apart from it, / Not even one's own thoughts in terror."

In a long, slow, right-hand turn to the southeast, I have arrived at my foregone conclusion. The possibilities of the day have all expired, and action stands as the final test. I am in the Iraqis' space. They are not in mine. I am the sovereign nexus of ideology, weaponry, and a clash of civilizations.

Over Tharthar Lake, just up-country from Fallujah, the Sunni triangle

Don't punch out here. The orange sodium lights of the city crystallize as they approach, sliding down from the far horizon. The power grid is not targeted this night. Five million people mark time with the lights lit. The

Tigris is a black velvet ribbon scoring the city. High cirrus clouds reflect the lights above our altitude, wispy mares' tails. Maintain track right of course for winds, or the autopilot won't hack the turns and the bombs won't release. I would *never* live that down.

A flood of words over the intercom: "Pattern management, weapons ranging, tapes running, target number seven thousand, one GBU-37 on the command and control bunker, minute-forty to release." Right of course; tracking: "Checks—switches up, clean and green, auto; station L-8 is a go."

The small-caliber anti-aircraft artillery is difficult to spot in the glaring brightness of Baghdad—not that it matters. Only the largest rounds can reach us, and the one that could hit us, we won't see. I force my gaze up to the darker horizon and the clusters of sparkling air-defense rounds detonating closer to our altitude. Squeak 31, flight of three, is alone now, above the air-raid horns and journalists and people and confusion. Our support aircraft are marshaled around the southern borders of the city. Antiradiation missiles and massive amounts of communications and radar jamming cloud the electromagnetic spectrum. We are a whisper in a very noisy, very dark room. The colonel is stooped over his situation displays, tapping furiously.

The surface-to-air missile launches are starting. Three to our left on the east side of town and one off the nose. Un-aimed. Un-disciplined. We are—and remain—stealthy.

The colonel switches his focus to the weapons displays. I search my mental catalog for a Churchillian saying, something for the "squadron history books," a meager attempt at a redemptive appropriation of wisdom: nothing. We have our own radio frequency. It's scary quiet above the melee.

"Sixty seconds." The number-two wingman, Squeak 32, south of us, moving directly west to east, will have a weapon release in seventeen seconds.

I crank my lap belt tight and finger the grip of my pistol. Up to the horizon, look left, look right, left again, out of habit. Another surface-to-air missile to the east—brighter—probably an SA-2. I watch it detonate above our altitude, guessing ten miles away, its final act a steel rain on the Iraqis below, to be blamed on the Americans later, I'm sure.

"Thirty seconds, in the release corridor, stand by for doors on the left. Next release 7001, thirty-one seconds following, two GBU-37s on the bunkers below Uday's palace."

I am winding up. Breathe. Center. Work the routines. They can't find us. They'll know we're here when they see the explosions on Al Jazeera. "Doors in five, four, three, two, one. Weapon away, target 7000 at 1803:30 Zulu, doors closed. Impact at 1804:25. Shack timing, delta zero. In the corridor for 7001, L-6, R-8, clean and green, switches up, auto." Another SAM. More AAA. The eastern edge of the city is passing under the nose of the aircraft, but we will be lit from below for another two minutes. We are not producing contrails. I crave complete darkness. I want Plato's Cave. I want these missiles to be the shadows of perfect missiles, our bombs to be the shadows of bombs.

Sometimes you must do a bad thing to stop something even worse.

Make it so.

Two hundred eight seconds and out.

Tigris means *arrow* in Old Persian.

The air war was "victorious" in weeks: fixed targets destroyed, statues toppled, museums looted. Thus endeth the major fighting, but there are unclaimed dead throughout the buried bunkers and desert landscapes of Iraq. Babylon, Ninevah, Nippur, Ur, Uruk, Iraq—how many dead? In the aftermath of the air war, some now may be mine. Bodies disintegrated in holes, below once-lavish palaces, terrorist camps, command centers, and barracks. How to think on these things?

Three years later, and I have not yet gathered the memories surrounding my three-week war. I tallied two missions, the first and the last for the B-2s flying from Missouri. These are the barest of facts.

My war memories start here: fifteen years ago I had a writing teacher who made—in my mind—a manifest and abiding link between great reading, writing, and a life lived well, a life that recognized and rewarded gentleness, empathy, artistry, and grace. After becoming an officer and, during the twelve years following, as an aviator and student of aviation, I read when I was able and wrote little. I flew F-16s and B-2s all over the world, with brief periods of combat action in both. In six months on the ground in the Middle East, I witnessed one terrorist bomb detonate and

I came upon the aftermath of two others. One—Khobar Towers in Saudi Arabia—was monstrous. Then 9/11. I was roused to fight.

As a pilot, I have fallen into bed for years hoping that I know enough, that I'm skilled enough to keep myself and my wingman alive through whatever imagined tragedy awaits us during the next day's flying: engine fire, midair collision, spatial disorientation, G-induced loss of consciousness, hypoxia. It can be easier to compartmentalize these morbid notions and train and train and train until you have acquired the expertise—even the art—of supersonic violence. But don't imagine that you might not compartmentalize your humanity in the process just because survival is paramount.

For years, I worked desperately to *not* be the lieutenant in northern Japan who made a late decision to eject from a miserably executed takeoff-abort due to a minor engine problem—a cascading series of errors and indecisions that ultimately had him parachute into the fireball of his own tumbling F-16. He died eight weeks later from a staph infection. His wife was twenty-three, and his picture now hangs in a fighter squadron bar. Six years later, new lieutenants ask, "What's his story?"

The story daunts them, daunts their sense of confidence in themselves, but they charge on. Later, at their homes, in bathroom mirrors, they lecture themselves: "That won't be me. I'm good. I'm better." At the bar, they raise their glasses and quote one of the most common axioms among pilots: "I'd rather be lucky than good." There is that, but that is not nearly all, and it's no comfort to those who loved, and love, the dead.

I've seen literature, faith, family, and friends equip those peripheral to a sudden loss as harrowing as this with the armaments necessary to defend their souls. Choice lies mainly in the first two—faith and art—for trials like death and war and what comes after. Conviction is personal and art is communal. Problem is, you must constantly strive for their possession *before* you need them.

Walking into the local market in my uniform, I avert my eyes from those I suspect will acknowledge me for service to the country. "Thank you for what you do" is difficult to hear. I am confounded by their innocence. I smile and nod—no words. I am embarrassed because troops are dying and I am here, buying fresh asparagus, wine, and apples. These people are kind and gracious, but I can't tell them what I have done because I don't know what's buried in the bunkers of an ex-tyrant's palace. I know I left more than thirty-six tons of high-explosive and weapons-grade steel in Iraq: buildings destroyed, bunkers mangled beyond recognition, airfields once bombed to submission, and now in use by our own forces. It is conceivable that I killed no one. It is, however, very unlikely.

I turn back to the *words*, words I would like the people in local markets to read and own, own and live. I read and write and read.

Hemingway wrote that "there are worse things than war and all of them come with defeat." I believe that. But just because one thing is worse than another, it doesn't make the lesser good—just less bad.

Once more to Heraclitus, twenty-six hundred years ago:

War, as father
of all things, and king,
names few to serve as gods,
and of the rest makes
these men slaves, those free.

Even the free then, are subject to war, and dying for freedom is easy, at least for the dead.

This is no boast. Killing's something apart.

I sit on an overturned canoe among budding wild rose bushes on the bank of a mountain lake that is named on no map. My son and daughter are fishing for trout and throwing pinecones at mallards. My wife is seven months pregnant. She sleeps on a couch in our small cabin with our youngest daughter. They are warmed by the late-morning sun piercing a picture window. I look up from Victor Davis Hanson's *Ripples of Battle*. My daughter beckons me to untangle a snag in her fishing line. I grab my fly rod and stride down the thorny bank to help her. The last paragraph I read before placing the opened book on the boat says this:

So battle is a great leveler of human aspiration when it most surely should not be. Stray bullets kill brave men and miss cowards. They tear open great doctors-to-be and yet merely nick soldiers who have a criminal past, pulverizing flesh when there is nothing to be gained and passing harmlessly by when the fate of whole nations is at stake. And that confusion, inexplicability, and deadliness have a tendency to rob us of the talented, inflate the mediocre, and ruin or improve the survivors—but always at least making young men who survive not forget what they have been through.

From a kneel in the cold water, I roll-cast to a trout rising from the shadows of an overhanging cottonwood. Stealthy even now. A slow retrieve and . . . nothing.

I have begun a new bow, bamboo and cherry wood.

I will hunt elk in the fall.

I will make rosehip jam with my children.

Colorado, 9 April 2006

Canon Fodder *An Epilogue*

Aircraft scattered thousands of mines along the Ho Chi Minh Trail and other infiltration routes into South Vietnam. Dale Ritterbusch was an army officer responsible for coordinating shipments of those mines—a responsibility that detonated his innocence about war. Any residual naiveté about the human drive toward belligerence vanished during a lifetime of the study of war through literature and the arts. As an invited panelist at the War, Poetry and Ethics Symposium, convened at the United States Air Force Academy in 1998, Ritterbusch referred to Picasso's painting *Massacre in Korea*, based on Goya's disturbing series of war paintings. "You see the terrible beauty of art conjoined with war. It is a strikingly fine work of art, although not nearly as well known nor as highly regarded as his war painting *Guernica*." Then:

> Pablo Neruda says in one of his poems that there are people who are going to ask him why he doesn't write about the sunlight on the sea or the flowers that are growing outside his window. And the reason he doesn't deal with these things in his poetry is because of the refrain in the poem where he says, "Come and see the blood in the streets." And he repeats that a couple of times. "Come and see the blood in the streets." What he is getting at, then, is that it is very disingenuous to create poetry that is not in any way mindful of the political realities in which one lives. It would be very disingenuous, I suppose, too, to think that the prescriptions for a poet are so constrained that one is only to deal with leaves changing color in the fall or dew on the grass.

Ritterbusch is himself the author of two collections of poetry. His collection *Lessons Learned*, centered on the Vietnam War and its aftermath, won the 1996 Council for Wisconsin Writers' Posner Award, a prize given to a Wisconsin author for the finest book of poetry written the previous year. His second collection, *Far from the Temple of Heaven*, was published in 2005. He is currently at work on a book about the history of war poetry. A professor of English at the University of Wisconsin–Whitewater, Ritterbusch served, during 2004–2005, as distinguished visiting professor in the Department of English and Fine Arts at the United States Air Force Academy.

In this epilogue, Ritterbusch does more than reiterate; he distills the necessity of personal accounts of the dread, baggage, and fallout of war.

—Donald Anderson

Within the academic world, the literature of war has been marginalized, relegated to a provincial outpost where a few stalwart readers and practitioners of the arts of poetry, of memoir, of storytelling, station themselves to repel the forces of willful ignorance. Perhaps this skirmish was lost long ago, and perhaps that is justification for the exclusion of war literature from any required curriculum. Perhaps this is a way of avoiding the critical nature of self-examination, both individual and collective. If we were, individually and as a nation, to engage in such examination, we would learn more than we want to know; certainly any pretense to innocence would be destroyed. But it is within the confines of war literature that we also find a parable of redemption, of salvation, for despite all attempts at dehumanization, the recording of some triumph over inexorable geopolitical, ideological, and other multifarious, repressive forces contributes to an acute understanding of human possibility: we are better than we pretend to be, despite the contrary evidence that we are far worse.

Academic skittishness, the fervent embrace of a traditional but misguided canon, some natural repellency to dealing with real-world issues, relegates war literature to the province of pulp fiction, lowbrow literature that offers little of intellectual value, never mind the extraordinary exceptions—the great works of world literature that have dealt with war since the inception of storytelling as an art. Such misperceptions abound, ironically, at all levels of our warrior culture. As the Vietnam War memoirist and poet John Balaban frequently reminds us, Dante considered the primary themes of poetry to be love, virtue, and memories of war. Despite Dante's instructive prescription, we respond otherwise.

Similarly, in the realms of history there are historians who believe the Vietnam War was of little consequence to our nation's history, a mere blip on the radar screen, there but briefly, and like any meteorological anomaly, gone and forgotten. Our history textbooks spend more time on the War of 1812 than on the wars in Korea and Vietnam. The culture vows to disown the bad wars and embrace the good ones. We are as disingenuous with our histories as we are with our literary studies.

So the literature of war stands apart, the literature primarily produced by those who were there. They provide no distanced perspective, no big picture; their stories are personal, but, in applying the greater-good formula, these stories are critically considered of little consequence; what can one person's story tell us when the error in logic consists of generalizing from a particular and when the historians' perspective must necessarily, according to established methodology, abstract general principles from higher authority, those who determine policy and who force subordinates to accept their argument without question? Such kowtowing to higher authority, embracing a fixed hierarchical structure at the expense of an individual's sentient perception, governs and determines acceptance in the canon.

But even those who have learned from their experience (and not that many do), and who record that experience for the gristmill of consideration by those who follow, are mindful that they will have little effect, for their task smacks against the fact of who we are, what we believe, and how we behave as a singular species on this planet. Wilfred Owen considered his experience in the trenches of World War I and surmised, "All a poet can do is warn." Kurt Vonnegut laconically wrote, of his survival of the Dresden firebombing, that "there is nothing intelligent to say about a massacre."

Speaking of his memoir *A Rumor of War*, Philip Caputo projects the effect he believes his book will have: "It might, perhaps, prevent the next generation from being crucified in the next war. But I don't think so."

So if little can be learned or taught, if there will be little appreciable effect and that effect may be deleterious, why consider writing on war to be other than an exercise in futility? But of course, there is a simple defense of remembrancing, as is found in a reverential, elegiac poem by W. D. Ehrhart entitled "Song for Leela, Bobby and Me." Ehrhart wrote this poem for a fellow marine killed in Vietnam, a man named Robert Ross:

I still have that photo of you
standing by the bunker door, smiling shyly,
rifle, helmet, cigarette, green uniform
you hadn't been there long enough to fade
somewhere in an album I don't have
to look at any more. I already know
you just keep getting younger. In the middle
of this poem, my daughter woke up crying.
I lay down beside her, softly singing;
soon she drifted back to sleep.
But I kept singing anyway.
I wanted you to hear.

And so the memoirists in this volume want us to hear their eloquence, their stories being the one legacy of war that just might offer a note of grace.

Donald Anderson, editor of the international journal *War, Literature and the Arts*, has culled—from some twenty years' worth of material printed in that journal—a remarkable compendium of selected memoirs of the highest quality, the most acute understanding. Ironically, as evidenced in other venues, many who return from war show little evidence that they have learned from that most extreme experience. It is as if they had merely taken a trip to the hardware store. But others, the ones possessed of exceptional powers of perception, record their glimpses into the mysteries of life-engaging experience of the most demanding order. Think of John Wolfe's elegant defense of art, visual but literary as well, in "A Different Species of Time":

Understandably, because I am a painter, a large part of a picture's value to me is the amount of this religio-aesthetic warmth that emanates from it and the degree to which it reflects the depth of human experience. Ultimately, the many hidden structures, the overlapping gestalts that hide behind and interpenetrate with the subject matter and the passion, feeling, and purity of its execution become a metaphor for humanity itself. It seems to me that when confronting a work of art, one should feel awakened in oneself a capacity for complexity, mystery, and an extraordinary intensity of feeling. Only through my experiences in Vietnam, my wounding, and my recovery did I come to understand this.

Or consider Joseph Cox's *Notes from Ban Me Thuot*, a perfect example of the grace and wisdom that comes out of the weird serendipity that often defines the experience of war. Cox relinquishes his seat on a flight north and later listens to the radio traffic concerning the crash of that flight into a mountain. It is the recollection of those lost, their memory, that burns deep so many decades later, evidence of the cost and the transformative effect of war. In the same way that those searching the aircraft's wreckage had to solve "the puzzle of mangled flesh," Cox sorts out recalled images, seemingly disparate, attempting to make sense of it all, noting, "What do we carry from that wreck? Memory and monument. Time and death fold in on themselves." Searching illuminations such as this characterize not just Cox's piece but the best that memoir has to offer.

A curiously interesting point concerning the selections included in this volume: a goodly number of the pieces are not directly related to the experience of combat. One might think a temptation would be to capitalize on the more sensationalistic aspects of war and war's experiences, but here we have thoughtful recollections of Civil War battlefield visits a hundred years after the war was fought, visits that linger and define our personal destinies. And we have childhood memories (as in "A Boy's Blitz," by Paul West) balancing youthful bravado, unaffected by any real knowledge of the world, against the adult world of waging war, just another means of excluding the very young from knowledge required to gain entry into that forbidden geography:

> We all wanted to know, but we were no doubt going to be killed before we found out. War, like peace, kept so much of what really mattered away from us. We were growing up on rumor and soft soap, buttered up by genial parents and austere teachers, never having our noses rammed in what mattered, what had driven the Germans to occupy France and Belgium, and God knew what else.

Ultimately, the pieces in this volume consider the dynamic of exclusion versus inclusion, a tension that defines so much of everything. What we want in our trivialized, materialistic culture is the experience of war without having to suffer the real and unintended consequences of that experience. In our warrior culture, we want the heroism (as evidenced in our Hollywood movies and the posturing of politicians) without experiencing any trauma, without any lingering battle scars that negatively affect our daily lives. We want to be ennobled but unbroken, to retain some innocence when that innocence is blasphemy. These works destroy our pompous punditry: they provoke our sensibilities as we would expect from the best of our literary tradition.

There are profound arguments here on matters of great consequence. When one considers the inconsequentialities given so much attention in the American diet of mass media nonsense, these arguments on politics, history, military strategy, and so forth make one ashamed of our propensity to trivialize, to render banal, our responsibilities in a democracy. This literature works, then, as moral discourse, allowing us to engage the most difficult and terrible questions we must face, such engagement defined by intelligence and grace.

There is poetry in this volume—not poetry as it is typically understood and is found in excellent abundance in *War, Literature and the Arts*, but the poetry of the perfect word or line or insight or truth contained within exchanges such as the following between Paul West and his father, a veteran who says little to his son about the war:

> "You're far away," my father said, or something like that.
> "I am dreaming," I answered, "a dream of soldier's stripes."
> "Never mind those," he said, "just a bauble. The real good conduct's in how you manage to control your breathing when the game is up."
> "Like taking an examination."
> "No never. Blood on the moon, my boy, and no questions asked."

And there is the poetry of philosophical observation, as when West surmises, "If you have gone down with the Lusitania, you know the names of the fish." The evidence abounds. Pure poetry of the reflective image is contained in this passage, also by Paul West: "My father did not live long enough to discover how grains of sand, fiercely spun by the rubbery throb of a helicopter's seething blades, turn into sparks like prim iotas in the early visions of philosopher Democritus."

One of the more pernicious effects of war is that veterans believe their particular war was unique in the annals of warfare, that their battles were the only ones worth fighting, that no other war compares with theirs; but each historical moment is eclipsed by the next, and every war is relegated to diminution by the latest conflict, which always superintends the last.

So soldiers and their stories are quickly relics and of little concern to anyone except vestigial students of the war and a few fellow comrades in arms. That few students in the present generation know, for example, of the exploits of Audie Murphy is evidence of how quickly heroism is compromised by the passage of time and by the unconcern bestowed by our temporal culture on even the most crucial events of the recent past, let alone the vast reach of history. Veterans, then, are little different from the rest of our society and are willingly complicit in compromising even the illustrious histories of those with whom they served. They prefer their own ideological bent to that of a veteran possessed of different understandings (so many political examples could be brought to mind here), and thus the process of marginalization, sanitization, and exploitation obtains. But from those few veterans who possess a capacity to learn from their experience and who desire to record that experience, we are given a literature that is commanding and deserving of attention. It should be the responsibility of the culture to provide an audience, and it should be an expectation that the formal study of the humanities would include such works for elucidation and reflection, for the inculcation of humane values in the face of other doctrinal social demands.

War literature addresses a series of essential human mysteries, not the least of which is a rendering of the cognitive transformation that inevitably results from the experience of war. One function of war literature is a retelling of that transformation, as when the messengers recount to the beleaguered Job stories of the destruction of his family and worldly possessions, saying, "And I only am escaped alone to tell thee." Just so, war memoirists have escaped to tell us their stories of redemption and salvation, answering the question Ishmael posed in the epilogue of *Moby Dick*: "The drama's done. Why then here does anyone step forth?" For both Ishmael and the universal soldier, the answer is the same.

Ironically, our ethical constructs now forbid conducting various experiments on the human psyche—such experiments as those done by Stanley Milgram, Philip Zimbardo, and others. Yet, the crucible of war memoir provides such psychological insights that one comes away with an understanding, often revelatory, concerning reactions to stress and to extreme, life-threatening situations. The psychological determinants are such that one engages the core of human experience: memoir is a mechanism of engagement with those determinants, an experiment with one's own psychology. All writing may be a form of self-discovery, but the impetus behind these memoirs is not merely of record but of evaluative discrimination. Think of *Moby Dick* as a memoir of war, a war with inexorable forces beyond human knowledge or understanding. That undercurrent of rage against one's mortality—emblematized, perhaps, in Ahab's line, "I would strike the sun if it insulted me!"—governs war memoir, for there is injustice in fate, in the serendipitous nature of war, culling by random chance those left living from those dead, those able to critically engage this spectacle from those who learn nothing from it. The fact of war causes one to confront and differentiate power from powerlessness, moral complexity from simple moral platitude, the dull and stupid from wisdom and humanity. There is both grace and redemption in such loss.

Differentiation, evaluation, and judgment are endemic to the critical process of examining war experience. Discriminating assessments, regardless of the cost, even to the point of slaughtering sacred cows, are at the heart of the story, and once memoir breaks through, it reaches places unreachable by other means. The disingenuous, the self-serving, the proselytizing are easy to spot, and they indicate inauthenticity in the evaluative process. The true memoirist knows the instructive value is negligible because of the human practice of deliberate misreading; but for those who are receptive, those possessed of a desire to search the depths of human complexity, war memoir provides some small, embryonic light to follow, to embrace, to hold on to when understanding slips into the shadows.

If a major objection to memoir involves bias against veracity as opposed to fictional truth, then the retelling of war stories is subjected to criticism that reflects more on the reader than on the writing itself. All arguments involving the fog of war aside, interpretation of personal experience is always selective, but this process of selectivity is a positive determinant, not a negative. The long-term argument concerning Tim O'Brien's work and whether it is fiction or memoir or any combination thereof became tiresome after so many newspapers reworked this topic, as if it were the only means of engagement of such work. A war story, as O'Brien explained in *The Things They Carried*, works this way: "In any war story, but especially a true one, it's difficult to separate what happened from what seemed to happen. What seems to happen becomes its own happening and has to be told that way. The angles of vision are skewed."

Similarly, literature of the highest order is multidimensional, existing on several perceptual planes at the same time, each level skillfully blending imagination and veridical fact; and whereas the reader may apprehend, perhaps, only one level, the others enrich—if only subliminally—the experience of a reader's engagement. Since a criticism of memoir is that it is one-dimensional with only the import of anecdote, it is interesting to note that the pieces included in this volume resonate insightfully on various planes of perception and apprehension. One wonders at the dismissal of the war story genre when it provides such extraordinary penetration into so many areas of human complexity—existential confrontation with forces beyond our comprehension and control, moments of triumph (gestalts) over extreme trauma and adversity, the lingering awareness of the serendipity of chance and how it falls unequally on the just and unjust alike. And just so, unmistakably, the stories work metaphorically, untraditionally in the literary sense of metaphor, approaching the more philosophical understanding of metaphor as proposed by Hannah Arendt in *The Life of the Mind*: "Language, by lending itself to metaphorical usage, enables us to think, that is, to have traffic with nonsensory matters, because it permits a carrying-over, *metapherein*, of our sense experiences. There are not two worlds because metaphor unites them." Within the war literature represented in this volume we find the metaphor of affirmation and grace—what we desire if we are at all sentient and wish for some measure of revelatory transcendence.

So many studies of memoir focus on what should be included, what should be left out, that both student and professional writer rely only on that point of concern when crafting their various essays. But there is an element of shortsighted foolishness in this role. When Annie Dillard writes of the process she employed in writing *An American Childhood*, she says, "I tried to leave out anything that might trouble my family." If one were to consider the removal of all materials that were troubling, there would not be much left to write about, and certainly memories of war are by definition "troubling." Dillard, praised for her honest and direct recounting, defends what for the memoirist of war would be disingenuous: "I have no temptation to air grievances; in fact, I have no grievances left. Unfortunately, I seem to have written the story of my impassioned adolescence so convincingly that my parents (after reading that section of my book) think I still feel that way. It's a problem that I have to solve—one of many in this delicate area. My parents and my younger sister still live in Pittsburgh; I have to handle it with tongs."

This smacks of sanitization, the means by which innumerable historians and journalists managed to record their various wars without concern for the truth, even if it were impossible to record. In wars such as Vietnam, sanitization was the operative principle in many quarters, and no memoirist could employ such techniques and expect to justly present the experience of war.

Memoir, easily dismissed by traditional historians because it does not contend with "the big picture," and similarly disdained by students of the literary arts because this genre does not seemingly assail the creative, imaginary heights of the novel, contains elements crucial to contemporary understanding: within that rubric of understanding is found an array of psychological, social, historical, and political insights uncolored by the limits of these individual disciplines. In Hannah Arendt's terms in *The Life of the Mind*, the modern "dismantling" of tradition has created its own ethos: "What has been lost is the continuity of the past as it seemed to be handed down from generation to generation, developing in the process its own consistency. The dismantling process has its own technique. . . . What you then are left with is still the past, but a fragmented past, which has lost its certainty of evaluation."

One thinks, however, of how little certainty there is—uncertainty, as the physicists explain, being the fundament of the universe.

Certitude and the embrace of an admirable tradition may be positive values profoundly desired, but fragmentation and uncertainty are more characteristic of the contemporary world. War memoirs reestablish a hold on what matters, and the mere act of writing, of recording these stories, is in itself a mechanism for ordering the chaos, just as natural, chaotic, forces are a mechanism for creating beautiful and intricate artistic patterns. There is, in fact, some philosophical reconciliation present in the act of writing memoirs, as both seeing (experiencing) and reasoning are assimilated in the process of creation. The act of seeing and then recording that visual determinant creates a higher order of apprehension, explication insufficient to convey the relative truth of that experience. This is not to denigrate the idea of Coleridge's "esemplastic imagination" but to refine it according to a different prescription. Epistemologically the memoir holds true; against rationalism, the events recorded transcend a logical existence. Traditional dimensionality does not obtain, and it is a mistake often made to consider the genre of memoir limited by parameters that cordon off the retelling. Again, such reasoning is suspect. The percipient is controlled, unmercifully, by the experience as deterministic forces have their sway, but the experience of war rendered into literature provides a degree of counterbalance, allowing the writer (and by extension the reader) a measure of control, a redirecting or deflecting of those deterministic forces. Transcending grace and affirmation result. I have relied on those terms because I have few others and because the only legacy of war that matters is derived from those experiences, those memoirs, which contain these values. One could consider others: memoir as prayer, perhaps, but that would still turn back to transcendence and grace. One thinks of John Wolfe's encounter, narrated in "A Different Species of Time," with another wounded vet when they both were undergoing rehabilitation:

> Semiconscious and strapped into a wheelchair, I was wheeled down to a physical therapy room with various exercise bars, tables, and gym equipment around. . . . Just a few feet away, a physical therapist was busy balancing something on a table that at first looked like a sack of potatoes. When I focused, I saw that it was a young Asian man, probably Korean, who had lost both arms and both legs close to the torso. No sooner would the therapist balance the torso on its buttocks than it would topple over on its face with a painful-looking impact, and then the process would be repeated.
>
> The Korean's eyes met mine, and for a long moment the presence of everything and everybody else in the room blurred, faded out, dematerialized, leaving only his mind and mine on that spatial plane in an uninterrupted convergence. And then we both started to laugh hysterically.

This laughter both defines and mitigates the shock of recognition. There is more humanity in that laughter than in any philosophical dialectic or exercise in deconstruction.

So memoir need not be myopic and self-centered, though there are certainly many representations of the genre that exhibit these traits in abundance. Works by those highest up in the chain of command are often ideologically based defenses of actions that are questionable. But for those in the trenches with no fixed position to exploit, there are phenomenologically based observations presented of considerable value. And where there are discrete differences in perspective and understanding, one finds that argumentative or contesting discourse provides particular illumination.

War memoir is representative of collective experience, that experience shared by others subject to the same social, historical, and political forces. Sociological disciplines consider the nature of communal experience, organized social behavior that patterns our existence. As such, war memoirs are particularly instructive. Military culture and the experience of war emblematize essential social values reflective of individual sacrifice for the greater good, fulfilling, in the extreme, provisions of the social contract: rights and responsibilities, expectations and obligations, rightfully tested. Too often memoir is regarded as confessional rather than as an expression of the social order. One could extend this argument existentially to consider the role of the individual within a social context reflective of humanity's ontological fate. Regardless, personal narrative is not inconsequential and merely concerned with the self. At the highest level, narrative modes of thinking yield meaning and knowledge unattainable by other means.

Narrative as a means of gaining and transmitting knowledge ranks formidably high in the process of human cognitive development, given that storytelling is a singular biocultural attribute of our species. Whereas the individual process of constructing a personal narrative is an act of self-realization, a more important consideration involves the more distanced assimilation and evaluation of personal experience. Experiential factors govern or influence cognition; as Jerome Bruner has explained in "Keeping the Conversation Going: An Interview with Jerome Bruner," "you organize and construct knowledge on the basis of encounters with the world." Robert MacGowan writes in this volume of such constructed transformations regarding family relationships:

> My brother, my father, myself—in some fundamental way we are now the same. My brother went to war three times to gain our father's love; I went once and put the hope away. It came to me in a dream: my father is standing beside me, and we are looking down on the Khe Sanh Valley. He

does not look at me, nor I at him. We are both looking down at the battered red earth below us. He says, "Now that you have returned, I can love you." I respond, "It's not worth it."

A familiar defense of imaginative literature is that it vicariously expands our personal experience by injecting the reader into various and disparate experiential worlds. The resultant knowledge is an invaluable shortcut to constructing a firm epistemological framework upon which to build a personal and communal identity. A similar argument can be made for memoir that is artfully constructed. It may be as multidimensional as fiction and certainly no more self-deceptive or disingenuous. In the case of MacGowan, an empathetic reader contends with the effects of war experience on otherwise unassailable relationships. Not just the individual soldier, but others close to him are profoundly affected; by extension, the entire culture is defined by such rending.

It is, perhaps, the interpenetration of imagination with concrete experience that develops and defines the successful exposition of memoir. Such conjoining achieves metaphorical resonance, and the resultant memoir is both expressive and emblematic of universal experience. Certain penetrations occur from one war to another, forming intricate patterns that inform the corpus of war literature. These works contain and convey various strategies of engagement with fundamental questions at the core of human existence. And so war memoir stands as remonstrance to our willful ignorance and foolish pretense. Currently, within the ongoing culture wars, a prejudicial curriculum ensures a compliant, uncritical population, and that curriculum excludes war memoir while it includes a palatable, sanitized history: the desire is to eradicate the social memory and replace it with a fairy tale. War memoirists included in this volume work against the extirpation of those truths contained within their stories. For their courage and their art we should be grateful, accepting their affirmation and grace as a profoundly human gift.

Contributors

DONALD ANDERSON has edited *War, Literature & the Arts: An International Journal of the Humanities* since 1989. He is editor, too, of *Aftermath: An Anthology of Post-Vietnam Fiction* and *Andre Dubus: Tributes*. His own collection *Fire Road* won the John Simmons Short Fiction Award. He is professor of English and writer in residence at the United States Air Force Academy.

JASON ARMAGOST is a graduate of the United States Air Force Academy and the University of Colorado. He was in the lead aircraft on the first air strikes of Baghdad during Gulf War II. This is his first publication.

For his service in Vietnam, DONALD CLAY was awarded three medals for valor: the Bronze Star, the Bronze Star w/gold star, and the Navy Commendation Medal. He was also awarded the Purple Heart. During his incarceration, Donald Clay completed an associate degree. He was released from prison during the spring of 1995, the twentieth anniversary of the fall of Saigon. He now lives in Michigan.

ALVORD WHITE CLEMENTS served in his own war—World War II —with the 503rd Parachute Infantry Regimental Combat Team. He served later during the occupation of Japan with the 11th Airborne Division. Following the war, he attended the University of Maine, graduating with a degree in forestry in 1947. He has been married for sixty years to Pauline S. Clements. Until his retirement in 1979, Mr. Clements worked for the National Foundation March of Dimes. The Civil War memoir he contributed to this collection was written by his paternal grandfather.

JOSEPH T. COX, PH.D., is headmaster of the Haverford School in Haverford, Pennsylvania. A thirty-year army veteran, he commanded from the platoon to the battalion level and served as an academy professor at the United States Military Academy. Several of his poems have appeared in *WLA*, and he is the author of *The Written Wars: An Anthology of Early American Prose*. His collection of poetry, *Garden's Close*, was published by Thirteenth Angel Press.

Coeditor of *Visions of War, Dreams of Peace*, JOAN A. FUREY served as a nurse in Vietnam. Now retired as director of the Center for Women Veterans, she lives in upstate New York.

DOUG HECKMAN is a graduate of the United States Air Force Academy; he later received his MFA from the University of Washington. His stories have been published in *WLA*, the *Beloit Fiction Journal*, *Other Voices*, and *Weber Studies*. He and his wife split their time between Grand Teton National Park, where they are park rangers, and Omaha, where the two of them teach at Creighton University.

WAYNE KARLIN is the author of six novels and two memoirs. He has won the Paterson Prize in Fiction, the Excellence in the Arts Award from the Vietnam Veterans of America, and two fellowships from the National Endowment for the Arts. A marine veteran of the Vietnam War, he teaches at the College of Southern Maryland and is the American editor of the Curbstone Press Voices from Vietnam series, which publishes translated works by contemporary Vietnamese authors. He is working on an expanded version of "Wandering Souls."

ALFRED KERN is a World War II veteran. He is the author of three novels, including *Made in USA*, a seminal novel of the world of organized labor. Educated at Allegheny College and New York University, Kern was, for years, a member of the Allegheny College faculty. He also served as distinguished visiting professor at the United States Air Force Academy.

ROBERT MACGOWAN is a pseudonym, designed to protect the author's privacy and that of the veterans about whom he has written. He served in Quang Tri Province as a 26th marine rifleman from December 1966 through February 1968.

JAMES H. MEREDITH served in the United States Air Force for twenty-five years. He retired in 2004 as a lieutenant colonel, while serving as professor of English at the United States Air Force Academy. Among his many war-related publications, his books include *Understanding the Literature of World War I* and *Understanding the Literature of World War II*. He also edited a special edition of *WLA*, *Stephen Crane in War and Peace* (1999). He is president of the Ernest Hemingway Foundation and Society.

WILLIAM NEWMILLER teaches composition and literature at the United States Air Force Academy, where he is also *WLA*'s editor for electronic publishing. He retired from the air force in 1993 after serving twenty-three years as a pilot of trainer and transport aircraft. He has become a frequent contributor to *WLA*, and his work has also appeared in *Letters to J. D. Salinger*, the *North Dakota Quarterly*, and the *North American Review*.

A frequent contributor to *WLA*, DALE RITTERBUSCH is author of the poetry collections *Lessons Learned* and *Far from the Temple of Heaven*. He is professor of languages and literature at the University of Wisconsin–Whitewater. During 2004–2005, he was distinguished visiting professor in the Department of English and Fine Arts at the United States Air Force Academy. He is a Vietnam veteran.

The author of more than forty books, PAUL WEST'S recent *My Father's War* is a memoir of his World War I veteran father. The two essays that appear here are reprised in a slightly altered form in that book. Other recent books are *Tea with Osiris*, *Sheer Fiction IV*, and *The Shadow Factory*—an account of West's experience with aphasia. His war-related novels include *Rat Man of Paris*, *The Very Rich Hours of Count von Stauffenberg*, *The Place in Flowers Where Pollen Rests*, *The Tent of Orange Mist*, *The Immensity of the Here and Now*, and *The Dry Danube*.

After leaving the army, JOHN WOLFE returned to New York City, where he attended drawing and painting classes at the Art Students League of New York. Since graduating in 1974, he has exhibited his paintings in galleries and universities throughout the United States. He lives in upstate New York and maintains his studio in New Paltz, New York.